ETHICAL AND SOCIAL ISSUES
IN PROFESSIONAL EDUCATION

ETHICAL AND SOCIAL ISSUES
IN PROFESSIONAL EDUCATION

Celeste M. Brody
and James Wallace, Editors

STATE UNIVERSITY OF NEW YORK PRESS

Published by
State University of New York Press, Albany

© 1994 State University of New York

For information, address State University of New York
Press, State University Plaza, Albany, N.Y. 12246

Production by Diane Ganeles
Marketing by Fran Keneston

Library of Congress Cataloging-in-Publication Data

Ethical and social issues in professional education /   Celeste M. Brody
    and James Wallace, editors.
        p.   cm.
    Includes bibliographical references and index.
    ISBN 0-7914-1915-0. — ISBN 0-7914-1916-9 (pbk.)
        1. Professional education—United States—Moral and ethical
aspects.   2. Professional education—Social aspects—United States.
3. Education, Humanistic—United States.   I. Brody, Celeste M.
II. Wallace, James, 1929-
LC1059.E87   1994   93-26783
378'.013-dc20   CIP

To our staff and students,
who continue to teach us
about the meaning of serving others.

Contents

Foreword   ix
  NEL NODDINGS

Acknowledgments   xi

Introduction   1
  JAMES WALLACE AND CELESTE M. BRODY

Part I: Challenges to Professional Education

1. The Role of Liberal Arts in Professional Education   13
   DOUGLAS F. MORGAN

2. Interdisciplinary Studies and the Possibilities of Community 29
   CELESTE M. BRODY

3. Collaborative Learning: Fostering Dialogue
   Across the Professions   49
   CELESTE M. BRODY

Part II: Thematic Responses to Ethical and Social Issues in Professional Education

4. Story and Voice in the Education of Professionals   69
   CELESTE BRODY and CAROL WITHERELL
   with KEN DONALD and RUTH LUNDBLAD

5. Reflection and Adult Development: A Pedagogical Process   89
   ROBERT R. KLEIN

6. Digging, Daring, and Discovering: Sifting the Soil of
   Professional Life through Journal Writing   103
   JOANNE E. COOPER

7. Self-interest and its Relation to an Ethic of Care   117
   TERRENCE R. WHALEY

8. Liberation, Multiculturalism, and Professional Education   133
   ZAHER WAHAB

9. Citizens and the Conduct of Ecological Science:
   A Response to the "Tragedy of the Commons"   147
   CHARLES R. AULT, JR.

10. The Internationalization of Professional Education   169
    JACK CORBETT

Part III: Reflections on a Graduate Core Program

11. The Feminine in Public Service Professions: Implications
    for Graduate Instruction   189
    MARY HENNING-STOUT

12. Gender and Professional/Liberal Knowledge:
    Men's Perspectives   207
    JAMES WALLACE

13. Learning about Organizational Cultures and
    Professional Competence   219
    GORDON LINDBLOOM

14. The Evolution of a Graduate School:
    The Effects of Developing a Liberal Arts Core   237
    CAROLYN L. BULLARD

Afterword: The Search for Personal and Professional Meaning   247
   KEN KEMPNER

References   259

Contributors   275

Index   279

FOREWORD

NEL NODDINGS

This book is unique in several ways. First, it is addressed to professionals and those preparing to be professionals across a broad range of public service; it is certainly valuable for educators but also for nurses, social workers, and administrators in all social agencies. Second, its authors have worked together to build an educational program, and they enrich their theoretical discussion by reporting generously on their personal experience in creating and teaching in this program. Third, although they advertise their program as drawing heavily on the liberal arts (and it does), the authors make an even more important contribution by challenging the standard material of the liberal arts.

The program described here acknowledges that professionals must be well trained to perform the particular tasks of their occupation. But, beyond that obvious layer of preparation, professionals should also have a deep understanding of the ethical and social problems that abound in their fields and in the environment surrounding their professional work. In addition, they should be enabled by an appropriate program of education to seek self-actualization. They should be able to explore intelligently questions concerning their obligations not only to clients and society but to themselves as developing human beings.

The authors ask explicitly about the connection between professional education and the liberal arts curriculum that usually precedes it. They set out to explore the question: "to what degree should this education [professional education] be plain-and-simple task training and to what degree should it continue the liberal education that has supposedly permeated earlier education in schools and colleges?" Their unequivocal answer is to continue the approach they associate with the liberal arts:

> We ask students to confront fundamental questions which are at the core of a liberal arts approach to professional education: What *should* I do with my life?" "What *can* I do with my life?" "What kind of society do I wish to live in?"

ix

Notice that these questions are indeed among the basic questions associated with liberal arts. A liberal education is supposed to free people—to prepare them—to think deeply and reflectively about the most fundamental problems of human life. But observe carefully as you read this book and reflect: There is almost never any mention of the role of particular disciplines in the study of professional problems. These writers do not look at the professional scene through the lens of literature, philosophy, or any other discrete discipline. Instead, they consistently use the avowed purposes of liberal education to challenge readers to go beyond the narrow boundaries of particular disciplines and specialized training. This, I think, is a great contribution. It is a subtle and effective challenge to liberal education to abandon the pursuit of narrow specialties and take up, once again, the questions that are implied in its name.

Readers will encounter many themes here—all approached from the perspective of the liberal arts as described above. Among them are multicultural perspectives, cultural transformation, the needs of children, voice, perceptions on peace, capitalism, racism, cooperation, and caring. Themes also attend to issues of personal development: writing for critical inquiry and balancing work and family life. As these themes are discussed, it will be clear that the authors really do draw "heavily on the humanities, arts, and social sciences." Within the themes, there is an emphasis on "ethical, gender, cultural, and international perceptions."

In this book, "liberal arts" refers to an approach, to a set of vital questions; it does not refer to a set of disciplines. Some readers may be disappointed to find no chapters on "Literature and the Professions," or "History and the Meaning of Social Agency," or like titles. But persevere. You will find reason to celebrate the contribution of the disciplines to professional thought. Best of all, you will find reasons to rethink not only what professional education should look like but, just as important, how the liberal arts themselves should be redefined.

ACKNOWLEDGMENTS

One of the many pleasures of editing this book, based as it is in a common experience of the authors, has been the opportunity it has given us to continue a dialogue through the writing and thus to strengthen the sense of community among us. We have enjoyed getting to know our fellow authors better and have developed an increased appreciation for their commitment and competence. We are grateful to all of them for sharing with us their interests, knowledge, and expertise. We acknowledge their help, while retaining responsibility for the inevitable limitations of this book.

The support staff in higher education play a central role in helping faculty maintain healthy connections with each other and with their students. So it is appropriate for us to extend our first and greatest thanks to Aileen Fisher, who cheerfully and skillfully typed several drafts of the book and who gave us useful advice on various technical matters. We have enjoyed her good-humored, insightful, and candid comments as she has worked patiently with us.

We also want to thank staff members in our different graduate programs who helped faculty as they worked on their chapters. We appreciate the help of Barbara Roady, Kelly Wainwright, and various student workers in the Lewis & Clark Academic Technologies office for their help with various computer problems.

We are grateful to our authors, both for their willingness to write their chapters and for their patience and goodwill as we proposed revisions. Our authors have many important things to say and would prefer to express them at length; one of the hardest parts of our task was asking authors to shorten their excellent manuscripts in order to keep the book within a reasonable length.

We want to thank the many people who were involved in the development of our core program, who have taught in it, and who have participated in it as students. Mary Kay Tetreault was instrumental in writing the original grant to the Fund for the Improvement of Post-Secondary Education (FIPSE), under which planning for the core program was done; she also participated actively in planning and teaching as the program was implemented. We are grateful to FIPSE for supporting our efforts.

We thank the hundreds of students who participated in core classes and seminars and who gave us honest and useful responses to them. Some students have become our valued colleagues as they have completed their degrees and gone on to team teach core classes with us. The excellent writing that students have done is represented in some of the chapters that follow.

We thank administrators and faculty committees in the Graduate School of Professional Studies for travel and research grants and academic leaves that facilitated our work. We are grateful to colleagues in the American Educational Research Association and the Lewis & Clark Gender Studies Symposium for giving us opportunities to present our ideas and to get useful responses from program participants.

We are very grateful to Lois Patton, our editor at the State University of New York Press, for answering our many questions and for timely advice as we have worked our way from prospectus to publication.

We thank our spouses, John and Mary, for support, encouragement, tolerance, and patience during the many months we have worked on this book.

Finally, we want to thank our readers in advance for their time and interest. The ideas in this book, like the core program itself, are constantly under development and revision. We invite our readers to write to us with their questions, disagreements, and suggestions and to continue the dialogue of which this book is a part.

Celeste M. Brody and James Wallace

Introduction

JAMES WALLACE AND CELESTE M. BRODY

In 1899 Thorstein Veblen wrote:

> Institutions are products of the past process, are adapted to past circumstance, and are therefore never in full accord with the requirements of the present.... The readjustment of institutions and habitual views to an altered environment is made in response to pressure from without... If any portion or class of society is sheltered from the action of the environment in any essential respect, that portion of the community, or that class, will adapt its views and its scheme of life more tardily to the altered general situation; it will in so far tend to retard the process of social transformation. (Veblen, 1918, p. 191–93)

Veblen was one of America's most insightful social critics, but his recommendations for social change are often seen as elitist and unrealistic. Veblen's contemporary, John Dewey, was an equally profound critic, but his recommendations for institutional and social change have better stood the test of time.

John Dewey described one institution—education—as "the growing edge of culture." Education is the institution and process through which society organizes itself to shape the future. This is true at all levels, from nursery school through graduate school. And it is at that growing edge of culture that the most significant controversies occur. Indeed, if education is not controversial, it is not fulfilling its function. If education is not disputed territory, it is not dealing with those issues about which people feel most deeply.

In the last decade the wisdom of Veblen's insights has been confirmed by the experience of those working in professional education. We struggle in a number of arenas to keep up with the needs of our rapidly changing environment. We are charged with—among other sins of omission—failing to prepare individuals to make sound ethical judgments in the confusing, complex world of work in the United States. The results of this failure are evident daily in business, government, and other settings. Abuses of knowledge in the business world create huge fortunes for the few and increasing poverty for the

1

many. In government we see repeated scandals, further signs of weak moral judgment.

Practitioners report that their professional education programs do not prepare them to deal with the profound moral conflicts and developmental challenges of their working lives. They experience tensions between personal and professional values, organizational mores and individual commitments, and bureaucratic expectations and their own standards, and they feel ill-prepared to work productively amidst these dilemmas.

Conservatives and liberals agree that we have focused too exclusively on narrow technical competence and have failed to teach students how to deal with the complexities and ambiguities of late twentieth-century American life. Robert Bellah writes:

> There is a profound gap in our culture between technical reason, the knowledge with which we design computers or analyze the structure of DNA, and the practical or moral reason, the ways we understand how we should live. We often hear that only technical reason can really be taught, and our educational commitments from primary school to university seem to embody that belief. But technical reason alone is insufficient to manage our social difficulties or make sense of our lives. (Bellah et al., 1991, p. 429).

The 1980s and 1990s in America have seen an unusual amount of argument over education at all levels. The conservative hegemony in politics was accompanied by efforts to effect what Ira Shor calls "the conservative restoration" in education (Shor, p. 111). Conservative politicians, experiencing success in the political arena, attempted to institutionalize that success through the judicial system, in the broad social realm, and in education. They had substantial success in the federal courts, where the appointive power of the president encountered much protest, but few effective limits. They had somewhat less success in the social domain, where Congress and state governments held back some of the conservative tide. And, in spite of massive rhetorical assaults, they had even less impact on education, where the organized opposition, as well as the institutional inertia that Veblen described, provided effective resistance to the most reactionary efforts of the conservative movement.

The effort to impose conservative values on schools and colleges has been widely publicized and can only be summarized here. Beginning with *A Nation at Risk* in 1983 and continuing through a series of conservative articles, reports, and books by such writers as William Bennett (1984), Allen Bloom (1987), and Dinesh d'Souza (1991), there has been an outpouring of attacks on education. While their targets and their anger vary, these authors have generally asserted that American society is failing economically, politically, socially, and spiritually, and that to return to a better America we must restore "traditional" educational values and practices.

Specifically, these books and authors have called for "back to the basics" in content and methods and for abandoning government meddling in the form of affirmative action, bilingual education, compensatory education, gender studies, and multicultural education. They stridently call for giving families educational "choice" (among public, private, and religious schools), assuming that market forces will create positive educational competition. For these writers, the world and education were better places when there was a consensus on a canon of a predominantly traditional, patriarchal, Western curriculum. Even lifetime liberals like Arthur Schlesinger, Jr. support parts of this traditional message (Schlesinger, Jr., 1992).

Educational institutions are porous; controversies at any level tend to seep upward and downward to other tiers and to change as they move. As these dialogues penetrate into the arena of professional education the question becomes: to what degree should this education be plain-and-simple task- training and to what degree should it continue and extend the liberal education that has supposedly permeated earlier education in schools and colleges? Meetings and journals of professional educators are replete with arguments, manifestos, and proposals on all sides of this critical issue (Mann, 1988).

In this book—which is intended primarily for teachers of adults—we present dialogues and case studies on this topic. Lewis & Clark College faces these issues as they are formulated in the setting of small liberal arts colleges. A bit of history here may help readers see the applicability of our experience to their own thinking, planning, and teaching. In 1985 (just as the current educational debate was catching fire), Lewis & Clark, Oregon's largest private college, integrated several professional preparation programs into a graduate school of professional studies. The act of creating such a school thrust our faculty into the midst of the liberal/technical debate.

Our programs in teacher education, educational administration, special education, public administration, and counseling psychology had previously focused primarily on technical training for specific professional roles. We recognized, however, the urgent need for education to assist professionals to deal with issues that transcend their specialties. Professionals continue to mature and develop personally throughout their careers and work in organizations and environments that pose important sociocultural concerns and dilemmas. The question of how individuals might thrive and continue to develop within organizational contexts receives little attention in most professional education programs. Yet how people respond to these challenges profoundly affects their work in public service.

Integrating our programs caused the faculty to ask what might hold them together. What do these professions have in common? All are primarily public service occupations, and those who work in them face issues of ethical practice, of bureaucracy, of personal development, and of the place of the professions in the larger social order.

Our faculty made a conscious decision to extend liberal education processes into professional education—although we drastically revised the content of that education. While students in our programs have had sound undergraduate liberal arts preparation, they have not had the opportunity to face "liberal" issues in the context of professional education and practice. The faculty insisted that effective teachers, counselors, and administrators must be responsive to pressing problems: the power and purpose of high technology, emerging issues of gender, and the challenges of working in diverse cultural and international communities.

We designed a series of seminars and classes that require students to consider deep personal, ethical, intellectual, and social dilemmas as they manifest themselves in professional work. And, since all our students are in public service occupations with some similar problems, we require students to undertake these "core" studies together, while taking most of their professional courses within their separate programs. Thus people working at different levels and in varied jobs in public service share their perspectives with a range of colleagues.

We invite students to join a learning community in which we confront fundamental questions that are at the core of a liberal arts approach to professional education: "What *should* I do with my life?" "What *can* I do with my life?" "What kind of society do I wish to live in?" These questions turn into particular commitments that we make as we design and teach our classes. Our curriculum must help students deal with the conflicting moral claims that they encounter in their personal and professional lives, prepare them to deal with the ethical ambiguities involved in their choices, assist them to live with the uncertainties that surround their decision making, and encourage the deep and continuous self-criticism that enables professionals to adapt to changing circumstances. (See Morgan, chapter 1, for elaboration on these questions and commitments.)

We recognized also that we needed a broader epistemology and methodology that reflected inherent tensions between professional knowledge and the contexts—psychological, social, cultural—in which it is applied. We tried to realize collaborative possibilities among faculty by requiring that core classes be team taught and that the pedagogy support multiple forms of inquiry, ways of knowing, and knowledge creation among students and teachers. We work continuously to challenge the traditional classroom pattern through which future professionals are usually inducted and in which teachers are authoritative transmitters of knowledge. We maintain that learning is a process of co-construction, which emerges out of dialogue between teacher and student and student and student. We recognize the contribution of adult learners to their own reflective inquiry and to the creation of a community of learners.

We made another equally significant decision: to resist conservative calls for an orthodox definition of this continued liberal education. We rejected appeals to narrow the liberal curriculum, and we designed programs with firm commitments to gender studies, to multicultural and global education, and to straightforward attention to ethical and political issues. This did not mean that we agreed on a party line to be imposed on students—although as we will note later, some perceived parts of our curriculum that way. It did mean that we required new and experienced professionals to confront major social issues in the context of their professional work. For example, how do all of us handle our own inclinations to stereotype, to classify and sort our clients by race, gender, sexual identity, and social class? How can we overcome these habits so that we can serve our clients and society in ways that honor diversity and promote equity?

Without making a conscious decision to do so, our own planning and the responses of our students led us to "teach the conflicts," as Gerald Graff proposes (1992). Our students are sufficiently perceptive and confident to resist efforts to mold them according to some liberal/ professional ideology. The honest and effective way to help them deal with these issues is to provide them with materials and activities that immerse them emotionally and intellectually in major social, political, and educational controversies, and this we try to do.

How do we achieve this when our faculty members have their own generally liberal-to-radical political and social commitments? Our teachers are personally and publicly committed to gender equity, to multicultural education, and to fair treatment for all persons in our society. We hope that our students have similar convictions, and most do, but they all face the challenge of expressing their commitments in complex, often conservative and patriarchal bureaucracies. Our decision, in effect, has been—as one instructor put it—to be "objective but not neutral." We can teach students representing a range of religious, social, and political backgrounds without demeaning them or their ideas. And we can help them move beyond the dichotomous thinking to which some are accustomed toward more complex and sophisticated analyses of important issues.

Anyone reading our course titles, descriptions, and bibliographies might understandably accuse us of the liberal sin of "political correctness" (PC). Our response to such charges must be mixed. If "political correctness" means that we are committed to principles of equity, diversity, and justice, we must plead guilty as charged. If, however, PC connotes indoctrinating our students with our beliefs, we declare ourselves innocent in intention, if not always in action. Challenges by occasional students to our approach to controversial issues shows that we are sometimes perceived as "moving from preaching to meddling," as the old Southern saying goes. A recent seminar on demilitarizing the economy, for example, brought objections from some students that we presented a one-sided, antimilitary point of view. Our students occasionally pull us up short and make us reflect on our own commitments, those of the college of which we are a part, and of the professions within which we work.

While we struggle not to fall into a doctrinaire PC trap on the left, we have no trouble avoiding what Robert Hughes identifies as the other PC ("Patriotic Correctness") snare on the right (Hughes, p.28). The narrow, strident, dogmatic calls by Patrick Buchanan and others for reimposing a supposed earlier consensus in politics and education have little appeal or relevance for us or for our students. We believe that we must help our students and their clients to move toward a broader global patriotism that unites, rather than divides, the people of the world.

With Frederick Crews, we reject the "'transfusion' model of education, whereby the stored-up wisdom of the classics is considered a kind of plasma that will drip beneficially into our veins if we only stay sufficiently passive in its presence." We share his vision of learning as "keen debate, not reverence for great books; historical consciousness and self-reflection, not supposedly timeless values; and continual expansion of our national canon to match a necessarily unsettled sense of who 'we' are and what we ultimately care about" (quoted in Hughes, p. 109).

So our vision of education is not that of Bennett, Bloom, d'Souza and other conservatives. It is, rather, the broader, more humane, more liberal vision of people like Carol Gilligan, John Dewey, Nel Noddings, Robert Coles, Jerome Bruner, Michael Harrington, Robert Bellah, James Banks, and James Comer. Our vision is of a society and of institutions that celebrate diversity, promote equity, acknowledge the contributions of all groups, and broaden conceptions of human growth and development. Education is inevitably political; any educational decision explicitly or implicitly promotes a political agenda, and ours can be no different. We have chosen in our small way, to help our students become part of Dewey's "growing edge of culture."

These issues and commitments will become clearer, we hope, in the chapters that follow. We will describe and interpret our own work in professional education, but we think that our setting and our experiences are typical enough so that others can find in our experiences ideas, support, encouragement, and perhaps even some measure of inspiration. We can resist the calls of those who would drag us back to a more elitist and less equal world; we can, instead, move humanely and realistically toward a liberal and professional education worthy of our heritage.

A Description of the Core Program

This book grew out of the experiences of a graduate faculty working to develop and implement a core program. This is a multidisciplinary liberal arts curriculum that challenges adult students and practicing professionals to confront and engage with issues and concerns of their specialties from individual, professional, and societal perspectives.

Our graduate programs require students to design and complete a selection of core courses and critical issues seminars. The seminars are organized around annual themes that address current sociocultural issues faced by professionals in the broader community. Students, practitioners, community members, and international, national, and regional experts spend one to two days exploring issues through presentations, exercises, small-group discussions, and faculty-guided projects. These seminars confront current questions from multiple perspectives and act as learning laboratories for participants. Seminar themes have included: Multicultural Perspectives on the Re-making of America; Global and Cultural Diversity; Societies and Cultures in Transformation; Advocating for Children; Giving Voice to Children's Needs; and Cross-Cultural Perspectives on Peace.

Within these themes, seminars have addressed such specific topics as Reassessing American Capitalism, Racism in America, American Attitudes Toward Immigration, Mutual Aid and Self-Help, Living and Working in Small Communities, Ethical Dilemmas of the

Modern Professional, Caring as a Moral Dimension of the Professions, Comparable Worth as A Gender Issue in the Workplace, The Culture of the Deaf, Writing for Critical Inquiry in the Professions, and Balancing Work and Family Life.

Courses and seminars are team taught and interdisciplinary, drawing heavily on the humanities, arts, and social sciences, and emphasizing ethical, gender, cultural, and international perspectives. One central course, offered every term, is Adult Development and Organizational Life, which creates a context for examining intersecting issues of personal and professional life. Participants explore ideas about adult and organizational development by considering the interplay of cultural mores and the norms of their families, peers, and workplaces. This involves an examination of individual choices and commitments in the context of organizational life.

Faculty also develop innovative and experimental courses that integrate their own interests and expertise with the perceived needs of graduate students. Examples of such courses are Cross-cultural Perspectives on the Family; Cross-national Perspectives on Organizational Culture; Ecological Knowledge for Environmental Problem-solving; Gender and Education; Leadership and Collaboration; The Life-span—An Interdisciplinary Approach; Narrative and Voice: Themes of Gender and Culture; Professional Authority in Organizations—An International Perspective; Professional Ethics and Organizational Authority; Racism and the Law; Ways of Seeing, Ways of Knowing; and Women at Midlife.

The Organization of this Book

Three themes recur throughout this volume: first, that new and experienced professionals should confront issues of their specialties from individual, occupational, and social perspectives within interdisciplinary contexts; second, that students and faculty together must question traditional sources of knowledge so that question-posing, as well as answer-seeking, becomes part of our practice; and third, that there are unanticipated issues of faculty development and organizational culture that emerge during the implementation of programs like ours.

The nature of ethical and social issues depends on the history of the particular context and the ability of professionals to see anew—to be able to define the issue itself. This book explains how teachers and students in one program grapple with questions and dilemmas familiar to most members of higher education in western societies. The contributors offer analyses of the concerns that drove their thinking and practice as they developed a core curriculum in a professional development program. They provide descriptions of their experiences in designing educational activities that foster critical and self-reflective inquiry. The authors discuss the ways in which curriculum and pedagogy can expand ways of knowing, the structure of knowledge, and the practice of teaching and learning for professionals. Each author has participated as a teacher and learner in the graduate core program.

Our authors are generous in integrating student writing into their chapters. We take pride in the voices of our students, whose needs and interests are at the heart of the program. In several chapters their words and ideas exemplify the pivotal role that student thinking can have in professional education.

We have organized the book in three sections based on the contributors' approach to our central concerns: ethical and social issues in professional education. In Part I, "Challenges to Professional Education," Douglas Morgan and Celeste Brody explore the theoretical and practical concerns of faculty who are redefining their work as an expression of a liberal arts perspective for professional education. The authors examine the tensions between professionals' interest in self and career and their larger duty to serve the public and their communities. They invite the reader to consider the value of dialogue about questions of meaning and purpose that are at the very heart of a liberally educated professional.

Part II, "Thematic Responses to Ethical and Social Issues in Professional Education," includes chapters by Celeste Brody and Carol Witherell (with Ken Donald and Ruth Lundblad), Robert Klein, Joanne E. Cooper, Terrence Whaley, Zaher Wahab, Charles Ault, and Jack Corbett. Each of these authors examines possibilities for classroom dialogue and curriculum construction in professional education. These chapters include the voices of both teachers and students as they work with particular themes from various professional areas. They demonstrate how faculty in a graduate school, from different disciplines and orientations, can implement the goals of a professional liberal arts program.

Part III, "Reflections on a Graduate Core Program," examines what happens when a professional school faculty develops an issue-oriented curriculum. The writers give particular attention to the organizational considerations involved in creating interdisciplinary programs and suggest that the ideas we ask students to grapple with in relation to their own organizations apply equally to the assessment of our own faculty interaction. Writers reflect on their own teaching, learning, and administering in a liberal arts core program. Contributors are Mary Henning-Stout, James Wallace, Gordon Lindbloom, and Carolyn Bullard. Ken Kempner concludes with an outside observer's perspective on the applicability of this experience to other higher education organizations, and he challenges other institutions to examine themselves in similar ways.

John Dewey defined education as "that reconstruction or reorganization of experience which adds to the meaning of experience and which increases the ability to direct the course of subsequent experience" (Dewey, 1916, p. 76). As Lawrence Cremin wrote in 1989, Dewey "lamented the conflict and confusion that characterized the world of learning, but he sought solutions not in what he saw as a retreat into traditionalism but rather in a radical reconstruction of liberal education that would unite it with vocational and professional education and render it burningly relevant to the flux of the present" (Cremin, 1989, p. 8). We hope that this book will help us and our readers to productively direct our future endeavors as we assist our students to integrate and enrich their professional lives. The ethical challenge facing those of us who educate professionals is to create organizational contexts that encourage us to reframe the questions we ask and answer with our students. Writing and editing this book has helped the editors and authors to add meaning to their own educational experiences. We invite our readers to join us in this important dialogue as we all work to make professional education more meaningful and more transformative.

For more information about the Lewis & Clark College graduate core program, contact: Coordinator, Graduate Core Program, Campus Box 93, Lewis & Clark College, Portland, Oregon, 97219. Phone: 503-768-7701; Fax: 503-768-7715.

Part I

Challenges to Professional Education

This section explores how instructors, as they face contemporary demands on professional life, can redefine and apply the liberal arts to their teaching. The authors reflect the tensions that exist between the traditional expectations of higher education and the ethical demands of professional practice. Amidst daunting social, educational, and political challenges, instructors in professional programs must acknowledge the limits of merely technical approaches to problem solving. We must reexamine our organizational lives, the values inherent in our programs, and our commitments to one another. Students and faculty alike find themselves in conflict-filled situations that require choices among competing values. The authors in this section examine the idea that a core curriculum can help professionals resolve the competing demands of the self, the broader expectations of their work, and the greater needs of the public. Their arguments set the stage for realizing structural and curricular responses to these challenges. The authors in this book share a common commitment to and experience with these pedagogical principles.

In chapter 1, "The Role of Liberal Arts in Professional Education," Douglas Morgan situates the current debate about professional education in a historical context and confronts professionals with questions that reflect the moral tensions of professional practice: "How should I live my life? Are the requirements of being an effective professional consistent with personal virtue, organizational loyalty, and good citizenship?" He discusses what a liberal education can mean within the context of our contemporary democratic order, and he supports the continuation of the liberal arts into professional training as a means of strengthening both liberal and professional education.

Celeste Brody, in chapter 2, "Interdisciplinary Studies and the Possibilities of Community," introduces as a case study Lewis & Clark's graduate core program, in which faculty develop interdisciplinary insights through co-teaching. This program brings a liberal arts perspective to the challenges of professional life. She argues that

11

higher education has a responsibility to create structures committed
to community life in which teaching and learning become praxis both
for faculty members and for present and future professionals.

In chapter 3, "Collaborative Learning: Fostering Dialogue Across
the Professions," Celeste Brody argues for a pedagogy of collaboration
that creates dialogue among different professions around the common
conflicts and tensions of professional life. She discusses the particular
character of adult learners and applies principles of social
constructivism to a classroom discourse that challenges traditional
assumptions about professional knowledge. The resulting pedagogy
rises out of a commitment to create processes and structures that
reflect our values about professional change and about participating
in the transformation of the social order.

1

The Role of Liberal Arts in Professional Education[1]

DOUGLAS F. MORGAN

I hold every man a debtor to his profession; from [which] as men of course do seek to receive countenance and profit, so ought they of duty to endeavor themselves by way of amends to be a help and ornament....

——Sir Francis Bacon
Maxims of the Laws (1630)

In some ways the professions have come a long way since the days of Sir Francis Bacon when they were viewed as a mere "help and ornament." Today professionals serve as vanguards of almost all that we do. In law, medicine, business, government, mental health, and education, professionals are treated by peers and clients alike as the keepers and gatekeepers of the skills and knowledge necessary to function effectively in our emerging postindustrial era. So strong is their hold on our personal destinies and so powerful is their influence over our collective well-being that a countermovement has been spawned by consumers and clients who are demanding drastic remedies to correct the abuses of creeping cartels parading under the guise of various professional labels. Medicine, law, education, and most of the other major professions have witnessed the rise of organized and angry clients demanding the demystification of practice and greater participation with professionals in the assessment of their needs. These developments both reflect and contribute to the erosion of the legitimacy of professional practice.

The growing crisis of professional legitimacy arises in part from the inability of practitioners successfully to reconcile what Sir Francis Bacon described as the "countenance and profit" of the practitioner with the duty to provide "help and ornament" to the inquiring client. But professional legitimacy is also undermined by two other developments: the emergence of large complex organizations as the primary instruments of professional practice and a prevailing public philosophy of ethical individualism. Both of these modern developments place professionals in the unenviable position of having to reconcile their own personal sense of meaning with the competing claims of clients, the organizations for whom they work, and the professional associations that control their right to practice.

These kinds of moral tensions are ideal grist for the liberal arts mill. They, in fact, are contemporary versions of the age-old questions at the heart of liberal education: How should I live my life? To what extent are the requirements of being a good professional consistent with the goals of good citizenship, personal virtue, and organizational loyalty? In this paper I will argue that the recovery of a liberal arts perspective that confronts aspiring professionals with such questions is essential for successfully coping with the moral tensions of professional practice. I will also advance the more controversial proposition that the incorporation of some attention to career preparation into the liberal arts is necessary to make a liberal education meaningful. I will begin in Part I with a discussion of what a liberal education can mean within the context of our contemporary liberal democratic order. In Part II, I will review the major signs of discontent with both professional practice and professional education and argue that the recovery of a liberal arts perspective can help to address these sources of discontent. Finally, in Part III, I will argue that the recovery of the liberal arts perspective in the training of professionals can also be used to strengthen the ends of liberal education.

Part I: What Liberal Education Can Mean in the Twentieth Century

According to the oldest understanding originating first with the Greek polis and continuing through the middle ages, liberal education was the cultivation of the mind in accordance with the nature of the mind (Strauss, 1959, pp. 3-5; 1968, pp. 78-94). It was the process of liberating the mind from prejudice, parochialism, and unreflective opinions. Such liberation, however, required an uncommon amount of leisure and equipment not in possession of the many. Even among the few capable of liberal education, a distinction was drawn between those who accepted on trust certain of the most weighty things and those who treated these weighty things as themes of investigation and questioning. The former were the artisans, professionals, and those who accepted the responsibilities of governing. The latter were the philosophers who frequently endangered and undermined the foundations of the professions and of public life.

There was, then, a fundamental disproportion between liberal education, on the one hand, and professional and public service preparation, on the other. Those involved in professional and political activities followed the sound political rule of letting sleeping dogs lie. Philosophers stood and fell by their disregard of this rule. Nevertheless, both groups lived side by side, grateful (at their best) for what the other provided. From the caretakers of practical affairs, philosophers obtained a protected space in which to undertake their questioning and investigating. In turn, these caretakers needed the philosophers to clarify the ends they pursued, in particular, to help clarify and distinguish the pursuit of decent ends from indecent ends. The clear distinction between ends that are decent and those that are not is, in a way, presupposed by those engaged in practical affairs. For example, a doctor does not need to question whether life is preferable to death. A political leader in the United States need not question whether liberty is preferable to slavery. The philosophical task seeks to clarify what is presupposed. In the light of professional and political practice, then, liberal education aimed at fostering civic and professional responsibility. In the light of philosophy, however, liberal education was a preparation for living the life of the mind, for becoming a philosopher.

This traditional understanding of liberal education underwent a far-reaching transformation long before the demands for more "relevance" and career preparation in higher education. Three factors contributing to this transformation deserve special recognition (Strauss, 1968, pp. 9-55). First, the distinction between the philosophers and nonphilosophers has disappeared as human beings (including the philosophers themselves) no longer believe in the possibility and/or value of disinterested contemplation of the eternal. Instead, we have lowered our sights to seek longer, healthier, and more abundant life. Education, including liberal education, has now become a means to achieve this very worldly end. Second, the traditional distinction between the few and the many has been dissolved by the rise of our modern liberal democratic belief that all are equally capable of governing and leading a fully autonomous life. In the light of this belief liberal education loses most of its special role in the preparation for civic and professional responsibility. Finally, modern science and enlightenment have combined to overcome any sense of limits as to what is within our power. We are our own makers, and education, at its best, need only transform unenlightened to enlightened self-interest in order to ensure that our scientific creations are used decently and humanely.

In the face of these three major developments, liberal education no longer dares assert its traditional claims of teaching that knowledge is choice-worthy for its own sake, that our words and deeds must be measured against a standard that transcends the value of long and comfortable life, and that political and professional rule are arts best reserved for those trained to decent and selfless judgment. If the reaction to two recent defenses of liberal education is any indication (Bloom, 1987; Hirsch, 1987) it is doubtful that the "old view" can serve as the legitimate template for educating professionals in our postmodern world (Aronowitz, 1988; Urban, 1988).

If the counterelite forces of greater equality of condition, cultural diversity, increased global interdependence, and the instrumentalism of modern science preclude us from looking upon liberal arts simply as a preparation for ruling over others or philosophic understanding, where does this leave us, then, regarding the role of liberal arts in the preparation of professionals? One possibility might be to view liberal education as preparation for civic responsibility. After all, there is a growing disenchantment with our Lockean individualism and the consequent loss of civic mindedness (Bellah et al., 1991). While preparation for civic responsibility might be a viable option for a few undergraduate disciplines, it is likely to be rejected by most institutions as an appropriate educational focus, especially given increasing uncertainties as to the proper bounds of the public realm and the curricular commitment of most colleges to providing students with a smorgasbord sampling of minimally structured choices. The existence of these systemic barriers means that those of us concerned about the role of the liberal arts in professional education must find our solution close to home, in the classroom and in our daily interactions with colleagues. It is to be found in the questions we presuppose and pose to ourselves and our students in selecting and teaching our course materials.

The question most on the minds of our students, whether they be freshman or career professionals returning for some course work to renew professional certificates, is "What *should* I do with my life?" This question, however, can not be addressed without also asking another: What *can* I do with my life? Together, these questions embody the traditional elements of liberal education, namely the need to pay some attention to the cultivation of moral character and one's place within a larger community but without the classical overtones of the distinction between the few and the many. It is a way of recognizing the claim of liberal arts within a context that reflects the forces of modernity sketched out above.[2]

The liberal arts approach I am advocating shifts the debate away from the purposes of liberal education or its content to the questions that guide the educational process itself. This is not to suggest that the purposes and content of a liberal education are not relevant. In fact, they are critical, but they are critical only as a means of initiating an ongoing conversation our students will continue to have the rest of their lives as they seek to answer the question, "How should I live my life? The viability of this understanding of the liberal arts is further reinforced by the lessons learned by our colleagues in developmental psychology. According to their research, students entering college tend to think dichotomously, in terms of moral absolutes without much toleration for ambiguity (Kohlberg, 1981). While Kohlberg's developmental stages have been seriously challenged by feminist critiques (Gilligan, 1982), developmental psychologists on both sides of the gender debate seem to share a similar understanding of the chief goal of liberal education: to cultivate the capacity of individuals to apply abstract thinking to concrete choices so that these choices become integrated into a seamless web of personal meaning. This is what we have come to understand as a healthy autonomous individual (Berthoff, 1981). It is precisely this capacity for integrating policentric patterns of meaning into an integrated whole that the gender debate over the last decade has contributed most to our rethinking of professional education (Gilligan, 1982; Lyons, 1983).

In theory, all human beings are capable of passing from an initial world of passive, simplistic dichotomous thinking, through a stage of potentially incapacitating relativism, to an integrated comprehensive worldview. When individuals fail to achieve this potential, the theory emphasizes defects in the curricular design of the educational institution and inadequate pedagogical techniques of instructors rather than inherent and insurmountable weakness in the students. The secret to successful teaching with this model, then, requires two things. First, students must be taught how to appropriate abstract theories to their personal experience and sensibilities. Second, they must be confronted at appropriate stages with a wide array of intellectually and morally stimulating experiences so that grist can be continually fed into the ever-moving developmental mill.

The lessons of developmental psychology seem to coincide with the lessons of history. Students should be systematically confronted with the question "How should I live my life?" Colleges and teachers cannot succeed in helping students emotionally and intellectually prepare for this quest unless every opportunity is taken to expose the theoretically rich issues that lie buried just beneath the surface of the ordinary, the mundane, and the practical. A recognition of this fact has some important implications for seeing how the liberal arts can be used to enhance professional preparation and vice versa.

Part II: Why the Liberal Arts Perspective is Essential for Professional Education

Those who carry a "professional" label are under growing assault for their continued failure to meet the expectations of their critics. Whether it is the high professions of law and medicine or the aspiring professions of paralegals and nurse practitioners, no one seems happy either with how professionals are being trained or with how they practice. But who are these critics? What are they saying?

Criticisms can be divided into three categories of concern: the character of professional practice, the nature of the knowledge suitable to this practice, and the ends that ought to guide its application. First, there is an *ontological* debate over the nature of the reality of professional practice. For example, can or should professionals be neutral and autonomous agents of their specialized knowledge, or are they inevitably and inextricably a part of a socially constructed reality? In short, to what extent are the professions and individual practitioners instruments and agents of social control and political power? Second, there is an *epistemological* debate that focuses on the nature and adequacy of professional expertise and knowledge. What are the special knowledge claims of professionals? Where and how is this knowledge acquired? How much can be learned from formal classroom training and how much from clinical practice? Finally, there is a *teleological* debate over the proper purposes or ends that ought to be served by practitioners. What fiduciary responsibilities do professionals have to the larger community beyond those of serving individual clients?

The Ontological Debate: What is the Context of Professional Practice?

At the risk of some oversimplification, debate over the context of professional practice turns on whether the creation of a profession is primarily a matter of politics or sociology (Haskell, 1984). Both perspectives agree that the rise and fall of the professions are dependent on, and interactive with, the larger social setting. It is the character of this interaction that is in dispute. The sociological perspective places primary emphasis on those social preconditions that *pull* a set of practices into professional status. According to this view, professions are created to meet the specialized knowledge and skill needs of society. However, if specialized knowledge and skills were sufficient to acquire a professional label, then plumbers, carpenters, and bricklayers would be considered professions rather than crafts. What distinguishes the two, according to the sociological perspective, is the possession of "knowledge to which the professionals are privy by virtue of long study and by initiation and apprenticeship under masters already members of the profession." While plumbers, carpenters, and bricklayers undergo apprenticeship to masters, they do not possess skills that "are supported by a fund of knowledge that has been organized into an internally consistent system, called a body of theory (Greenwood in Nosow and Form, 1962, p. 208).

In summary, the sociological perspective emphasizes three sets of factors that *pull* a practice along the professional status continuum (Etzioni, 1969; Larson, 1977; Haskell, 1984). First, professions arise in response to a social demand for a body of esoteric knowledge and skills. The more esoteric the knowledge and skills and the higher the social demand, the greater the likelihood that a practice can acquire the status of a profession. Second, the knowledge must flow from a body of consistent and integrated theory. Finally, a guild is created to monitor the creation and application of the special fund of esoteric knowledge and skills.

While sociologists emphasize the factors that *pull* a set of practices toward professional status, political scientists emphasize the use of instrumental power that is needed to *push* a set of practices into the status of a profession. According to this view, a practice acquires the status of a profession once the group successfully mobilizes sufficient political power to be delegated the authority to monopolize control over the marketplace. Pushed to its extreme, this view reduces professional associations to just another vested interest group.

The Epistemological Debate: What is the Nature of Professional Knowledge?

Professional knowledge traditionally has been divided into two categories, theoretical and applied, with the former standing on a higher plane than the latter. This paradigm leads to the familiar status hierarchy found in most professional schools, where the applied professions and those engaged in applied research have a lower status than those attending to the higher-order activities of pure thought (Schon, 1983, chapter 2).

Over the last decade this conventional view has undergone serious challenge from critical theorists (Habermas, 1973), humanists (Hummel, 1987), feminists (Gilligan, 1982), and organizational theorists (Lipsky, 1980; Argyris and Schon, 1974) who emphasize at least three forms of tacit knowledge that are inseparable from action but yet stand on a separate, if not equal, footing with theoretical principles. There is, first, the prudential understanding that is acquired by undertaking an activity over a long period of time. The subtlety to nuances and complex interactions among the particulars of materials, people, and setting acquired by master artisans and craftsman through a long period of "hands-on" experience is an example of this kind of tacit knowledge.

A second kind of tacit knowledge, what might be called a "feel for the whole," is also critically important to successful professional practice. This kind of knowledge has been likened to the "transitory knowledge of witnesses to an automobile accident; no one sees it all, but each account contributes to a richer picture" (Schmidt, 1992, p. 78). Those who are considered masters at their profession have a much greater capacity to apprehend the fullness and richness of the whole than do journeymen and apprentices.

Finally, there is passive or critical knowledge that gives skilled practitioners a sense of when things are not quite right, even though their judgment may not be supported by any known theoretical principles and may even be contrary to such principles. It is not unlike understanding a language or appreciating good music even when we cannot read/speak it fluently or write it (Schmidt, p, 79).

What is at stake in this debate over the nature and character of professional knowledge is the viability of two major assumptions that undergird the training of professionals. The first assumption is that we can separate knowledge of causes from knowledge about their effects. This assumption is essential for manipulating and controlling the outcomes that professionals are trained to undertake. The second major assumption we make is that ordinary opinion is inferior to scientific knowledge that has passed the proper empirical tests of verification and validation. Together these assumptions fuel the modern scientific paradigm upon which almost all of our professional training has been constructed. It is precisely these assumptions that are challenged by the various forms of tacit knowledge set forth above. And it is precisely these forms of knowledge that are cultivated by a liberal arts perspective.

The Teleological Debate: What is the Purpose of Professional Practice?

The variability of ends that can be served by professional practice creates a twofold paradox. There is, first, the paradox that arises from being an agent of an independent body of professional expertise and traditions while also serving as an agent of the wishes and desires of individual clients (Baumrin, 1982). There is a second paradox that arises from being a responsible agent of one's profession while also carrying out a larger fiduciary trust on behalf of the public that legitimizes the monopolistic exercise of professional authority (Hastings Center, 1987; Starr, 1982; Sullivan and Bellah, 1987). Both of these paradoxes are framed by a liberal democratic order that is uncompromisingly committed to ethical individualism (MacPherson, 1962; Bellah, et al., 1986).3 This public ethos is the mighty engine that shapes the way in which the two teleological paradoxes of professional practice tend to be resolved on a day-to-day basis. This can be illustrated by examining the approach to the teaching of professional ethics in most graduate programs.

The professional ethics materials I have examined over the years from a variety of institutions and professional schools assume that the most frequent ethical problems faced by practicing professionals arise from the difficulties of using their specialized knowledge on behalf of others. The possession of such knowledge potentially places clients at the practitioner's mercy. This gives rise to a host of conflict-of-interest issues that are at the heart of professional codes of ethics. Most attempts to deal with professional ethics begin and end with a discussion of these problems. When is it appropriate to keep knowledge from the client? When is it appropriate to reveal knowledge about your client to others? Such questions go to the heart of the special relationship of trust that develops between professionals and their clients.

But there is a more public dimension of professional ethics that grows out of a recognition that professionals not only exercise power through their knowledge but through the collective action of their professional associations. When are professional associations taking positions that undermine the autonomy of the practitioner to the detriment of the client? When is the collective power of an association being legitimately used to place restrictions on the autonomy of professional judgment and practice in order to protect the client against unscrupulous and/or incompetent practitioners? Such questions point to the larger fact that an increasing amount of professional practice occurs through the collective activities of complex organizations. These organizations have agendas, standard operating procedures, and policy objectives that frequently create ethical problems for the practicing professional.

The organizational dimensions of professional practice bring us back, full circle, to the larger public purposes of professional life. It is not sufficient for doctors, lawyers, educators, counselors, and administrators to be instructed in their respective codes of professional ethics. Such codes, while a useful starting point, tend to focus on the negative merit of preventing private gain at the expense of individual clients. Such a focus tends to leave our public ethos of ethical individualism largely unchallenged (Cooper, 1991; Rohr, 1989). Once we recognize that professionals exercise a fiduciary public trust, we further enlarge the role that liberal education can play in preparing practitioners for the tension-ridden world they will occupy.

The Role of the Liberal Arts

The systematic incorporation of a liberal arts perspective within a professional education curriculum prepares practitioners to confront the previous set of ontological, epistemological, and teleological issues in the following four ways. First, a liberal arts approach directly confronts students with the problem of _conflicting moral claims_. This is essential if professionals are to successfully juggle the sometimes competing claims inherent in their practice: the demands of large complex organizations, the needs of individual clients, prevailing standards of accepted professional practice, and the needs of a social order largely devoted to a public philosophy of ethical individualism.

A second role played by the liberal arts in the education of professionals is the preparation it provides, not only for living in a world of moral conflict but for living in a world where moral choices may be _ambiguous_ even in the absence of conflict. Whether it is an issue of student tracking for teachers, a choice of diagnostic protocols for counselors, or the selection of an appropriate organizational design model for administrators, the exercise of professional discretion is suffused with moral ambiguity.

A third advantage of a liberal arts perspective is the preparation it provides for making decisions in the face of _uncertainty_. The liberal arts approach develops an appreciation for the multiple, tentative, and emergent nature of our knowledge of the human condition. While some might argue that such an appreciation fosters an incapacity to act, I have found that, instead, it fosters the courage to act in the face of uncertainty. It is precisely this courage that professionals need in order to act in settings where they seldom have all of the facts necessary to dictate a choice (Benjamin, 1990).

A final advantage of the liberal arts perspective is the self-critical capacity it fosters. By this I mean the capacity to step outside one's own views, or the situational urgencies of the moment, or the dominant organizational and peer-group paradigm to critically assess what Donald Schon and others have called "the situation for action" (Argyris and Schon, 1974; Schon, 1983). This capacity to be simultaneously absorbed by the moment while still maintaining a critical perspective is essential for the well-being of both clients and professional practitioners. It is also essential for the well-being of the bureaucratic structures of authority within which we work and the larger social order these structures serve.

To summarize, the systematic incorporation of the liberal arts perspective into the education of professionals prepares them to participate more responsibly in the ontological, epistemological, and teleological debates surrounding their lives by: (1) Enabling them to cope with the conflict, uncertainty, and moral ambiguity inherent in their day-to-day practice; (2) Developing an appreciation for multiple sources of knowledge; and (3) Cultivating a critical capacity constantly to reassess the ends to be served by professional practice.

Part III: How Professional Preparation Can Be Used to Enhance the Goals of Liberal Education

While many are increasingly acknowledging the important contributions the liberal arts can make to professional education, we do not so easily acknowledge the role of professional education in helping the liberal arts achieve its objectives. In fact, there is growing doubt in most liberal arts institutions about the appropriateness of their role in undertaking professional preparation. This doubt frequently grows out of three sets of assumptions.

First, most assume that the liberal arts involves the acquisition of generic writing and computational skills and broadening one's perspective through exposure to a traditional and classic body of subject matter in the *basic* disciplines. Second, most believe that professional and career preparation narrows rather than broadens a student's perspective. Finally, in the face of economic pressures to "do more with less" many traditional liberal arts institutions assume that they must "get back to basics," "narrow their market niche," or "improve quality." Frequently, these are code phrases to justify eliminating applied arts programs. I will give three reasons why this may well be a serious educational mistake. I will argue that liberal arts faculty members experienced in career preparation issues can use professional education to be a "help and ornament" to the liberal arts.

Learning How to Confront the Tensions
Between Theory and Practice

Liberal arts institutions throughout the nation have an obligation to keep alive questions central to a liberal arts education. What is and/or ought to be the appropriate relationship between theory and practice? How do the claims of the world of work and a life of action bear upon the life of the mind and a cultivation of the intellectual virtues? Are the two worlds ultimately reconcilable, and if so, upon what grounds? These questions do not necessarily require liberal arts academics to become practitioners, but they do require that scholars/ teachers actively and routinely confront such questions in their professional work. We owe it to our students and require it for our own self-renewal.

There is an unhealthy tendency in most institutions—liberal arts or otherwise—for the *vita activa* (Arendt, 1959) and the world of *homo faber* to become balkanized, both institutionally and intellectually, from the ongoing commitment to the life of the mind. This frequently results in second-class citizenship for the applied arts and professional graduate programs while depriving the liberal arts faculty of a necessary stimulus constantly to rethink the appropriate relationship between theory and practice in a liberal arts education. But this need not occur. The curriculum can be structured to force each of the universes of discourse to confront the claims of the other on a routine basis. This includes the appropriate use of postgraduate professional education as a useful vehicle for stimulating a constant reconsideration of questions of first principle with respect to a liberal arts education. If nothing else, professional studies serve to remind us of our responsibilities as teachers of not only preparing students to *think about* the world but the difficulties of *living* and *working* in a world we did not create and probably cannot fundamentally remake. It is the old question of getting students to consider what it means to live a life that is personally self-fulfilling and improves one's soul (the object of a liberal education) versus what it means to live a fully active life of good works (the object of career and professional education).

Whether one accepts *this* formulation of the distinction or not, the appropriate relationship between theory and practice is a necessary question to be asked by all those in a liberal arts college, a question that is also central to the preparation of practicing professionals.

Learning to Confront the Tensions within the World of Work

One of the most frequently heard questions during recent years is whether it is possible to live a fully integrated and satisfying life in the world of work. There is good reason to wonder about this. The functional differentiation and specialization of the world in which we work calls for managerial and professional skills of control and coordination. We are all seemingly under constant pressure to resist being treated as mere functionaries. But this pressure and the propensity and opportunity to resist varies with the context. Work is not a whole cloth (Morgan, 1987). The rhythmic and routinized labor of the Trappist Monk is not the same as the labor of those on the automobile assembly line. In addition, we know from our own experience that assembly line labor is distinguishable from bureaucratic labor informed by visions of career ladders. The distinctions are reflected in the kinds of friends one makes, how one spends one's leisure, and one's general aspirations for self and family. Professionals live in yet another world of work that is governed by its own *raison d'être*. For example, professionals tend to emphasize discretion and moral autonomy over routine and technique.

These distinctions can be usefully appropriated to serve the ends of liberal education. For example, do these differences add up to distinctions of significance? Are some forms of work more fully consistent with living the fully human life than others? What makes the routine and labor of the Trappist Monk more attractive for some than the routine and labor of the assembly-line worker? Is the discretionary autonomy we tend to associate with professionals preferable to the discretionless automatism we tend to wrongly associate with the career bureaucrat? While all of these questions are raised in every liberal arts college worth its salt, unless the questions arise out of and are informed by life experience, they tend to remain at the level of idle school talk. Successful education requires that we take students beyond idle school talk and engage their passions and sensibilities. In doing so, we can take advantage of their natural and preexisting concern for acquiring practical salable skills and use it to foster liberal education. But we cannot do this unless we are prepared to engage students on their own terms, and this means getting down in the work-pit world that many of them inhabit.

Learning How to Confront the Tension Between a Concern for Self and a Larger Duty to Serve the Public

Most liberal arts institutions are concerned about how to prepare students intellectually, morally, and practically to sacrifice narrow self-interests to serve a larger community of interests. While some institutions give more explicit attention to this goal than others, all take seriously the need to enlarge the moral vision and duty of its graduates. Even if this is not an explicit part of an institution's mission, it can hardly be avoided if we are to take liberal education seriously. The question "How should I live?" cannot be answered without consideration of its social implications—that is to say, without asking "How should *we* live?" Short of opting for a hermit's life, we all live in some sort of community and probably in a great number of overlapping communities. Reflection on how (or whether) our living together can realize the good life or justice is an unavoidable component of a liberal education. Professional preparation helps to achieve this goal in at least the following ways.

First, professional education forces students to take seriously community standards of judgment. The community standards of the professional, of course, are not sufficient, but as a starting point they force students to distinguish mere personal choice from a larger, if not more objective, standard. By seeing how their personal preferences do not always coincide with professional judgment, students are prepared to take the larger public interest more seriously. In short, by helping students see the connection between their professional responsibility and their individual well-being, we better prepare them to exercise civic responsibility by seeing the difference between being a good citizen and being a good person. This difference is a necessary part of a liberal arts education.

Second, by giving serious attention to the professional and career interests of our students, we begin with their convictions, with the stock of their received opinions and habits. To do otherwise would empty their minds before understanding had time to mature, lead them to question the very basis of all morality, and leave them on a sea of nihilism and/or confusion that would incapacitate them from acting and judging as citizens. By capitalizing on their interest in professional education, we can moderate the dangers of liberal education, avoiding the possibility of leaving our students more disoriented, less decent, and less capable of common sense than we found them. In short, if we take professional preparation seriously, our students will all be in a better position to take from their liberal arts education what each is capable of receiving.

Conclusion

Professional education and the liberal arts need one another to successfully address the central educational question they share in common: "How should I live?" The failure to recover the common ground upon which both can make use of one another is especially urgent, given two major social forces that are driving an ever-widening wedge between the two universes of discourse. Not only are liberal arts institutions trimming their sails away from applied programs and disciplines, but this move is occurring at the very time that an increasing number of students are making market choices among expensive educational alternatives with an eye to "relevance" and to advancing their own career aspirations.

Without ongoing dialogue between the two universes of discourse we run the danger of developing educational institutions that are either islands of esoteric irrelevance or are devoted exclusively to mundane trivia. We must recognize that both the liberal arts and professional education have a mutually reinforcing role to play in helping our students seriously consider what it means to live a fully human life. Whether this life is informed by the vision of the philosopher devoted to the contemplative pursuit of truth, the artisan dedicated to the creative task of fabrication, the laborer committed to producing basic human necessities, or the professional presuming to know the needs of strangers (Ignatieff, 1984), all will be well served by the kind of critical self-examination we should expect of *both* professional and liberal education.

Notes

1. An earlier version of this manuscript served as a discussion paper to justify the creation of Lewis & Clark's graduate school of professional studies and a set of common liberal arts core requirements for all students in the several professional programs.

2. By uncompromising I do not mean that we do not recognize and embrace the need for correctives to the excesses of ethical individualism. Our collective indignation at the recent scandals on Wall Street, in the corporate boardrooms and in high and low offices of public trust confirms our belief in a sense of enforceable limits to the pursuit of private gain. But this indignation is informed and guided by a desire to temper excess, not to replace our commitment to ethical individualism with a set of common communitarian principles.

3. I recognize that the instrumental premise of my argument undermines the view that the disciplines, traditional bodies of knowledge, and even education itself is an end in itself, worthy of being pursued and preserved for its own sake. While I personally hold to this view and hopefully model it in my work, I think it is possible, even necessary, to approach learning and the acquisition of understanding as an end in itself without prematurely prejudicing other more instrumental views that may be the very "soul-stuff" that makes our students who they are. I believe good pedagogy, our liberal democratic principles, and equanimity all require temperance in riding our knowledge horses in the academic arena.

2

Interdisciplinary Studies and the Possibilities of Community

CELESTE M. BRODY

Professional education is at a unique juncture in its collective histories. As never before, we are seeking those outside our fields and wondering together about our common purposes. This may be the result of our recognition that we have been cast in the perennial predicament that touches everyone in higher education. As both scholars and practitioners we make quiet compromises among ourselves to reconcile the competing values of scholarship, teaching and practice. Our chief compromise has been the unharnessed growth of specialization in our professions that ensures our continued *raison d'être* in the face of burgeoning knowledge and technical advancements. We have felt the uneasy sway of the peculiar patterns of inquiry and modes of knowing that mark our disciplines and our professions, as Clifford Geertz describes them: patterns "that start at the center of things and then move toward the edges" (quoted in Gabelnick, et al., 1990, p. 7). This means that we live with the same dilemmas that our students face in their careers. In higher education we face the limits and legacy of our cultural values that have created messy conflicts and dilemmas in our own organizations. In his essay, "Managing dilemmas by building professional communities," Larry Cuban attributes the heart of these dilemmas to "the failure of the quiet accommodations that we have fashioned over the last century. In professional education we are still adrift between 'practicality and prestige....' The one obvious outcome has been a stunted sense of community among educators engaged in preparing professionals at all levels" (1992, p. 8).

I will examine the idea that community is the foundation for a successful reexamination of our work in our professional schools, discussing two organizational structures that reflect a commitment to that community—interdisciplinary studies, which bring different professions together and draw from the liberal arts, and co-teaching. I will cite our own case at Lewis & Clark College, which suggests that these structures allow faculty to explore their work as a form of praxis. This involves programmatic goals that sustain a commitment to the creation and recreation of a community bent on fostering multiple forms of inquiry, ways of knowing, and knowledge creation between participants—students and teachers alike (Belenky et al., 1986; Grumet, 1987; Martin, 1985).

Communities as Contexts:
Nurture Faculty and Educate Future Professionals

Building promising communities begins with the acknowledgment of our failure to resolve or even frame the questions for debate around the profound ethical and social dilemmas facing all of us. It starts with the desire to find meaning and wisdom in the practice of teaching, which enlarges the conversations between professionals who work in the service of others. There is a scarcity of conversations among scholars and practitioners about these teaching commonalties—the uncertainties, the ambiguities, and moral dilemmas of teaching, as well as the developmental and organizational challenges we hold in common. Our language, research orientations, individual and collective histories have forged deep habits of both heart and mind within the requirements of our particular fields, which have made it difficult to seek others in our own organizations to address the common moral purpose we share: the impulse to serve others. The questions we must address together through our professional education programs are: How can we create communities within our universities that bridge the gaps between our professional fields? Can we develop shared understandings of teaching—goals, objectives, and pedagogy—and engage in sustained conversations about our common ethical dilemmas, our shared humanity and life-course challenges, and our organizational life?

A Commitment to Community

I will explore the connections between the commitment to create community and the organizational structures and pedagogy that support this, but I will suggest at this point that community is both the striving toward and the result of a group of people committed to a common purpose. The paradox of community is that it involves a consciousness about differences between individuals and groups while working for that common purpose to impart understanding and appreciation of those differences. When we are able to recognize it through shared meanings, it becomes the context for each participant's continual striving for autonomy and inclusion, for independence and connection. Community is the acknowledgment on the part of all involved that they are pursuing a vision that is individually defined but collectively embraced. It is, therefore, not so much of an achievement as a course of action that provides the context for developing mutual regard and shared understandings, as well as a commitment to certain concepts and ideas against which we can stretch and evaluate our growth. Professional schools achieve community when they strive to create a profound sense of belonging to a profession through rich and vibrant connections among members based on commonalties in the moral imperatives of their work, the ideals of service and learning, as well as the honest respect for the power of multiple perspectives that come from embracing and understanding differences. And, as intellectual communities, professional schools should foster interactive and collaborative approaches to learning; encourage interdisciplinary connections and understandings; provide a forum for risk-taking, experimentation, and active manipulation of structures and models; and provide a social setting that promotes and values both individual achievement and group cooperation (Lieberman, 1992; Marshall 1992, p. 6).

We do not come to a sense of community in our organizations and our professional networks without both the conceptual commitment to it and the actual experience of it. It is only within consciously constructed choices to build communities that we will be able to surmount our "unbridled passion for specialization and higher prestige" (Cuban, 1992, p. 9). The paradox is that there are no formulas for creating and maintaining these sustained conversations and no assurances that even when we do realize a sense of community we will also be able to achieve our goals. For communities must be continually tended and nurtured, and there is too often a price extracted in terms of prestige and other rewards for those who make it their work to provide the relational glue within organizations (Noddings, 1984).

The Case for a Professional, Interdisciplinary Core Curriculum

In the case of the newly formed graduate school of professional studies at Lewis & Clark College, the faculty would not have independently chosen to face these issues. (See Introduction for a more complete discussion of the Graduate School's history.) It is often organizational exigencies that force us to change, and like any other group of professors in higher education we had, and still have, our skeptics and our resisters to change. When we began by asking ourselves, "What do we all have in common about our fields of endeavor?" our response as well as the process of creating the dialogue began to forge a sense of community. But no one experiences any shared moment the same way; even though our knowledge is socially constructed, it is also personally meaning-driven. Some of us still settle for loose affiliations in which the notion and the experience of community is expediency in the face of institutional demands. Those who have worked in such areas as the social construction of knowledge, collaborative learning, writing and critical thinking, feminist pedagogy, and cognitive and intellectual development find that their work supports and resonates with the idea of community, because these all stand on the common ground of learning *as* development, the value of building connections and the power of shared inquiry (Gabelnick et al., 1992, p. 17). Academicians in professional education still struggle with the meaning and the application of this concept throughout all their relationships and activities. The challenge remains whether any orientation—positivist or transformative—will find ways to enfold the other within common ground that holds those differences as a source of strength and continual renewal. And it is important to argue that this diversity may actually teach all of us about unexamined possibilities and potential of community, because how we come to embrace difference in the face of criticism is still a critical developmental challenge for us throughout adult life. It is certainly the collective challenge within our organizations.

To imagine that professors in different professional fields could work together in a professional program, studying, creating, and considering commonalties in the dilemmas of their practice was not entirely new in the 1980s. It was occurring elsewhere. But we imagined that teachers and students from across disciplines could come together to engage in serious discussions and conduct jointly designed courses and projects. We imagined that we could consciously and actively draw from the liberal arts and humanities to understand and reflect upon our persistent human developmental challenges and our common ethical dilemmas, and we could enjoy team teaching our students through collaborative approaches to inquiry. We imagined that these collaborative teaching experiences would yield creative new ways of teaching. Most important, we imagined that whatever programmatic response we created to the question of what held us together, the faculty, our students, and the larger community would be beneficiaries.

Program Goals Support Community

I will examine the beliefs and programmatic goals that provide the impetus toward community in this liberal arts interdisciplinary program. Others who consider similar questions may arrive at different conclusions, if not comparable structures and program configurations. These goals continue to be curricular and pedagogical challenges because a commitment to such goals often overlooks the most important element: time for faculty to learn to adapt to the new practices in such a way that the values are expressed through a commitment to faculty renewal.

Interdisciplinary programs need to go through a process of developing a set of beliefs that bind them together. In our case the seemingly disparate graduate programs in counseling psychology, educational administration, special education for the hearing impaired, public administration, and teacher education, after two years of intense discussion, agreed on the following:

- A truly professional education combines the best of the liberal arts traditions with the most advanced theoretical and practical technologies.
- Our mission is to educate leaders not simply train specialists or technocrats.
- A true teacher, counselor, or administrator in the world is sensitive to the pressing issues of the world: for example, the power and purpose of high technology, the emerging importance of gender issues that influence all areas of society, and the need to apply a diverse cultural and international perspective to one's professional and personal life.

Most importantly, we believe that community has *value* in organizational life. For students, to participate in a community in their professional education gives them a model for their work life. Professionals are better community members for having struggled with the issues about how to create community while they are in the experience of trying to live it. We think there are positive outcomes for students relating to effective organizations and organizational citizenship that require professional education to constitute organizational structures that force the issues regarding community life.

Beliefs shape program goals; however, goals do not emerge easily out of initial discussions. They must evolve over time and may crystallize only through careful reflection on the mission of the larger institution and the practice of teaching this particular body of adult students within the resources and philosophies of this faculty. Thus the following program goals evolved from our institutional mission and our own commitments as seasoned teachers. They apply equally to faculty development and student learning, as well as to the value of community in organizational life:

1. Enhance interdisciplinary study at the graduate level.
2. Foster reflective inquiry and dialogue across the professions.
3. Enhance awareness of developmental themes in the human life cycle as they connect with personal and professional decision-making.
4. Explore the practical and ethical dilemmas of professional life and organizational cultures.
5. Explore the connections between thinking, writing, and speaking as modes of inquiry and creative expression.
6. Enhance intercultural and international understanding.
7. Address issues of equity in the realms of social class, physical limitations, gender, race, and social justice as they relate to professional practice and leadership.

Most of the chapters in this book are devoted to discussions of how these goals give shape to both curriculum and pedagogy and the ethical and social issues that they raise. I will limit my discussion to two of the goals: enhancing interdisciplinary study at the graduate level and fostering reflective inquiry and dialogue across the professions. These two goals capture most clearly the inherent tensions between professional knowledge and process and between outcomes attentive to student and faculty development. These goals drive the pedagogy for fostering community through the structural arrangements of interdisciplinary studies and co-teaching.

Enhancing Interdisciplinary Study
Across the Professions

Once a faculty realizes that there is a common ideal and commitment that binds professionals together (in our case, that we are all working as public service professionals), then discussions follow the question, "What are the issues we face in common?" Our faculty continues to return to these central questions: What is the purpose of my work? Is it possible to sustain a set of fully human values as a practicing professional? As a member of a public organization, how do I deal with dilemmas involving conflicting values and ambiguous goals? How do I survive in a large, complex, bureaucratic organization where my behavior is circumscribed by official policies and practices? We acknowledged that we share the same dilemmas as our students and future colleagues: concern with life course issues as they affect ability to maintain proper balance between personal and professional demands and concern with the nature of modern organizations as they influence ability to remain effective in work or to remain in work at all.

To provide the individual with a foundation for answering these questions, it becomes clear that a broader epistemology is needed than can be offered by one field of study. We consciously draw from the humanities and the liberal arts disciplines, such as literature, biography, film, history, and anthropology and the natural sciences in order to illuminate questions regarding human development and ethical dilemmas confronting the individual in personal, professional, and community life. At the same time, we engage in cross-disciplinary inquiry into professional life—ethics, gender, intercultural and international understanding, and human development—using research and scholarship from education, psychology, sociology, and other social sciences. Pedagogically, it means bringing students and faculty from different programs to address common moral, ethical, intellectual, and personal concerns facing us regardless of our fields. We seek sensitivity to how multiple perspectives emerge from different life, cultural, and disciplinary backgrounds and gender experiences and how we can develop a language, experience, and a regard that will forge further problem solving across disciplines. Within a classroom environment the tensions that differences promote can be a creative source of reflection upon both overt and implicit values that participants bring to their professions.

These beliefs remain as goals because they are difficult to realize. They become pedagogical challenges for teachers who have had few models of their own and are accustomed to traditional didactic methods of teaching. Drawing faculty to co-teach from different disciplines is often a scheduling impossibility. And, finding and using literature, film, ethnographies, and biographies can be very difficult for some faculty in considering, for example, themes of organizational culture. We ask faculty and students to rediscover and revisit their earlier, liberal arts education and to use genres that may have been discarded or forgotten, as well as pedagogies that may be yet beyond their comprehension or comfort.

For example, faculty who teach in the graduate core program have evolved approaches to exploring the theme, Individual Learning Histories: Ways of Knowing, Voice and Empowerment. Faculty and students seek to answer such questions as: How do culture, gender, and life histories affect the way we construct meaning and articulate values regarding self, knowledge, power, and possibilities? Are there different values regarding ways of knowing derived from different cultures? (See Henning-Stout, chapter 11, for a fuller discussion of this topic.)

Examining organizational life and culture through interdisciplinary study has been somewhat problematic for faculty. Robert Coles has written about his successes in using great novels and literature to uncover fundamental ethical dilemmas between individuals and communities and between leaders and their organizations. His *Call of Stories* illuminates the power of narrative in realizing the fundamental character of practice in the helping professions (1989). But frequently our faculty are tentative about and resistant to approaching questions about leadership, professional development, and organizational life through literature, biography, or drama, perhaps because material from the liberal arts and humanities is unfamiliar or because they do not have instructional strategies that raise questions rather than present answers. It may also be the result of our inability to consider these themes as questions for our own lives within our organizations and of a reticence faculty have for self-disclosure through sharing our own personal stories.

When considering tensions between individuals and organizations, students invariably question whether conflict is an inevitable part of community and organizational life. How have tensions between individuals and communities shaped individual development and organizational change? How are values shaped by these tensions? How do individuals deal with the stress produced in organizations and environments? What alternatives are there for handling conflicts and dilemmas? How does change occur? *Habits of the Heart: Individualism and Commitment in American Life* (Bellah, et al., 1985) is an obvious choice for reflecting on these questions. Sophocles' *Antigone* questions the requirements of individual moral responsibility in the face of a larger context or government, and Marc Reisman's *Cadillac Desert* offers a compelling narrative about the limits of bureaucratic decision-making and the failures of individual responsibility (1986). (See Lindbloom, chapter 13, for more discussion on this topic.)

Teaching in an Interdisciplinary Program

Faculty must be equal beneficiaries in an interdisciplinary program in order for the program to be successful. When we began discussions about those beliefs that we held in common across professional programs, a few faculty wondered how we could consider teaching in a core program as a unique opportunity for our own renewal and the foundation of a dynamic, evolving "community of learners." A commitment to gender and cross-cultural perspectives and to reflective practice ought to draw attention to the process through which knowledge is produced as well as to the broader political context within which the participants are situated (Lusted, 1986). In classrooms as well as in faculty meeting rooms, knowledge is constructed from the interactions of different perspectives. Dialogue and collaboration are critical to students' learning on their own terms and for the cultivation of their own voice and authority. Unless students experience the process of how their questions and activities are constructed they will not be able to evaluate the source and implications of their authority in their own professional work. The same is true for the faculty. They must experience the shift in perspective as they struggle with hierarchical relationships to knowledge and scholarly expertise. Each time they collaborate with another instructor, they must be willing to juxtapose their differing perspectives to create new texts and new perspectives. Teachers need to be supported and encouraged to attend to their pedagogy in such a way that their own perspectives are truly valued and respected while holding to the promise of experiencing new teaching and learning possibilities. This notion of renewal asserts that only through collaborative forms of relationship and dialogue can we hope to create intellectual communities in which all students and teachers are knowers. How can we do this in a manner that is supportive, resolute, and earnest in the same desire to build a community of learners? Co-teaching holds the possibility of altering student and teacher roles, reconceiving content, and fostering cross-disciplinary connections.

Co-Teaching: The Organizational Expression of Community

Most teachers in higher education have experienced collaborative forms of teaching at some time during their careers. Professional collaboration practices take many forms in education. Ideas and experiences such as collegial sharing, collaboration, partnerships, interdisciplinary teaching, and peer coaching have for years supported our quest for collegiality and professional learning communities. But nothing penetrates the classroom and holds the potential for affecting the growth of an individual or the organization more than the practice of co-teaching.

There are numerous studies on the positive effects of team teaching on professional growth and student learning. Teaming has had a checkered past in American higher education. It has been rediscovered as a pedagogical innovation during almost every recent curriculum or restructuring reform but has easily shifted to the wayside when persistent problems remained. It achieved a lively renaissance during the 1950s and 1960s when educators reconfigured programs to ameliorate overspecialization and forged interdisciplinary general studies programs, such as American studies or core curricula. Team teaching emerged as the organizational expression of a commitment to develop intellectual communities engaged in collaborative conversations and inquiry (Hollingsworth, 1992).

Understanding Co-teaching: Defining the Possible

I distinguish co-teaching from the many forms that team teaching takes and the many interests it serves, although our graduate faculty still refer to their collaborative processes as team teaching. (I will use the term "co-teaching" when the relationship I am discussing meets the conditions I describe in this section or when a teacher consciously chooses this term. I will use the term "team teaching" when talking about or quoting faculty who refer to collaborative teaching in this way. Many collaborative relationships are not committed to the kind of pedagogy that co-teaching implies, although I hold it as both an ideal and a possibility; I have observed co-teaching among a number of colleagues, and have experienced it myself.)

Co-teaching enlarges the collaborative conversation. It is a process where two or more teachers plan for, teach and assess the same students in order to create a learning community. They consciously commit to model, that is, live collaboration with and through the students and each other. One of the goals of co-teaching is learning from one another through reflection together and with students. In our ideal world, co-teaching would mirror the concerns of teachers who seek to explore the possible in education: creating communities of learners who respect differences, cast questions rather than answers, and reconstruct the nature of knowledge and knowing. These communities are charged with developing and nurturing professionals who could, themselves, foster and support caring relationships and collaborative possibilities within their own spheres of influence. If the co-teaching relationship is truly collaborative, that is, mutual, personal, and enduring (Hargreaves, 1992), it has the potential to transform and change the teachers significantly, as well as the organizational culture.

Although others have described those practical qualities that mark successful collaborative relationships (Wallace and Loudin, 1991; Gabelnick, et al., 1990), students still need personal models that draw attention to the processes of collaboration, not as formulas, but as guideposts. A graduate student who participated in a co-taught course said to the instructors, "Your relationship and the way the two of you interacted with each other defined what was possible for us in our own interactions as students in this class." But co-teaching is like marriage; there is no map for what will unfold or how the parties will make sense out of the relationship.

Conditions Supporting Co-Teaching

One of the most important conditions for co-teaching is the evolution of trust within the relationship, so that each party will take risks in sharing who they are and what matters to them as teachers, and be willing to set goals for their own learning within the relationship. Hollingsworth calls this equal vulnerability (1992, p. 376). Klein refers to this as the capacity for self-disclosure between the teachers and with students (See Klein, chapter 5). Not everyone values the qualities of trust, support, and caring and the time and attention it takes to develop these in professional relationships. Indeed, as our faculty would attest, even when colleagues are aware of and cultivate the conditions necessary to support collaboration, relationships are not always successful. Teaching styles, personality and developmental factors, and other outside forces can inhibit even the best of intentions. What does happen in a relationship that all parties deem successful? What are the hidden inequities that must be understood and resolved? What are the tensions that differences create for teachers and how does one resolve them?

We conducted a study to examine faculty perceptions of the value and importance of the core program in the graduate school (Rusch, 1989). All the faculty interviewed who had taught in the program (seventeen out of twenty-seven full-time faculty) said that team teaching was the most significant aspect of the program, and that the experience created a heightened sense of community. Five, including three who had taught in the core program, noted that the intended collegiality was not evident to them, indeed, two who did teach in core would not consider participating again. Interdisciplinary programs need to know how teachers construct knowledge within collaborative relationships and how this affects their professional growth and ultimately the students. Collaboration is more complex, contextual, and unpredictable in its direction, form, and results than had been appreciated.

I examined the interviews for the themes that emerged from the faculty about those aspects of the co-teaching experience that they considered conducive to their own professional growth. Did the team relationship create a sense of self-renewal for the teacher? How did the experience of teaming provide a sense of the larger community in the graduate school? Faculty talked about three ideas related to their desire for community that were significant: (1) the importance of faculty and students learning together, creating the texts for the courses out of the dialogue that emerged from the relationships in the class, (2) the significance of stories and metaphors as expressions of beliefs, and (3) reflection together about pedagogy.

Faculty Relationships and Student Experiences as Text

One of the most significant changes in our faculty's thinking has been that the experiences of students as expressed through the narratives and stories become the "living curriculum" or text of the class. For some this was a shift to a new paradigm of knowledge construction that locates truth as the intersection of multiple perspectives. For others this was experienced more as the unfolding of a deeply held belief in the learning process. The ideas brought into the discussion and writing by students work to create the grounds for a dialogical pedagogy when they are regarded as the text of the class and as material for personal and professional growth.

Drawing from the liberal arts and humanities encourages faculty to use story and narrative. It gives teachers encouragement to share their own personal stories as they explore the themes of the course. As one instructor said, "The reason core works for many faculty is the opportunity for a special relationship among the faculty." She viewed teaching, research, and curriculum as reciprocal processes:

> In team teaching you risk mocking the very values and goals which core seeks to emulate. The unfolding of the team relationship is a model for students. The course (i.e., Individual and Societal Perspectives on Adulthood) is really about relationships and what is happening between adults. The challenge is in allowing the relationship to become text for the course. Not every aspect of the relationship should be public and open to view, but there is a great fear in academia of letting other people into our lives. How we structure our knowledge in our disciplines is always filtered through life experience.

Another teacher said, "There is the opportunity to balance newness to a team relationship with experience in re-creating the knowledge for the course. The interpersonal nature of core breeds closeness and the sharing of life experience between teachers." One teacher described the "living curriculum. If you do it well, you have to do the sharing."

Stories and Metaphors as Expressions of Beliefs

In arguing for the fundamental narrative character of pedagogical knowledge, Gudmundsdottir offers this:

> Values and narrative are inexorably intertwined (because) they have one fundamental principle in common, a principle that is basic to the narrative nature of pedagogical content knowledge—values and narrative are interpretive tools that constitute a practical but highly selective perspective with which we look at the world around us and use it to make sense of facts, various kinds of text or whatever experience we meet as teachers (1991).

To participate in a relationship is to know and use a range of shared meanings, and it is the narrative quality of this shared knowledge that allows it to be known, interpreted, reflected upon and ultimately transformed (Connelly and Clandinin, 1990). Narratives form the basis for the constructed text of a co-teaching arrangement. We bring our perceptions of the shared event in the form of vignettes and stories offered to make a point, to test perceptions and to achieve a consensus about a further course of action, in the hope of achieving a new praxis, that is, a new understanding of our practical knowledge.

Teachers need to be supported in recognizing the power of stories for navigating the murky seas of co-teaching. Stories wrap around our values and judgments, making our beliefs understandable to ourselves, each other, our students, and to others. They rise out of dialogue and form narratives of self, of the milieu of teaching, of subject matter, and of pedagogy. In collaborative relationships the fundamental character of those values and beliefs cannot be fully appreciated by the other unless the narrative is offered through dialogue. While narrative and dialogue are interconnected but different modes of expression, dialogue is at the heart of collaboration. When we seek to tell our stories, it is in dialogue where we create the possibilities to hear and be heard. Dialogue insists on an empathetic awareness of the repeated patterns of our beliefs and those of the other, because it is through the structure of these core beliefs that we make our fundamental assessments of students and their knowledge and our basic choices about the structure of authority and control within the classroom. In this process we model the possible to our students.

Making Beliefs Explicit—Equal Vulnerability

By listening to and working with faculty who have team taught, I have found that the greatest obstacle to creating a collaborative environment is the failure of teachers to recognize the importance of making their implicit beliefs explicit to each other and to their students. Central to this is the willingness to explore the meaning of "equal vulnerability," self-closure, or openness and trust with each other and the students, as well as the commitment to listen to our students' assessments of whether and how we are doing it. Even so, differences in how the idea of self-disclosure is expressed through actual teaching moments can cause one member of a team to feel more frustrated or satisfied than the other. One teacher may believe in consistently opening herself up emotionally to the students and therefore takes the full force of the interpersonal struggles that it implies. The other teacher may be only too willing to let her do that and play that role for the team and the class. But the willingness to reflect on and "process" what the experience means to them, and what they could learn from this, always holds the promise that the struggle can eventually be perceived as worthwhile or that the differences in roles within the teaching relationship are experienced equitably and to the satisfaction of each. Whether these teachers would be willing to co-teach again often depends on the outcome of this sharing and reflection.

Teachers in higher education pride themselves on their ability to bridge theoretical and philosophical differences. This is often the case for those teachers who take the time to reflect upon their relationship, or "process," that is, look back on the actions (Schon, 1987) they created and shared as text. Differences can become a source of wonderful insight and opportunity for learning, and often they test the limits of our ability to demonstrate unconditional regard for the other. Modeling these for students is the basis for understanding the role of collaborative talk in building community and student learning. Differences in understanding collaborative learning can put one teacher more "out there" for student recognition or criticism. (See Brody, chapter 3 in this volume for a discussion of collaborative learning.) The beliefs teachers hold about the nature of knowledge and the process of knowledge acquisition play a powerful role in determining the design and outcome of collaborative relationships in the classroom (Palincear, Stevens, and Gavelek, 1988). Faculty must attend to these beliefs and the way in which they construct their pedagogical knowledge while they are in the process of implementing these new learning arrangements. They must take the time to reflect together.

Constraints and Challenges of Co-Teaching in an Interdisciplinary Program

Other writers have documented the issues faculty encounter teaching in interdisciplinary, learning communities. Our experience and findings are consistent with others (Gabelnick, et al., 1990), but warrant sharing. Although establishing an interdisciplinary, team-taught program seemed natural given our histories, espousing the values expressed earlier, however, was easier than realizing them. For some faculty, the co-teaching experience ameliorated the considerable student resistance to this new program requirement. For a few others, the realization that their pedagogy was inadequate for the challenges of this program turned them away from the core program. Teaming alone did not ensure a successful learning experience for either students and faculty. Faculty knew that team teaching took time, but their own models were few and traditional didactic methods of teaching sometimes translated into "turn-teaching." At first course syllabi were simply passed along and the instructors did their best together to understand the new domains of the course content.

Within a year it was apparent that recruiting faculty to teach a new course, developing curricula, and assisting faculty to prepare for these courses required more than we had bargained for. Looking back to the onset of the program, we admitted that we had made classic mistakes in program implementation. We had moved too quickly from designating the course of study into the actual teaching without proper time for discussion and preparation among faculty as to how to develop the pedagogy we wanted for building a learning community. The courses simply "happened" without much consensus about how we could promote collaborative conversations. We had not defined what team teaching, much less co-teaching, meant. But we carefully reviewed student course evaluations, and systematically catalogued their suggestions in the program evaluation reports. We convened the faculty for self-study using insider- and outsider-generated data on the program. The lessons we learned derive from a conscious commitment to focus upon co-teaching as the organizational expression of our commitment to developing a sense of community and renewing faculty.

Who Should Teach in an Interdisciplinary Program

Within professional school faculties, the success of new, interdisciplinary programs depends on the leadership and on the senior faculty's willingness to be the vanguard in the teaching of the program. When we started we enjoyed unanimous support from program directors, the dean, and the president of the college, each of whom were active in the program's development. The first instructors in such programs ought to be established, senior faculty who are more able to be vulnerable and who engender the positive regard of other faculty. At first, we hoped to require all faculty to teach in the core as part of their commitment to the new graduate school and as a basis for their own professional renewal. But faculty must be recruited within the conditions that the opportunities afford, and they must perceive a fit with the program. Everyone cannot or should not teach in an interdisciplinary program.

Thus there is the continuing tension about the prestige of teaching within such a program and the weight such teaching will lend to promotion and tenure dossiers. Interdisciplinary core programs can divide regular core faculty from those who have not taught in the program. Faculty must consider ways to reward faculty for teaching in such programs because to do so requires more time and holds the potential for failure, since it may take teachers outside their areas of expertise. In our case, we try to maintain a ratio of one teacher to every 15 students in a course. Faculty may choose to teach alone, although one of the attractions of the core program, particularly for new or adjunct faculty, is the opportunity to co-teach. And at the level of the dean's review, teaching in the program has been considered a strong and positive contribution to teaching and service within the organization.

Multiple Partners and Initiating New Faculty into the Program

Working with multiple partners provides important lessons about the teaming process. Instituting the practice of pairing people who have already co-taught with teachers who have not yet taught in the program means that faculty have to be even more generous and patient with their time. Faculty will view this experience quite differently. For example, the following statement reflects a teacher who invites new partners: "You ought to celebrate people as agents of your own transformation." Other teachers raised concerns, "A good team teaching experience makes me realize that I wouldn't want to team with just anyone." Another teacher who has worked with five different faculty has experienced it as a strain to reinvent the curriculum to accommodate others each time. This points out the advantage, at least in the beginning phases of a program, of having course outlines that guide the development of syllabi and allow faculty new to the program to master the content. It also demonstrates the need to honor faculty choice, wherever possible, in establishing teams.

For faculty new to an interdisciplinary program, there is always the issue of equality and domination. Some faculty are conscious of these realities and talk freely about the importance of both people valuing equal participation despite different academic preparation and previous teaching experience. This is a sensitive topic; most new faculty welcome the experience that a seasoned teacher can bring to the course. When inducting new faculty into the ethos of a program, I see it as particularly critical to have a new instructor paired with someone who has not only had a personally successful teaching experience in the program but shares program values. On the other hand, new teachers must make each course their own, and to do that they must experience the program as a forum for the expression for their own personal and professional concerns and expertise as well. While the benefits accrued by those who have had successful experiences ought to be the basis for extending this opportunity and responsibility to others, relationships take time to develop.

Gender-balanced teams, or teams of two female faculty, seem to be the most successful according to student evaluations and faculty self-reports. This may be because many of the courses in the core program address issues of gender and social justice, and male-female teams offer the opportunity for considering divergent perspectives between the two teachers. More likely, however, is the fact that our women teachers are open to the relational aspects of teaching, creative in their approaches to pedagogy, and likely to understand the practicalities involved in working cooperatively. This bears further study, but other schools ought to give serious attention to the potential that gender plays in such programs.

Viewing Program Challenges Organically

The emphasis on community-building, active dialogue, and collegiality among course participants leads some faculty to question whether there is adequate content in interdisciplinary courses. This reflects the continual tension between the ideas of knowledge and the value of process. There is also the question of how to continue the construction of knowledge from the interaction of different perspectives among the faculty. Interdisciplinary, core programs need curriculum continuity and stability in order to evaluate what they are doing and to recruit new faculty members. Thus, faculty may need to ask each other to give up a certain amount of individual freedom in constructing course content and to try out a new curriculum. The challenge is to invite but not impose. How faculty conduct their work together through the construction of their relationship, the planning of the course, and the creation of community in the classroom is as critical to the success of the program as how they frame the nature of learning, inquiry, curriculum, and pedagogical processes. It remains a challenge to assist faculty to achieve congruence between the values of the program and their own biographies, teaching styles, and deeply held pedagogical beliefs without imposing another form of external authority not derived from their experience. There is a paradox, as Apple argued, between the democratic ideal of change from the ground up and the need to suggest possibilities in order to move people (1986).

We must pay attention to the way teachers make sense and the manner in which they construct knowledge that is relevant to their roles as teachers. The kind of knowing that occurs for teachers is a function of the joint interaction of teachers' and students' ways of knowing. The teacher joins the students in co-constructing meaning and new knowledge, ending with a product that is the interaction between these multiple epistemological systems (Lyons, 1990). This joint interaction also occurs within collaborative relationships among teachers who share the same teaching/learning context and who develop a common language and a shared, even collective, knowledge.

Conclusions: Affirming the Possibilities of Community

A commitment to community can become the foundation for a successful reexamination of our work in our professional schools. I have discussed two structures that we have developed at Lewis & Clark College to give institutional expression to that commitment—interdisciplinary studies, which brings different professions together and draws from the liberal arts, and co-teaching. These structures have encouraged faculty to explore their work as a form of praxis. Programmatic goals sustain a commitment to the creation and recreation of a community when they foster multiple forms of inquiry, ways of knowing, and knowledge creation between participants—students and teachers alike. The student data from our core program convinces us that this kind of experience does make a difference in their professional lives. Our students need to experience the making of community in order to create effective organizations and participate as citizens in their organizations and communities.

Interdisciplinary professional studies can create an invaluable context in which teachers and students give meaning to their experiences in relationships. We value the potential of co-teaching in uncovering values and beliefs, stories of struggle and accomplishment, and dilemmas of practice and vision, enabling those who are ready to participate in collaborative communities. Our experience in the core program allows us to frame the problems within our own organization differently, but we do not expect this knowledge to be useful in every context we encounter or that others may encounter. While our particular process may not work for others, each element moves out of the central commitment to relationship within community, toward developing collaborative relationships across disciplinary lines that are mutual, deep, and enduring.

3

Collaborative Learning: Fostering Dialogue Across the Professions

CELESTE M. BRODY

Collaborative learning means learning through joint intellectual effort. It has a rich and varied tradition over the last 50 years deriving from different epistemological traditions. Cooperative learning, a particular form of collaborative learning is most popular as a teaching tool in K–12 schools. Its purpose is to teach students social skills and to arrange groups of student to achieve cooperation, positive interdependence, and improved achievement (Cohen 1986; Cooper et al., 1990; Slavin, 1989). Since the 1980s cooperative learning has gained a ground swell of interest, indeed, it has been referred to as a social movement (Schmuck and Schmuck, 1992). In higher education, cooperative learning, or the larger frame collaborative learning, has not received as much attention and its purpose differs. Collaborative learning conveys a transformative potential; it provides a framework for thinking about how power is allocated, how decisions are made, and how multiple perspectives can be heard and validated (Sapon-Shavin, 1991). Collaborative learning is most often connected with the building of interpretive communities and writing groups within the creation of learning communities (Bruffee, 1984, 1985; Graves, 1983; Gabelnick, et al., 1990).

I will discuss collaborative learning in the context of this latter use—a particular epistemological orientation that distinguishes it from other forms of group work or contexts for collegial learning. We should not take these distinctions lightly, because the different historical roots of these practices give coherence and provide a framework for developing pedagogical processes that can help teachers evaluate the congruency between program philosophy and program goals.

Collaborative learning derives from the work of the twentieth century social constructivists, such as George Herbert Mead (1934),

Thomas Kuhn (1970), Richard Rorty (1979), John Dewey (1930, 1938), and more recently Lev Vygotsky (1978 a, b). These theorists emphasize the critical role of social interaction in learning, telling us that meanings—both personal and social—are socially constructed. In the field of psychology the works of Jean Piaget (1952, 1954), George Kelly (1955), and Robert Kegan (1982) parallel the social constructivists, although their constructivism tends to focus on personal meaning-making more than on the social process of knowledge construction. Collaborative learning has political and educational roots in the democratizing efforts of Kurt Lewin (1948) and Yael and Shlomo Sharan (1992) and has feminist proponents who have broadened our understanding of both theory and practice, such as Mary Belenky and colleagues (1986), Sandra Harding (1987), Sandra Hollingsworth (1992), Nona Lyons (1990), Janet Miller (1990), and Kathleen Weiler (1988).

One criticism of graduate professional education is that it offers too specialized and technocratic training. At Lewis & Clark we strive to initiate graduate students into their professional communities, to foster dialogue and inquiry within and across the professions, and to understand the human experience in organizations. Collaborative learning is a natural fit for these purposes. In this chapter I will address the ideas behind collaborative learning to understand the teaching contexts in which it can be a successful pedagogical strategy for interdisciplinary professional education programs.

The Justification for Collaborative Learning in Professional Education

(Collaborative learning within the social constructivist traditions, supports us with three reasons for constructing classroom contexts to educate our future colleagues: (1) organizational life requires professionals to work collaboratively with different people, while serving and interacting with a diverse clientele, (2) we must consider the adult developmental needs of our students in higher education, and (3) knowledge is socially constructed, thus collaborative learning challenges the theory and practice of the status quo.)

The Requirements of Organizational Life.

Organizational life requires professionals to work with professionals in different fields while serving and interacting with an increasingly diverse clientele. Graduate students are hungry for collaborative models of working relationships, since the traditional structure for professional education has rewarded individual efforts and promoted competitive forms of learning. Adults are aware of the demands for negotiation and conflict resolution skills within their own practice, but they are often novices at orchestrating team problem-solving, where they may be required to be part of an interagency or interdepartmental group that brings different perspectives to bear on problems they hold in common. Indeed, some of the newer members of our professions are often so bent on negotiating the language and technical competencies of their own field that they frequently eschew contact with other professionals. It is very demanding to learn how to talk *across* different professional cultures and different languages of experience, at just the time when the novice is mastering a new one. For example, I have found some counseling psychology students extraordinarily good at focusing on the individual, but resistant to or unskilled at applying another lens for considering other possibilities as explanations for a particular problem or dilemma. And many classroom teachers have never been asked to consider the organizational influences upon their work. When they are required to work with students from other professional fields, they find that their specialized language can pose barriers to effective problem solving.

Many adult learners enter professional programs not expecting to examine the orientations in which they are embedded. But we would have them, however, experience the wonderfully unexpected in terms of a sense of collegiality, the opportunity to break down age, ethnic, gender, and disciplinary stereotypes, and gain insights into problems that they had never considered before. (The first reason for collaborative learning is that it creates contexts where students address issues of practice within a community of peers, which mirrors the realities they face in their own organizations—how to foster dialogue and teamwork across the different professions.)

A Pedagogy for Adult Development

The second reason for adopting collaborative learning has to do with our responsibility as teachers to consider the adult developmental needs of our own students. We are connected to them as mutual agents of the public good, but they also bring their full, complex lives into our programs. We must recognize and assist them in understanding the interplay of their human lives upon their work.

Graduate professional students are a unique university clientele in several respects. Many of them are our colleagues at this very moment, studying for principalships, or superintendencies, or advanced degrees in teaching. They may be budget analysts in government agencies or accomplished adults who have returned to school to make a career change and a commitment to helping others. Our own students in the graduate school of professional studies at Lewis & Clark College reflect the national demographic trends. They are older; the average graduate student age is over thirty-four. They are focused in their studies, having developed their professional identification before they returned to school. They are, in general, instrumentally oriented, that is, they want to prepare for their professional life in an expedient and efficient manner, and because most of them pay their own tuition, they demand the best of their teachers within the possibilities of what is knowable to them. They are likely to be philosophically aligned with the programs they have chosen and that have carefully selected them; indeed, many of them have actively selected the program because of its explicit beliefs and values. Like most graduate students in professional programs they are within a commuting radius of their work or home, and as working adults they are usually trying to balance home, school, and professional activities.

The relevance of collaborative learning to these students is at first glance strictly pragmatic from the point of view of the research on adult learners. Adult learners are more likely to share these common approaches to learning: lower levels of competitiveness toward other students, more interest in participating with others, more inclination to assume personal responsibility for their learning, and more willingness to work independent of instructor supervision (Cuseo, 1992). Our experience echoes that of others who recognize that adults learn best through active, experiential contexts involving discussion and problem-solving, which allow them to draw on their personal and professional experiences (Brookfield, 1986). Furthermore, they have obvious differences that can provide rich opportunities for learning from one other. These differences become practical tensions within a collaborative learning environment because they cannot be ignored by the instructors or the students. These differences are developmental, representing different phases of meaning-making about self, work, and moral development; different historical perspectives due to the social milieu in which they were raised and came into adulthood; gender, race, and ethnic characteristics which allow them to construct different world views; and different real world perspectives, which derive from raising families, working, living, and loving, different people and experiences. By this time in their lives, they often have preferred learning styles. Some students need careful prodding to examine and expand these, while others honor and respect their limitations and accept support, if it is offered, for growing in new ways of learning. For example, one adult learner may inform me that he is dyslexic and would welcome patience and extensions for reading and writing assignments. Another will become upset unless every course expectation is outlined explicitly and can be defensive when a peer gently invites her to see this as a unique opportunity to explore her own boundaries and voice. They are, however, all people who have grabbed hold of their world and actively taken it in, and, to different degrees, they have considered how they have come to be who they are and how they uniquely construct the world.

Contexts for Engaging in the Conversations of Professional Life

The most important reason, however, for collaborative learning has to do with the theory of social constructivism that forms the basis of collaborative learning itself. In his essay, "Collaborative learning and the 'Conversation of Mankind,'" Kenneth Bruffee argues that, in its deepest sense, collaborative learning changes the social context in which learning takes place and challenges the theory and practice of traditional classroom teaching. This is because conversation and thought are related both causally and functionally; the mind is an artifact created by social interaction:

> To the extent that thought is internalized conversation, then, any effort to understand how we think requires us to understand the nature of conversation; and any effort to understand conversation requires us to understand the nature of community life that generates and maintains conversation. Furthermore, any effort to understand and cultivate in ourselves the kind of thought we value most requires us to understand and cultivate the kinds of community life that establish and maintain conversation that is the origin of that kind of thought. To think well as individuals we must learn to think well collectively, that is, we must learn to converse well. The first steps to learning to think better, therefore, are learning to converse better and learning to establish and maintain the sorts of social context, the sorts of community life, that foster the sorts of conversation members of the community value (1984, p. 638).

This argument has important implications for the education of professionals both within their normal communities of discourse and across disciplinary lines. Our task as teachers is to engage students in conversation among themselves through writing and reading processes, through collaborative conversations around problems of ethics, and through practice. The way our graduate students talk influences the way they will think and write and act with each other in their work communities. Collaborative learning is the general way in which we organize our students to experience and practice the kinds of conversation that we value as professionals. It provides a particular kind of social context for conversation, a particular kind of community of peers.

We are familiar with the discourse that marks our own particular community of knowledgeable peers. Richard Rorty calls this "'normal discourse'... a community of knowledgeable peers who accept, and whose work is guided by, the same paradigms and the same code of values and assumptions. It is within this normal discourse, that we learn 'what counts as relevant contribution, what counts as a question, what counts as having a good argument for that answer or a good criticism of it.'" (Rorty, quoted in Bruffee, pp. 642-43). We recognize this as the language in each profession—law, teaching, medicine, engineering, business, or counseling psychology.

In each field there are communities within communities who have developed their own special discourse, for example, the education of deaf children, or the education of children with other physical handicaps. It is this kind of discourse that requires such demanding attention by our students, particularly as it has become more technical, more specific and narrow. Within these communities, collaborative learning is particularly helpful because it allows a group of peers to pool the resources individuals bring with them to the "task of making accessible the normal discourse of the new community they hope to enter." (Bruffee, p. 644). It allows the individual the contexts for making sense out of the ideas that teachers are asking them to understand, test, and apply, and it supports their own constructions of knowledge as they negotiate the giving and receiving of help in mastering the particular forms of writing, speaking, and thinking that each field requires. Within these purposes our students are participating in communities of knowledgeable peers who maintain and establish knowledge, because they are engaged in a process of learning Bruffee calls "socially justifying belief."

> If we acknowledge the premise that knowledge is a social artifact created by a community of knowledgeable peers constituted by the language of that community, and that learning is a social and not an individual process, then to learn is not to assimilate information and improve our mental eyesight. To learn is to work collaboratively to establish and maintain knowledge among a community of knowledgeable peers through the process that Richard Rorty calls "socially justifying belief." (p. 646)

Collaborative learning models this process within the classroom and within the professional organization. Basically, we learn by explaining to others our way of understanding an idea. We build new knowledge by challenging each others' biases and assumptions, then negotiating new ways of perceiving, thinking, feeling, and expressing these. In this way we recruit each other into the larger, more experienced communities of our professions "by assenting to those communities' interests, values, language, and paradigms of perception and thought." (p. 646).)

But the significance of collaborative learning for professionals extends even further, and it is the more important reason for engaging these social contexts at every opportunity in our students' education: collaborative learning encourages participants to develop theories and ideas of their own that challenge and test the limits of traditional sources of knowledge. Ultimately, then, we are not just maintaining knowledge but generating new knowledge, and we want our students to engage in the fundamental responsibility of all communities of discourse in the professions—to challenge the authority of knowledge as we traditionally understand it. We have a responsibility as teachers to encourage future practitioners to resist the conservative tendency to maintain the authority of the professional by keeping the normal language of discourse to ourselves. We realize the tension inherent in this responsibility because we derive our authority as teachers of professionals from our established knowledge communities, and one of our fundamental responsibilities is to certify that our students are capable of becoming what they aspire to be—our peers within our established professional communities.

It is within this last argument for the necessity of collaborative learning that I make my case for creating contexts that purposely structure dialogue *across* professions, not just within professions. In this way, collaborative learning serves the larger community interest in bridging gaps among knowledge communities and opening them up to change. The case for collaborative, interdisciplinary studies derives not only from this social constructivist idea of knowledge and how we learn but from the need to create communities of discourse where established knowledge can be challenged and changed. Bringing heterogeneous groups of professionals together is a way of recognizing that knowledge is a social artifact that requires us to reexamine the premises of all of our education. Students and faculty alike have the potential to frame questions and engage in conversations that could lead to significant new understandings about problems that we hold in common. Within these contexts we have the responsibility to create openings for change, to leave ourselves as teachers vulnerable to criticism, to embrace those events that stimulate conflict as well as harmony, and to invite our students to engage in probing why this ought or ought not to be the way learning communities function and to realize what they can learn from this for their lives as professionals.

There is another consequence of collaborative learning relative to authority. As we encourage our students to question traditional sources of knowledge, and as they do this within collaborative circles, they will eventually challenge our authority as teachers—not so much about what we know and what we have experienced as adults and professionals. They will point out the contradictions in whether or not we are willing to do what we are asking them to do—construct texts through equal participation as *individuals* in the conversation. In this regard collaborative learning enables us to share a common experience with our students that creates a certain type of reflectivity, a mindfulness about our own knowledge and ways of knowing. These become new invitations to those of us who listen in order to continue the conversations among ourselves, with our students, and alone in the course of our thinking and writing.

It is at this point that collaborative learning gets messy and difficult. It is in the making of instructional practice, or pedagogy, which invites diversity in both process and content, and then requires us as teachers to participate in it along with our students, that we are likely to fail. Without a framework for understanding the purpose of collaborative learning as it relates to our communities of discourse, then collaborative learning can easily become just a tool or technique for bringing people together, but which avoids the personal and collective struggles for creating new knowledge. It can be put to use to serve traditional orientations to knowledge and knowing—positing the ideas of others, studying for tests, or producing answers to problems that we alone construct—all of these well and good sometimes within the approved limits of the normal discourses in our fields. If we are going to find ways out of the human and ethical dilemmas which face us, we are going to have to provide collective experiences for our professional students to live within our classrooms. These must be precisely the kind of inquiry that we really want them to go about in their professional and personal lives. We have to assist students to create their own collaborative conversations and teach them to recreate those contexts for others. We have a responsibility also to teach them that knowledge is in itself a social artifact. I know how difficult this is for some adult learners to grasp who do not want teachers to relinquish their "natural authority," and who firmly resist coming to grips with what this idea means for their very learning. Actually, we are less likely to simply fail, as we are to acknowledge how difficult and complex this process is and how attentive we must be to the process itself, because it is in examining and reflecting on the experience that we will catch insights into how to achieve our purposes.

I have witnessed the dynamics of students at work from different fields, with different life experiences, ages, and class backgrounds within collaborative learning groups. Most adult learners, when invited and actively recruited to trust the process, will work patiently with each other to develop a collective, shared language that embraces and transcends their commonalties and their differences. I recall the turning point for one group that realized the potential of their differing perspectives and were able from that moment to work creatively with this new idea. I was sitting in with a group of teachers, counselors, and public administrators who were exploring the meaning of Tillie Olsen's, "I Stand Here Ironing" (1976). It is a poignant story about a working-class mother who is asked by someone who "wants to help" to recall her eldest daughter's life experience. We never know quite who this person is, but the mother calls up and without self-pity recalls her memories of hardship, her lack of options as a single mother, and the effects of this on her daughter, who, the reader infers, is having some difficulties navigating her late adolescence. One parent of grown children, offered this insight into the meaning of this story:

> Now, at my age and with my perspective, I empathize with a mother as she remembers each phase of her child's growth. At the time, as each part of her life unfolded, she knew that it was not the best upbringing for the child, but she also knew it was the best she could do at that time, under those circumstances. She had to be content with that. She had to hope that the child had inner strengths, talents and sufficient resiliency to rise above the difficulties encountered in her early years. And the mother offers, "There is still enough left to live by."

Another student of counseling psychology did not consider the class background of the mother in her first reading on the story and insisted that the literary references indicated that the daughter was suicidal. This, she argued, was the result of the "failure of the mother-child bond." Now, it is more than easy for a group of adult learners to politely ignore differences in perspectives among themselves. They may be inexperienced in how social class, gender, age, and life experiences contributes to the way we frame problems. And they are less sure about how their normal communities of discourse influence how they see a problem and what solutions these offer. It is an opportunity, then, for the teacher to pose with wonder and enthusiasm a question that asks the participants in the group to consider whether and how their professional training has fostered ways of constructing a problem—in both enhancing and limiting ways. A teacher might suggest the following questions as the dialogue grows within the group: Assuming that each of you made that phone call to the mother, how do you account for your different views of this potential client or student—one view that moves out from the premise that the mother was inadequate and possibly even damaging to her daughter and the other view that the daughter is resilient and possibly creative in the face of diversity? Can we consider both perspectives without falling into relativism? Is it important that we all see the problem in the same way? If not, how do we begin to work together across the professions to assist this family or this young woman? *Should* we assist this family? And finally, can we learn something from one another about question-posing?

My point here, of course, is that no way of seeing holds the entire truth, but it is the teacher's responsibility to assist the students in capturing the areas of conflict and tension and to hold these up to the light of closer examination. And it is within interdisciplinary, hetero-geneous, small, collaborative groups that we offer the possibility of reflecting upon our own embeddedness, whether it be our fields of study, our own developmental challenges, or other.aspects of diversity. The theory of social constructivism, as this example illustrates, does not dictate a particular pedagogy, only the purposes that a pedagogy must serve and a means for evaluating the worth and value of what we are attempting to structure for and with our students.

The Practive of Collaborative Learning

Several conditions are necessary to establish collaborative learning environments that achieve an authentic community of discourse. They are (1) creating the small group seminar, (2) establishing a sense of community through shared norms, (3) using experiential learning, and (4) making the implicit, regarding the group process, explicit.

Creating the Small-Group Seminar

Collaborative learning can emerge within many different small-group structures—pairs, triads, and groups of four to six—depending upon the course, the problem at hand, the reason for collaborative talk, the particular group of students, and the size of the class. Our experience in the graduate core program suggests that the small-group seminar from five to seven people provides a structure that allows dialogue across the different professions and fosters the development of leadership and adult growth within caring and responsive communities. Within the larger commitment to build a learning community for the thirty students and two instructors in a course, seminar groups are the home base for students to simulate working communities and organizations. During each session a seminar group is led by a different class member for student voices to emerge. In these groups students gain insights into their learning styles and their ideas, and increase their ability to work as team members. The whole-class meetings and small-group seminars draw from fiction, biography, and film, and use discussion, writing for critical inquiry, self-reflection, and experiential learning to enhance the development of student ideas and provide contexts for designing questions for further inquiry.

Establishing a Sense of Community through Shared Norms

A sense of community is not easily defined or accomplished; it must be tended and nurtured continuously out of respect and regard for students' knowledge. They, with the teachers, are the co-learners and co-constructors of the text of the course. Teachers create community within classrooms by developing shared norms; these norms must be focused and reflected upon at each meeting, as they become gauges by which we compare our perceptions about our achievements and our failures. These norms include a commitment to working as a team, a willingness to take responsibility for one's learning and one's feelings, and a respect for the integrity of the others. For example, some adults have a difficult time shedding their "shoulds and oughts" in a required class despite the invitation for them to assist in creating a collaborative context. Teachers begin by acknowledging that their role is to recruit students into a community; that means taking their learning, their ideas, and their suggestions very seriously. The students' responsibility, in turn, is to let their peers and the instructors know what is on their minds, to engage in what Peter Elbow calls a willing suspension of disbelief, and to trust the process, which may seem foreign and uncomfortable at first (1986). If they do this, the group will create the common text from which everyone will learn. Furthermore, teachers ask students to trust that they will not be evaluated on their honesty in telling them what is on their minds nor on their point of view, politics, or opinions. They will be evaluated and they will also evaluate themselves on their seriousness of purpose in their written work, their journals, and their class participation. Teachers define what are the criteria for assignments; it is the students' responsibility to make their own meaning from these experiences.

Ethical guidelines for personal disclosure in journals and seminar groups are also important. The study of adult development, by adults of different ages and background, for example, creates inviting opportunities for participants to reflect upon their own lives as they examine developmental and social themes and life events in the lives of other adults. Participants must use their own judgment regarding the disclosure of personal information. A sense of ethical obligation to others should lead participants to agree to principles of respect and confidentiality when personal information is shared and the respect for privacy when an individual chooses not to disclose. These principles should hold for both oral and written work in the course. Participants should further agree to respect the privacy of clients and others not present in the class by not identifying them by name when discussion of professional or interpersonal dilemmas might be intrusive or harmful to those persons.

Using Experiential Learning

There is a strong bias within graduate education for intellectual, theoretical learning at the expense of narrative, expressive, or feeling modes of knowing and learning. These are tensions in ways of knowing, each with distinctive merits. Collaborative learning requires careful attention to the inclusion of both experiential, expressive, and logical, analytical activities (Bruner, 1986). Experiential learning allows adults to share common activities for bringing their different perspectives to bear on a problem. Collaborative learning fails more often than not because teachers do not want to take what they consider valuable time for both class-building and team-building experiences within seminar groups. In the long run, the more time spent up front on activities that create a basis for shared experience, albeit around the texts and ideas of the course, the more likely a group will coalesce. These activities range from short "people searches" for introducing everyone to the resources within the class, to all-day challenge courses designed to combine physical activities with cooperative group problem solving. (See Brody-Witherell, chapter 4 for further descriptions.)

A course might end with a group project that is presented orally and in writing by each seminar group. Topics and organization would be selected by each group, with the only stipulation that the paper and the presentation must address major issues and themes of the course.

Again, an additional expectation might be that the final presentation engage the rest of the class experientially, so that all participants learn from each other's group work.

Creating a Context for Collaborative Response: Roles and Reflection

In every case, the advice of group work facilitators remains steadfast: collaborative learning must attend to both the task and the maintenance aspects of community life and consider process *as* content (Schmuck and Schmuck, 1992). Despite the adult's sophistication as a learner, the forming of each new group is like any new relationship. This means that teachers have a responsibility to provide enough structure for groups to begin working together but that allows groups that are ready to move beyond that structure to define their own norms and ways of doing things. Simple structures provide contexts to develop shared norms and give many opportunities to reflect upon what is working or not working and why.

Group roles, for example, support both task and maintenance functions. Teachers commonly use the presenter, facilitator and process observer:

> The *presenter* prepares a working essay to present to the group as a starting point for discussion for that evening. The presenter plans one or two lead-in questions and discusses with the facilitator beforehand how the seminar can best be utilized. During the seminar the presenter asks the group to become consultants regarding his/her ideas presented in the essay. Group members listen and respond to the essay with affirming and stretching comments. These ideas may be incorporated into the finished essay.

Following this presentation, another member of the group acts as the *facilitator* for discussion of the presentation and issues identified by the presenter, instructors, or the group. The facilitator makes sure that all persons are heard and that the discussion is directed at the main questions and points of the presenter. The facilitator provides a brief summary of the salient ideas discussed in the group when it reconvenes. Sometimes the group is asked to define a question that captures an unresolved issue during the discussion. These questions should whet interest for continued reflection in journals. They also help the teachers understand what students are struggling with, and they give a framework for guiding thinking about how to respond.

Finally, one person within each group serves as the *processor* for the discussion. This person provides feedback to the group on how it handled the task and maintenance functions. The processor participates and observes and records interactions according to what the group decides to focus upon at the beginning of the session (Adapted from a course syllabus, Brody and Schmuck, 1992).

Even with the best of structures, a certain amount of practice, and much time for reflection, all groups do not operate as collaborative learning communities. Sometimes it is members who have very different expectations for learning and ask the instructors to intercede in the group process on their behalf. At other times, it is the watchful experience of the teachers who see that the group is having problems. Often these same groups will not agree with the perceptions of the teachers. Teachers need to use discretion in meeting with groups by participating in any number of ways that best serve their needs— modeling dialogue without dominating or sharing data from observations about what specific task and maintenance behaviors the group members are using.

Making the Implicit Explicit: Going Public about the Group Process

The final principle of collaborative group work stands, whether it is in the face of difficulties or success: it is important to share observation and evaluation data with the entire group. In order for students to reflect openly and together on what and how they are doing, they need good information if they are to be responsible for the group's direction. The following are three areas in which questions for reflection can be designed by teachers and students. A good and open discussion can provide enough information to alter the course of the group:

1. Consider the *content or ideas* under examination, for example, the movement of the development of your thinking as individuals and as a group: "How did the group discussion extend, change, revisit, or reaffirm the ideas which you presented?"
2. Reflect on the group discussion *process*: "What did you learn about your group's effectiveness as a working community?"
3. Consider the *metacognitive* aspects: "How did you come to know what you know and how has the group contributed to that understanding?"

Whether it is through extended narratives of self-inquiry within the journals or reflections on the group process to accompany their written essays, participants need structure, models, and encouragement for drawing their own tacit knowing to a new and purposeful consciousness. Teachers give students permission to raise the implicit and tentative understandings among them to the level of the explicit and public, so that hidden agendas are uncovered and differences in perceptions are tested against one another. Only within this context can conflict and difference become an opportunity for collective knowledge.

Some strategies for achieving this are straightforward and obvious, while others require great artistry, sensitivity, and skill. The straightforward, planned approach begins by teaching students simple data-gathering techniques about task and maintenance processes within groups, then asking students to take turns gathering data about how they did during any given seminar session and sharing it through a process observer. Then, at any number of points during the term, students are invited to anonymously answer a number of questions about their group functioning. This data is compiled for each group and presented to the class as a whole, with identifying group names purposely omitted. The class as a whole is then invited to make inferences from the data about how group work is proceeding, followed by time for each group to meet with the instructor and receive the specific data about their group and to consider the implications of this data for their further work with each other.

Any number of scenerios may unfold. Particular students who have been feeling vulnerable or outside the process, may now gather courage to air their feelings within their groups. Most groups have the resources to wonder honestly and in an inviting manner about the dissonant perceptions. On the other hand students who believe that all members of the class or group feel just as they do, may learn that they are a very small minority, and must then begin to wrestle with their own perceptions against those of the others. Other groups may revel in their shared and acknowledged harmony and take new license with each other, setting goals and desires which go far beyond minimum expectations. Professionals, when invited, will make connections about the value of this kind of reflection to their personal and professional lives in their unique ways.

The Impact of Collaborative Learning on Students

What students value most about collaborative learning is that it expands their thinking. They say they value their active involvement in the discourse with peers and faculty. They feel a sense of friendship and belonging and enjoy the intellectual energy and confidence emerging from their engagement. At the same time they are discovering the validity and limitations of their own ideas and experiences. Most importantly, they describe a new appreciation of other students' perspectives and the impact age, gender, and life experiences have on development. When they have experienced their collective ability to build new intellectual connections, the products that they create stand as testimony to their experience, and they are more willing to return to the reflections on their own learning.

There are, however, many difficulties in collaborative learning. It takes time to build trust and collegiality and to develop group work skills. And, in the hands of inexperienced teachers who are unwilling or unable to turn a difficult human relations experience into a powerful learning event, students are often left to their own devices to make sense out of what happens.

Sharon, a woman studying for her first principalship, exemplifies such a process. In this selection from her own narrative she relates the story of her group's development and then reflects upon what she has learned through the difficulties and challenges of becoming a cohesive seminar group. She demonstrates how professionals, when given permission and encouragement, draw new lessons from these experiences to their future roles.

> What began as a reluctant and a divided group has become a cohesive and fairly well-organized culture in less than four weeks. We have overcome differences in gender, age, interests, and strong personality variations to become a unified group. Our common philosophy of caring about children brought us together in exploring a common purpose and goal. Our values about the worth of helping children in need led us to really identify with the Dougy Center and its purpose, and the sharing of those values led us to work collaboratively with each other. Our norms changed from self-interest to an ethic of care, respect, and acceptance as our philosophy and values brought us together. The rules of our organizational culture changed as the women expressed a need for equality in decision-making. By the end, our rule was that everyone was needed for participation and that we would need to reach consensus for a group decision to be made. Our individual behaviors remained diverse, but as the group work progressed, everyone's behavior included more eye contact, more consideration, better listening and the practice of affirming others.
>
> This seminar group experience has taught me a great deal about being a school principal. Faculty members will never work together as a team unless they know each other. And unless they learn to work together as a team, they will not be able to create a common vision and common goals, which are necessary ingredients for an excellent and an effective school.
>
> Like many students, deep-down I prefer to work in isolation while taking classes. In this class, I would have preferred to read more and write a paper rather than have my destiny and success depend upon the joint work of a group that I didn't even choose. However, I learned

more about organizational culture from my hands-on group experience than I would have learned from merely reading and writing about it. I was forced into a group situation which I would not have chosen on my own, quite like most situations teachers find themselves within their own faculties. I am now convinced of the value of collaborative learning: When I am a principal, I will put my faculty into learning groups. At first, I'll bet that they won't like it. They might consider it a waste of their valuable time. But, by using these groups, I will model collaborative learning processes (as my seminar professor did for us) and encourage my teachers to use these approaches in their own classrooms. I will also ask them to work together to create common goals, e.g., writing a school vision or planning a faculty meeting. Their interpersonal interaction may be strained at first, as ours was, but ultimately, I envision a cohesiveness within my faculty born of active involvement, frequent interaction and demonstration of care for one another. If our group can succeed in creating a cohesive, caring, creative culture, then my school's faculty should be able to do the same.

Conclusions

In this chapter I have focused upon those aspects of collaborative learning that pertain to the success of adult learners who are working together in cross-disciplinary settings. These practices evolve from the pedagogical imperatives that social constructivism suggests for learning within communities of discourse. The reasons for this have to do with the requirements of organizational life itself, where professionals must be able to work cooperatively with different people, while serving and interacting with an increasingly diverse clientele, and with our responsibility as teachers to consider the adult developmental needs of our own students. We are connected to them as mutual agents of the public good, but just as important is the fact that they also bring their full, complex lives into our programs. We have a responsibility to recognize and assist them in understanding the interplay of their lives upon their work.

To the degree that we are going to find ways out of the human and ethical dilemmas that face us, we must provide collective experiences for our professional students within our classrooms. These ought to be precisely the kinds of inquiry that we want them to conduct in their professional and personal lives. We have to assist students to create their own collaborative conversations and teach them to be able to recreate those contexts for others. They must also realize that knowledge is in itself a social artifact. To this end we should encourage our students to question traditional sources of knowledge within collaborative circles and allow for the eventual challenge of our authority as teachers. In this way, we will create the means for our own transformation as teachers.

Part II

Thematic Responses to Ethical and Social Issues in Professional Education

This section deals with the evolution of a program and a pedagogy, which reflect the themes of this book: that new and experienced professionals must develop a common commitment to serve others and the community; that students and faculty together should question traditional sources of knowledge, so that question-posing rather than answer-giving becomes the norm of practice; and that professional programs have a responsibility to address the developmental needs of students through discussing and writing about issues of adult, moral, and ethical development. These themes continue the dialogue, begun in Part I, about redefining and reapplying liberal learning in professional education.

Chapter 4, "Story and Voice in the Education of Professionals," by Celeste Brody and Carol Witherell (with Ken Donald and Ruth Lundblad), describes the use of narrative and dialogue in a course on individual and societal perspectives on adulthood. The authors share their experience in developing a class that explores themes of culture, race, ethnicity, age, and gender as they shape identity through the life span and as they present both challenges and opportunities to professionals. Autobiographical writings by Donald and Lundblad reveal the power of narrative as a tool for addressing human and ethical dilemmas in the professions.

In chapter 5, "Reflection and Adult Development: A Pedagogical Process," Robert Klein addresses the need for professional programs to promote reflection about adult growth and change. Understanding adult development and how certain ideas and principles apply to personal and professional life promotes integration and growth and provides tools for assessing and managing conflicts and challenges.

Chapter 6, "Digging, Daring, and Discovering: Sifting the Soil of Professional Life through Journal Writing," by Joanne Cooper, underscores the importance of dialogue and journal writing as powerful, reflective practices that promote adult learning and context-embedded critical thinking. This chapter describes adult learners' use of journals to examine organizational and professional life. Using this process in professional education shows that facilitating personally relevant learning is essential if students are to reach some integration of personal and professional identity.

Terrence Whaley's chapter 7, "Self-interest and its Relation to an Ethic of Care," describes the evolution of a teacher's thinking as he and his students apply ideas from an ethic of care and an ethic of principle and the practical dilemmas that his students bring to this process. He argues that self-interest can provide a useful theoretical check to an ethic of care.

Zaher Wahab, in chapter 8, "Liberation, Multiculturalism, and Professional Education," challenges faculty in higher education to rethink and restructure the way we have been preparing professionals for human services. He argues that American higher education has pursued approaches to culturalism that have seriously inhibited professionals' understanding of race, culture, ethnicity, class, and gender. He proposes a multiculturalism which develops and cultivates the principles of universal humanism while redefining the nature of the liberal arts within professional education.

In chapter 9, "Citizens and the Conduct of Ecological Science: A Response to the 'Tragedy of the Commons,' " Charles Ault explains how education in science, environmentalism, and ecology can contribute to professional education, particularly in stimulating students from different fields to think clearly about tensions between individual interests and the common good. Ault draws on his experience as a teacher in a groundbreaking course that brings professionals together as citizens capable of affecting public policy.

Jack Corbett, in chapter 10, "The Internationalization of Professional Education," explains that professional education must address the increasingly insistent calls from business, government, and intellectual leaders for the internationalization of American education. He responds to three questions that represent major dilemmas for institutions of higher education: "What is internationalization?" "Whose interests should it serve?" and "How might it be implemented?" He interprets his own experience in teaching international study courses for professionals.

4

Story and Voice in the Education of Professionals

CELESTE BRODY AND CAROL WITHERELL WITH KEN DONALD AND RUTH LUNDBLAD

Stories go in circles. They don't go in straight lines. So it helps if you listen in circles because there are stories inside stories and stories between stories and finding your way through them is as easy and hard as finding your way home. And part of the finding is the getting lost. If you're lost, you really start to look around and listen. (Metzger, 1986, p. 104)

The story that follows is actually many stories. It is first the story about how a graduate school of professional studies has created a new vision of what it means to be a professional within a community of inquirers. It is also the story of how we as teachers have responded to the challenge of designing a curriculum and a pedagogy that speak to the special opportunities of teaching adults from five different professional programs. Most importantly, it is the stories and voices of our students themselves as they strive to construct new meaning out of their life experience and offer their teachers our most valuable lessons. It is a story of a shared journey; we are fellow travelers with our students as we attempt to integrate lessons from critical and feminist theory, life-span psychology, anthropology, and the humanities with discourse about our daily lives and the institutions in which we work.

We will describe the origins of our graduate core curriculum, highlight aspects of our co-teaching one of the core classes, and offer several of the stories written by our students as they speak to major

This chapter appeared in a slightly different version in Stories Lives Tell: Narrative and Dialogue in Education. Carol Witherell and Nel Noddings, editors, 1991. New York: Teachers College Press. Copyright 1991 TC Press. Adapted by permission.

life course themes in the adult years. Because it is predominantly our story, it is a hopeful story. We continue to be humbled in the face of our students' lives and the remarkable intelligence and caring that emerges from a single class experience. Finally, it is an unfinished story because the dialogue continues among the participants. Our understanding of even a single idea or moment in our lives continues to be transformed with each new experience as colleagues, teachers, and friends. We invite the readers of this chapter to do what we ask our students to do the first day we encounter them on this journey of self-discovery and meaning-making: to be willing to listen to your own stories as you hear those of others.

Andre Girard has observed that the greatest myth of the twentieth century is the myth of our own detachment. Extending this caution, we accept that one of the greatest challenges for professionals today is to guard against their own detachment—from themselves, from their community, and from those with whom they form particular relationships. The tendency of western cultures to overvalue individualism, autonomy, and competition has deeply defined the character of our nation's higher education and professional programs. These values have structured our social relations, the nature of our inquiry, and the norms that guide our professional lives. Creating a new professional school within a liberal arts college that would guard against such detachment and address the prominent ethical and social concerns of our era was far from a strictly intellectual endeavor. It tested the limits of our ability to create a deeper dialogue among ourselves and with our students, to be creative in our vision of what the curriculum would be, and to practice pedagogy which truly respected our students as adult learners and fellow teachers.

Teaching a Core Class

In 1984, when the five existing graduate programs at Lewis & Clark College were joined to form a new school, the Graduate School of Professional Studies, students and faculty were asked to identify the issues facing them as persons striving to seek satisfying personal and professional lives. Those concerns generally fell into two areas: concern with life course issues as they affected their ability to maintain a proper balance between personal and professional demands and concern with the nature of modern organizations as they influence our ability to remain effective in our work or to remain in our work at all. These discussions led to the creation of a common experience for students and faculty across programs. It soon came to be called the graduate core program (see Introduction and Chapter 2 for further descriptions).

One of the courses in the core program, Individual and Societal Perspectives on Adulthood," was to be designed with regard for the mature adult student, typically a returning professional, a life-long learner who would be invited to examine major themes of adult development. As team teachers of this course, our first task was to articulate the major themes that would guide our inquiry:

1. The expectations individuals have for their lives are based on an interplay of cultural norms, family patterns, and individual choices, commitments, dispositions, and personalities.
2. Individuals develop as adults as these factors interact with individual life experiences. The course of adult development is characterized by both continuity and discontinuity.
3. Throughout the life course, individuals strive to make sense out of their life experiences and choices in a number of domains: intellectual, aesthetic, ethical, psychological, social, and spiritual. In Robert Kegan's words, "the activity of being a person is the activity of meaning making." (1982)
4. The effects of life events depend upon how and when they occur within the context of social and cultural expectations. Gender, ethnicity, age, religious values, socioeconomic factors, and social support networks affect the way we interpret and respond to life events. A major challenge for professionals today is that of building a caring society and a peaceful, interdependent world.
5. The challenge of professional organizations and work environments is to create the conditions for their employees' continued professional and personal development and creativity.
6. Life transitions, relationships and commitments, career choices, and the balancing of one's personal, family, and professional life are persistent life course challenges. (Brody and Witherell, 1987)

We then assumed that adults, as well as children, are natural storytellers, though they have often learned to suppress their urge to tell stories as evidence of knowing (or even experiencing) because of the dominant theory of knowledge as "objectivity and generalizability" within the academic world. Jerome Bruner (1986) has characterized these two ways of knowing as the narrative mode and the paradigmatic (or logicoscientific) mode. While we acknowledge the distinctive merits of each mode, we designed our course in adult development with the assumption that narrative and story are powerful teachers of the themes and challenges of the adult years.

We regard our curriculum as a dynamic expression of instruction and method, as we intended to model and foster the values of dialogue and inclusion within the course. We gave careful thought to the practical implications of an ethic based upon care as well as justice, upon cooperation as well as individual success. We were particularly interested in expanding our ways of knowing as professionals and our capacity to live our lives in caring relation with others, both within our own community called the graduate school and the larger community called our profession.

Connectedness, trust, teamwork: these were easier to talk about in the true, detached academic tradition than they were to actualize as the norms for conducting a weekly three-hour seminar with 25-35 people from five professions. There was already considerable resistance to this new, additional course requirement for graduate students. What could we do to "break the set" of a typical college class and provide a context for people working creatively and honestly together? As educators, we held the belief that people learn about the life course not through their "seats bolted to the chairs" but by actually living it. One of us had a great deal of experience as a whitewater river rafter and had used the river experience to conduct training programs with women. She had used the shared camaraderie, the willingness of participants to move in and out of themselves as they reflected on the processes they used to solve problems and know what they should or should not do. We knew that the time honored practices of experiential education were important for adult learners. We wanted to provide a common, intense experience that would require people to solve problems, confront issues of trust when working in groups, explore the meaning of teamwork and examine the implicit understandings about handicaps, gender, culture and style they each brought to working with people. We needed that common, shared experience from which we could all draw as we moved through the course. We wanted to create a metaphor for life, much like a theater is a mirror for life, but one that could be completed within the confines of a weekly course. We instituted a single session "challenge course" offered by the North Portland Youth Service Center, as part of the course experience.

The challenge course consists of a series of physical activities and problems requiring group cooperation to be completed. Trained counselor-guides set up physical challenges for the group, including both real limitations and imaginary consequences. Then, our guides step back and observe the antics that follow. Leaping from 6-foot platforms into the arms of your colleagues and scaling a 10-foot wall successfully may be an awesome physical challenge for some, while for others it is not. Challenge may reside in the psychological dimension where articulating one's own needs or listening carefully to the suggestions of others may be more difficult. Reflective processing of the event is the most important aspect of the experience. While the challenge course is typically completed in no less than 6 hours, we designed a 3-hour course, offering at the end considerable guidance for self-reflection before the next class meeting. Processing was easy because people had more than enough to say about their experience. The week's reflection time worked particularly well with adults, who have developed their self-reflective capabilities. Conducting this event early in the term provided us with a powerful communal experience from which we could consider all the themes of the course. It also served to establish a climate of connectedness, teamwork, and caring toward each other.

The challenge course proved to offer the glue we were seeking. Indeed, the nature of the course themes and the topics we hoped to explore would not be easy to deal with openly with peers unless there was a significant level of trust. Experiential learning coupled with our emphasis upon narrative and the personal story as the thread of the life course proved to be an exhilarating combination.

Another early concern was: How do we organize the major themes from adult development in such a way that they release the participant's own voice through the activities of writing and speaking? How do we frame the issues in the life course in such a way that the professional will integrate these understandings into his or her cognitive framework? We drew heavily upon the work of Mary Belenky and her associates in *Women's Ways of Knowing* (1986), Carol Gilligan's *In a Different Voice* (1982), Nel Noddings's *Caring: A Feminine Approach to Ethics and Moral Education* (1984), Tillie Olsen's *Tell Me a Riddle* (1976/1956), and anthropologist Barbara Myerhoff's study of an aging Jewish community in *Number Our Days* (1978). The work of the developmental psychologist Robert Kegan in *The Evolving Self* (1982) provided the pivotal theoretical work, offering a dialectical and constructivist view of human development. Jerome Bruner's *Actual Minds, Possible Worlds* (1986) offered a view of growth as the con-struction of possibilities, and Mark Pilisuk and Susan Hillier Parks' *The Healing Web* (1986) explored the potency of community and social networks in both individual and societal development. These essays and stories created a set of ideas that we wove together as braided strands throughout the course through our written and spoken dialogues with students. We also asked our students to read a piece of fiction or a biography that explored issues of gender, ethnic, or cultural identity within the adult years.

Emphasizing narrative and the personal story as the predomi-nant schema for understanding the life course was a conscious decision about how best to create that particular context in which professionals can explore the paradoxes of human development. We often elaborated on how dialogue was a particular expression of the narrative mode of thought. Thus, our teaching methodology was guided by two interconnected but slightly different modes of expression: narrative and dialogue.

We were intent on modeling dialogue with our students as we believe that dialogue should be at the heart of a graduate education. We wanted our participants to experience dialogue as Ira Shor and Paulo Freire described it, "Dialogue is the moment where humans meet to reflect on their reality as they make it and remake it. It is the quintessential human act, the social moment wherein we establish ties, and where we have authentic recognition of the other" (Shor and Freire, 1987. p. 98-99). Dialogue is dialectical in that only through true dialogue, with oneself or the other, can a person be changed or change another. It is the essence of the egalitarian stance in that I have to be able to suspend my self and my constructs in order to receive and hear you, the other, who at this moment, is me. When we seek to tell our stories, to be heard, it is in dialogue where we create the possibilities to hear and be heard. Again, we continued to create the braided strand.

We conveyed to our students our belief that the narrative capacity is the way each one of us reorganizes, reassesses, realigns his or her life experience so that it is continually integrated into our present schema, a schema that includes rich cultural and historical features, and ultimately into the schema of the community and the historical context for the culture. Narrative ways of knowing have been devalued in western science, precisely because of their serendipitous ability to integrate the seemingly paradoxical. The power of narrative is that it allows the individual to continually locate and relocate his or her own voice within a social and cultural context. Narrative and dialogue give each person what Gilligan and Belenky call "voice."

The metaphor of "finding one's voice" soon became common language to the class participants. It was used in several ways in the course. Students described the experience of losing their voice when they returned to school, due to a lack of open dialogue in their classes. They identified and gave new value to the collective efforts of people outside mainstream society attempting to give shape and direction to their world, and they identified those personal, political, and professional dimensions of their lives that had special significance for them.

In concert with Nel Noddings's (1984) and Martin Buber's (1965) claims that dialogue is at the heart of nurturing the ethical ideal, the caring relation, we designed our class around active participant dialogue within discussion groups. Participants were encouraged to release their stories as anecdotes for exploration of the theories we were examining. We explained to them:

> Typically we'd like to begin the class with our own reflections on themes or issues from the readings assigned in preparation for the class. These reflections will be followed or interspersed with comments and questions from class participants. During the second half of the evening, we will break into seminar groups to be led by class members. Each class member will have the opportunity to lead at least one seminar during the term. The seminar leader should prepare, in writing, a five to ten minute reflective essay on an issue from the readings for that evening, to be presented as the topic for the discussion within the group. Following this presentation, the leader shifts to the role of facilitator for a discussion of his or her presentation (Brody and Witherell, 1987)

Participants were asked to keep a dialogical journal. Our instructions to them provided an opportunity for them to write and think independently yet responsively to the views of the authors we were reading and to other class participants.

> The journal offers you the opportunity to engage in critical and personal reflections on readings, class discussion, field exercises and potential applications of these to your professional life and growth. Think of this writing each week as a continuous process of reflection on both self and community. Try to write when you feel a sense of creative energy, even passion. (Brody and Witherell, 1987)

Students discussed their stories in their seminars and in their journals, relating their personal histories and dramas to those of characters in fiction or biographies that they were reading in the course, to each other's experiences, or to theories of development that we used as conceptual organizers.

We asked students to consider what they were learning from personal narratives about the significance of the life course. Kim Stafford tells us in *Having Everything Right* that "stories can save your life a little at a time" (1987, p. 55). The personal narratives of the participants in our graduate core class recorded in their journals, autobiographies, and reflective papers suggest that one of the ways that stories save life is through illuminating the power of connection— a powerful guard against detachment. Connections are forged within lives—that is, across time and context and between lives—across time, context, persons, generations, cultures, and gender. As the term unfolded, we observed our students with their diverse backgrounds and ages listening to each other with both humility and awe. We noted the respect they felt for the life experiences of each other and we read in their journals about the quiet, yet often profound, lessons they were learning from their peers.

Stories from Our Students

The story vignettes that follow offer voices that have made such connections within the human drama. They are stories of the human yearning for meaning-making. They are also stories of human caring: the memory of caring and being cared for and the conflicts and yearnings of caring.

We want to suggest that serious writing by students, when shared with class members in this way, can serve both as text and as grounded theory. Students' writing served to organize their concepts and ways of knowing within each seminar group in ways that prepared the groups for their final projects: presentations to the class that described a group action research project, a collective narrative, or a creative synthesis and application of major constructs developed in the course.

These stories join the worlds of thought and feeling. They connect the authors' analyses of self, gender, and culture with their feelings—feelings of joy, sadness, aloneness, anger, and the fullness of relation. They acknowledge the centrality of affect and subjectivity in human ways of knowing. We offer this language and these first-person narratives without apology, but rather with the hope that they will convey the power and richness experienced in our study of adult development and social networks.

With Nel Noddings, we feel that there is a great chasm that "divides the masculine and the feminine in all of us" (1984, p. 6). This may be especially true in the academic world, where, as in the rest of our daily life, our aim should be the full expression and reconciliation of these voices, for they are surely the partners in life's dance. Margaret, a 35-year-old counselor-in-training and a member of a religious order, shows how story and dialogue have helped her find her own voice.

Margaret

Hers is a story of one woman's personal healing through the growth of receptiveness and responsiveness, leading to a confidence in her own voice. Her growth in these areas occurs first through the world of nature, later through her work with a skilled therapist, and most recently through her discovery of female mentors in the case studies of Mary Belenky (1986) and Carol Gilligan (1982) and the fictional writings of Tillie Olsen (1956/1976). She begins her writing with an idea from Mary Belenky with which she personally identifies and continues to explore its meaning for herself in terms of her own history and her future life work as a therapist:

> In her book, *Women's Ways of Knowing*, Mary Belenky discusses how one must first begin to hear her own inner voice in order to understand the importance of drawing out the voices of others, whether the other is her child, spouse, student, client or friend. (Belenky et al., 1986)
>
> There was a big old tree in the backyard when I grew up. From the moment I was able to climb, that tree was my refuge, my home. I climbed higher each year until by the time I was 17 I would escape and sit in the high branches hidden in the leaves, riding on the eastern Oregon wind. I did a lot of thinking in the tree; the wind in the leaves was my only friend. One time in South Canyon with my dad and brothers I climbed way to the top of a very steep hillside and sat and listened to the wind. I was about 12 at the time. The wind listened to me and required nothing of me.
>
> On warm evenings I would wander around the fields near our house, and a wildness and longing would overcome me and I would think of running. I always knew there was something I wanted very badly, something I needed, someone to listen to me. And always, always there was that Eastern Oregon wind. I let the wind blow through me, calming me, crying for me. I could hear its voice in the trees and wild grasses, moaning and whispering, howling in February. I was so alone, but I had the wind. Yet that wind frightened me, too, because when I heard its cry I would feel things. When you grow up with an alcoholic parent, you do not want to feel things....
>
> There was nothing really dramatic in my home situation. My dad drank, withdrew, and we all kept quiet. The wind was a wonderful friend for many years, as was my journal for a while. The wind allowed me the space to think and feel, the journal helped me to begin to find my voice, and then I found a therapist who let me speak that voice and say aloud the things I'd only thought, felt or written for so long...
>
> That is why I want to be a therapist. There is a lot of beauty hidden in broken lives. There are many voices that have never spoken. Because of their wounds they may never be as strong as they could have been or as lovely, but as Tillie Olsen says, "There is still enough left to live by" (Olsen, 1956/1976, p. 21). In therapy the relationship between the therapist and the client is probably the most essential ingredient for good therapy. The trained therapist must make initial efforts at building that relationship and empathy is the starting point.

Empathy is a response that focuses on the other person's feelings in such a way that the person knows they are understood and accepted. It is very difficult to focus on someone else's feelings, thoughts and values if I am not comfortable with my own.

It has always been very important to me that I respond to others in a manner wherein I receive no criticism. This fear has caused me to block my own thoughts and feelings and to become what the listener wants me to be. Most of my life I have had no sense that what I think, feel or value is of any importance, and thus I have been unable to be at ease with myself, to go out of myself to be present to the other. My capacity for empathy is blocked because I have been unable to hear the truth of the inner voice of my own feelings and thoughts.

I now realize that the family situation from which I came was one which actively discouraged me from having my own thoughts and feelings. It was important for me to be quiet, and if I spoke, I was to reflect back what my mother felt and thought. My mother as well stood back from my father, who had the last and ultimately the final word. Mary Belenky describes this as a typical expectation in many women's lives and it was certainly in mine. Conventional feminine goodness means being voiceless as well as selfless (Belenky et al.,1986).

I feel my own voice beginning to be more sure and able to hold its own. At times I can express my feelings and thoughts without too much fear. I used to listen and enjoy, but now I can listen, express myself and enjoy. It's still amazing to me when someone listens to what I say!

Margaret's reflections demonstrate a pattern we found in our participants' writings: when given permission to use personal narratives to discover and reorganize the stories of their lives, adults will invariably explore themes of gender and culture. Certainly the readings of Tillie Olsen (1976), Belenky et al. (1986), and Gilligan (1982) stimulated the consideration of these themes as did our emphasis upon caring as the deeply feminine expression Nel Noddings describes (1984).

Ken

It is not a new assertion that telling stories can give an authenticity and power to the writings of a tender author. As teachers we have observed a few students who have a rich background in oral traditions. While they may be quite competent at the usual college writing discourse, they often excel when given permission to express themselves in the narrative mode. We have included the complete version of Ken Donald's story, "The ways of my mother: A Native American son's reflection of the oral tradition," because it so fully expresses the significance of the story in constructing "culture." Ken gives us a unique understanding of how the oral tradition provides the theme, symbol, structure, and motivation for the Native American tradition of connection to the land, to each other, and to a woman-centered social system (Allen, 1986). Without the story there is no cultural meaning for a people, indeed, there is no culture as Barbara Myerhoff learned from the elderly Jewish men and women she studied in *Number Our Days* (1978). It is often women who treasure the narrative as a way of knowing and a way of communicating. Ken shares the story of how a woman's birth changed the life of a people, bringing new meaning and wisdom to their culture as they struggled to survive. That Ken is now carrying on this legacy suggests to us lessons to be learned about connections between cultures and between men and women. This is Ken's story:

The Ways of my Mother: A Native American Son's Reflection on the Oral Tradition

"Sometimes you get so angry. Even worse, you know why you're angry. And you can't do a thing about it. The more you know, the more you don't see. The aches and pains of time: it rolls through you in quivering waves. The human conditions can hurt you."

My mom used to tell us this in her oral tales. My mother was born in the winter of the White-Buffalo. She knew her life was going to be hard—hard-work, hard-living, hard-luck and hard-to-ignore. My grandfather, her father, was the last of the Eagle Clan medicine men. In our tribe, these clans people are privy to the highest forms of healing arts. My grandmother was the daughter of the chief of our tribe, the head of the Bear Clan. A joining of the highest, most respected clan, the Eagle Clan (Grandfather), with the deep Earth symbol, the Bear Mother (Grandmother) produced a blessing: my mother.

It is January, 1929, in Northeastern Oklahoma, the dream season of our year. It's a time to open yourself, to open yourself bare to the wintery Earth and ask for life to begin again. The fruits of our tribe's dreams allow spring to realize itself. My mother stepped into this world early that snowy morning. Hundreds of pairs of eyes witnessed the birth as the tribe gathered around to experience the dream (i.e., second coming). The women's eyes misted with joy as a wailing female flung herself into life. The men's eyes blinked rapidly in disbelief. A female? This is the second coming?

This is wrong! Surely the Eagle Clan won't accept her. The White Buffalo won't come, not yet, not this year. The women reminded the men this blessing brings food to our hearths, "wherever our fires are lit."

My grandfather felt the eyes, the hopes upon him. He looked outside. It began to snow and snow. To the sweathouse the elders trudged. It kept snowing.

When the elders stepped out of the sweathouse into the early morning sun, before their disbelieving eyes stood a group of white buffalo. Buffalo are wily and stout, they are big with pride. They won't stand for any human's touch. They don't even like snow on their rangy manes. Staring at the elders was a herd of white buffalo, winter free buffalo; standing without looking; wispy, calm, with measured breathing. Not one out of breath. Not one was swaying with pride as does a buffalo. It was as if the buffalo appeared. The white buffalo showed our tribe what they could not see with their own eyes. My mom was as special as the second coming! Her birth called the "White Buffalo."

The White Buffalo brought us to this planet as caretakers of the Earth. The White Buffalo listens for the call only Mother Nature can make. When the time is ready, the White Buffalo will return and take us from this planet. The women of our tribe knew that events happen when they should. The men knew you live with time—not against it. The White Buffalo were talking to us.

My mother's birth coupled with the never-before-seen behavior of the snow-clad buffalo was interpreted by my grandfather as a sign. Never before in the memories of our people have we had a woman medicine man. Never before has the breath of the Earth (woman) been asked to walk where only spirits reside, where the eagles fly, the home of the medicine ways. The Eagle Clan did accept my mother. She became Chimi-Chimo, "The Wild Buffalo". Many in the tribe wondered, was this the direction our Great Spirits wanted us to go? A woman medicine man could tie us to the Earth preventing us from ever leaving (being saved). Many eyes watched my mom grow up. My mom said growing up she didn't feel different, but she saw that people felt different about her.

In retrospect, dropping out of school in the fifth grade freed up a lot of my mom's time. She spent most of her time learning the medicine ways from my grandfather and the rest of her time, "being wild with what I learned from Father." Many in the tribe shook their heads saying, "I told you so!" with their indifference. Many turned away from the hand reaching out to save them. Through it all, my mom's sunny disposition kept her detractors at bay, her supporters attentive.

My mother's special calling is her ability to call eagles to appear whenever she feels she needs their presence. She uses her knowledge of the medicine ways to heal sick spirits. Nowadays, tribal members go to clinics and hospitals for direct medical care, but still come to my mom for counseling and spiritual support.

Eight years ago, my mom developed stomach cancer. She went to a hospital in Tulsa, Oklahoma. The doctors wanted to take her to surgery immediately. They told her she wouldn't live one week. My mom said, "Not yet." She went back to her reservation and drove to a special spot she knew. This "spot" was where her father showed her how to step into both worlds—real and unreal, reality and magic. It was at this spot where she received her special calling of the eagles. She sat in her car and thought. She stayed there for days without food or water. My mom had a vision of eagles coming down to her. The eagles sat and watched her for a day. She says they, the eagles, wanted to see what foot she would follow—reality or magic. Eventually she felt a burning peace come over her. As she slept, she felt awakened by a fire in her stomach. She moved out of her body, floating above her car. The eagles were tearing at her stomach with their beaks. Even out of her body she felt the rolling waves of pain flow through her. Finally the eagles stopped, looked up at my mom and then my mom knew it wasn't her time to die yet.

When my mom awakened in the car she felt sick. Her stomach was swollen and the pain was great. She remembered her dreams and thought they were telling her to have the surgery. She drove to the hospital, checked in and was immediately prepped for surgery. When the doctors took x-rays to determine the spread of cancer before opening her up, they were shocked. No cancer was found anywhere. They did every test they could think of, always coming up with the same negative results. The hospital in Tulsa (Oral Roberts' territory) called the papers and told them of this miracle that had occurred. It was described as being done by God. My mom says she agreed it was done. She was a little wary of Oral's god having done it but agreed she had been healed by a power greater than her faith.

This brush with death didn't cause my mom to lead a "one foot in the grave" lifestyle. From her squalid trailer she exudes her special kind of magic. When you talk with her you can hear yourself think. Everyone's her sister or good friend. She pushes on your grips, your pillars of knowledge, your finely-tuned defenses until you can feel her loving acceptance of you. But paradoxically, she does not leave you to drift. Her pointed reminders present you with a way to see yourself while still holding out more possibilities.

My mom just found out she has a hole in her heart. Her heart can't pump enough to keep up sufficient pressure. She's had four heart attacks in the last six months. Doctors predict she won't last another six months. Coming to terms with her life and talking to each of us children will forever be an example of how to die to me. I'll never again be able to forget that significant people die. I'm sad for that. My mom's rich narrative, her stories, her reminder that life goes on, but that each of us has a special way to be with life is a knowing that is now integrated into my life.

My mom's understanding of her own life resounds with metaphors of the 'voice' we all strive to bring forth in ourselves and in our community and culture. Her oral stories were always meant to get us to see, as Native Americans, how to accept yourself. Her narratives were meant to bring us to the cliff but we had to decide when to jump. Jumping into "a way of knowing" is everyone's journey. I've had the pleasure of a loving guide, the pain of knowing what lay ahead. I am different as a man, as a Native American and as a counselor because of how I have come to "know" this.

My mom's message is simply, "Find the path to yourself and run to it." I'm still running. Thanks to my mom I have a clearer sense of where I'm running.

We view Ken's story as a wonderful example of the power of story in guiding both the life of an individual and the life of a culture. We are reminded of Cynthia Ozick's allusion to storytelling as a "kind of magic act" (1986).

One of the major themes for the course is derived from Robert Kegan's work on the nature of human psychological development (1982). He creates vivid metaphors to explain the human drive toward competency, toward increased differentiation, and toward the making of meaning as we continually strive to know the world. Many class participants were drawn to Kegan because of their intuitive sense of the paradoxical nature of life and the complexity of human development. They were relieved that his was not another cognitive stage theory that somehow did not accommodate their own experiences; rather they were intrigued by the notion that human development is a journey that involves striking balances between the fundamental yearnings of autonomy and inclusion. These balances are a kind of evolutionary truce where the person shifts onto new ground and revisits the old, continually realigning one's constructs while striving to make sense out of one's experiences. Our students appreciated a theory of development that considered that their own yearnings were not necessarily contradictions, but rather expressions of increasing complexity and possibility. Participants wrote and talked, putting their lives in a new order, finding new ways to make sense out of their experiences as they experimented with Kegan's language of meaning-making. For example, they connected Pilisuk and Park's (1986) notion of the healing web with Kegan's concept of embeddedness. Both metaphors speak to a social context that gives support and a culture of identity during a particular phase of development.

Ruth

Ruth Lundblad's writing is a particularly dramatic example of the connections students made out of the seemingly paradoxical tensions of the life course theme. Deeply touched by the fictional account of the old woman, Eva, in Tillie Olsen's story *Tell Me A Riddle* (1976/1956), Ruth applies Kegan's concepts in her analysis of the story as it speaks to her own life, while integrating the religious metaphors so personally meaningful.

A New Song

Grandaddy, Grandaddy don't cry. She is not there, she promised me. On the last day, she said she would go back to when she first heard music, a little girl on the road of the village where she was born. She promised me. It is a wedding and they dance, while the flutes, so joyous and vibrant, tremble in the air. Leave her there, Grandaddy, it is all right. She promised me. Come back, come back and help her poor body to die. (Olsen, 1956/1976 p.125)

Sitting here at the computer, trying to harmonize my brain cells into a wedding feast and dance, I resonate with Olsen's story, and with the plight of the dying woman, Eva, who, at her last moment faces point blank life's interplay, and melodious blend of some of their overtures in her life.

Both my song and Eva's song say this: that truth hides in paradox; that it cannot be embodied within either/or parameters, and that personal and sexual individuation serves an even greater pur-pose—that of renewing relationships between genders and across generations, and of teaching male and female, young and old, to step lively in the streets, in motion together to the trilling of Pan's flute, "so joyous and vibrant, and trembling in the air."

Because life, in its living, tightens the bowstring between radical opposites: between woman and man; between relation and separation; and between community chorus and long, lovely solos in the night. My status as a loner amid a chaotic family life, and Eva's stance in 'reconciled solitude' amid America's post-industrial society, become uneasy fortresses against what is instinctively known to be true—that we all swing spiderlike in the winds as members of a tightly knit life network, which begins darkly in the humus nature of our cultural history, continues above ground through the trunk of fierce individuality, and then reaches upward and outward into the sweet, sunlit branches of the Tree of Life; this is our "healing web."

We observe Eva in three life phases: (1) as a Russian peasant girl, drowning in poverty, yet singing about cultural meaning and about hope for a better tomorrow; (2) as a silent American mother, growing bark hard in isolation, and in the lop-sided nurturance of her growing, and then gone, young family; and (3) as a dying grandmother, blowing lonesome as a leaf upon autumn branches, and only just now regaining the power to sing, with the ability to hear her own voice, as she realizes her relationship to the oneness of life. She realizes it only perhaps as she drifts downward in death toward those mossy village roots and intertwining streets where she first heard music, first applauded the wedding, and first participated in the dance.

How could it be that the Old World, so deadly to individual autonomy, had yet harbored a culture which nurtured so well her ability to belong and believe? Because paradoxically, that was where Eva, as she thinks back, can place the feeling of connectedness, that sense of mattering, and of being one with the meaning of life.

But so much has changed. The passion for tending children in the New World had isolated this young mother from adjustment to the new culture, to a new form of inclusion, and to a new life through assimilation of a post-industrial way of belonging and believing. Moreover, her gift for relatedness (granted by virtue of gender) had isolated her from a male-dominated culture which overvalued individuality instead. So, therefore, Eva's very power to connect becomes her prison, a strangely silent prison with parallel bars which look not so unlike strands in social networks, yet lacking intersections.

Eva, then, as an old woman, has been rock dry for a long time. In these later years, life's tree trunk has become barkish, scarred over and defensive. And although she senses a more ancient truth within, authentic living water more powerful than blood, somehow joy, transport, and meaning have yet escaped. The sickness of loneliness invades her; still, it is a sickness she feels comfortable with. Connected in the near past only to babies and to blood, she remained silently aloof. But now, times have changed.

Now, stricken at once with cancer and with cacophony, she finds her voice, and clamors sullenly against the walls of a house she will not part with, a house symbolizing "excluded inclusion," plus a certain domestic detachment from society. Her husband, though, desires a more communal living arrangement instead. And, well, he only makes matters worse. During Eva's last illness he hauls her shrunken body helplessly between the homes of their grown children, as she groans and pleads for solitude instead. As this aged pair continue to roll so merrily along, the wife begins to cry bitterly against her husband in an overture toward dialogue, and toward a kind of understanding so long desired, yet never attempted before.

Bickering like magpies, then, they arrive on the peaceful Southern California coast amid other elderly folk who sit daily upon its shore, content in the gloaming, eyes silent upon the sea. But Eva, now, silent she cannot be. For the first time in a long while she begins to sing, a duet with death now, her new song for morning. I'll never forget Eva on the beach as she suddenly gathers strength and leaps hartlike into the sea; and then, when her long suffering husband gently tries to pull her out, and to wipe her dry with a handkerchief, she grabs the cloth and wraps up some sand to look at later with a strong glass—her womanly way of examining the ordinary for a hint of the eternal, and for the meaning of death, which rages and beats incessantly upon her shore.

Now enter Jeannie, their granddaughter, reality's nurse, yet imagination's artist, who presents the fulfillment of their Old World hopes, who ministers glowingly to her dying grandmother, who calls her lonely grandfather to the old woman's side in an affirmation of life even in confrontation with death, and who forms that healing link which, in balancing life's dichotomies, produces seedlings of promise, and of hope. Through Jeannie's ministrations, the Tree of Life fertilizes itself and the drifting movement downward ultimately becomes the movement up.

One extreme, then, Old World connectedness, represents the traditional female role; while New World individuality represents traditional masculinity. The important point to remember from this story is our need for the healing balance of both extremes; we must orchestrate life's cantata so that both male and female voices sound, and so that both solos and choral pieces flourish, or else harmony and health may be lost.

Whatever life guarantees, it is not the absolute answer. Paradox delivers oxymoronic truth. I desire the realization of this kind of truth in my life, an insight which can be utilized right now without waiting for the emergency of death to graciously point it out. As a college student, wife and as a mother of four, I often feel isolated and overwhelmed. My husband and children are lifesprings to me; yet also life draining. In confrontation with them, I step crazy into the sea, laughing furiously and wrapping up sand to examine later with my looking glass. The sand is my life; the looking glass, my story.

The truth is this: Masculinity and I make interesting music together. Together we cling to the vine, to the Tree of Life, to the ancient of days, so that we need not seek to revolutionize the other, but to harmonize with the other in a tremulous balance, a death defying rejuvenation, and an upward-spiraling flute song into the sky. This is the meaning of balance; and this, of grace.

The stories we have offered demonstrate the power of stories to heal, noted by Sam Keen:

Stories open you up to the stories of others, as common and singular as your own. That remains the best way we storytelling animals have found to overcome loneliness, develop compassion and create community. Indeed, if the unique stories of individuals are not cherished, a group of people may become a mass, or a collective, but never a healing community. (1988, pp. 46-47)

These writings of graduate students point out the collective power of a class experience and the responsibility of professional education to move beyond the traditional epistemological assumptions about knowledge and ways of knowing. They also attest to the legitimacy of student experience in the shaping of their professional curriculum. And, they demonstrate a way to practice and model an ethic of care.

The Lessons We Learned

These early experiences we had as teachers have now become the basis for the curriculum and pedagogy of the core program. What is particularly telling is that over each successive term and with new teams of teachers the course has been highly successful. Student writings and course evaluations indicate that we are doing something right. But what makes this experience so important to us as teachers are just those things that defy smugness and certainty.

Each successive course must be recreated anew, through dialogue between faculty and students. Because the nature of dialogue is to continually rediscover and revisit, we have found that there is no standard and efficient way to teach if the journey each term regards the participants as unique contributors to the living curriculum. Hence, a commitment to this kind of pedagogy is a commitment of time and energy, particularly on the part of the faculty. We have learned a lesson we always knew, that co-teaching takes time and more time. The ideas brought into the discussions and writings by the students must be considered by both instructors together as part of the text of the class and as material for their own personal and professional growth. Indeed, co-teaching offers the teachers the unique opportunity to reflect upon their own teaching, learning, and growth.

We further learned that if we are to come to know our students and understand the power of their ideas to shape the course then both instructors need to read the major writings of as many students as possible. This is a difficult arrangement to work out because of the numbers of participants in the course, but the benefits in terms of student trust and openness are worth the investment of time. Indeed, our own perceptions of each others' ideas were just as important for the evolving curriculum as our perceptions of our students' thinking.

We value experiential learning with a new level of certainty. The challenge course has become a standard part of the curriculum, and we continue to integrate more cooperative learning activities each term. The literature on adult learning tells us that adults are most willingly recruited as learners when they feel that their own life experiences will be affirmed and when they have the opportunity to revisit and make sense out of the new in light of the old (Aslanian and

Brickell, 1980; Brookfield, 1986; Chickering, 1981; Cross, 1981). Experiential learning supports what adults already know about their learning styles, and it creates opportunities for them to integrate new learning in the context of their previous experiences.

Narrative and personal story are powerful modes of knowing, and, while they are not exclusively for adults, we have observed the richness that these ways of knowing and telling have for adults who bring so many anecdotes and examples from life experience. We have seen the sureness with which our students continue to bring their voices into their other classes and have observed the benefits of this approach for our students in other classes. Students listen to others with greater interest and use narrative and personal stories in their other writing.

It is a pleasure for us to wander through the graduate school at night, meeting old friends from these classes and recognizing students from other programs than our own. We sense a camaraderie rooted in caring and take personal pleasure in experiencing a growing sense of community among graduate students and faculty.

We teach to change lives. Our experience teaching in this program has led to significant changes in our own and our students' ways of thinking and being. In the sharing of life stories and dilemmas of the workplace, we have come closer to understanding the "other" as ourselves, to "imagine the familiar hearts of strangers" (Ozick, 1986, p. 65). We have shared in a learning community that bridged many gaps and explored many paradoxes: feeling and thought; masculine and feminine; teacher and administrator; hearing and deaf; Anglo-Saxon and Native American; teacher and learner; individual and community. It has been a remarkable journey.

5

Reflection and Adult Development: A Pedagogical Process

ROBERT R. KLEIN

Reflection is essential for adult development in both the personal and professional spheres. It enables us to identify and correct distortions in our personal belief systems (Mezirow, 1990) and it allows us to evaluate successes and failures in the workplace, providing opportunities to improve our performance (Schon, 1988). But promoting critical reflection in the classroom can be a difficult task since people must analyze, evaluate, and possibly adjust their beliefs and behaviors within a group context. As Brookfield has pointed out, this process, which can bring into question deeply held assumptions, can be explosive, and educators who foster this learning are like psychological and cultural demolition experts. It requires care and sensitivity, for educators must ensure that if and when the foundations of an individual's assumptions are shaken, the framework of his or her self-esteem is left relatively intact. Only then can development be truly promoted (1990).

I will discuss a particular approach to fostering critical reflection as it relates to adult development that I developed with my professional students, colleagues, and co-teacher in a course, "Individual and Societal Perspectives on Adulthood." In this course we combined readings from history, anthropology, sociology, and literature with a dialectical group process to provide the kind of challenge and sensitivity Brookfield described. Readings rich in narrative furnished the raw materials for our critical reflection. We then set out to create a collaborative enterprise where dialogue was nurtured and all personal knowledge was valued. We intentionally raised ethical, social, and individual issues relating to adult development. But fundamental to this process was a belief in a caring community, where individuals could risk and be supported, where self-esteem remained intact, and where potentially difficult and divisive issues were handled with sensitivity and care (Noddings, 1986).

Central Elements in Course Design

When a teacher sets out to promote reflection in the classroom, it is important to select methods that are as approachable and nonthreatening for the learners as possible. I find that selecting literature from the liberal arts disciplines and the humanities met this prescription. Anthropological and historical accounts, sociological research, a psychological theory on adult development, and short stories provide very accessible materials for studying a variety of perspectives on developmental themes. We often begin each class by analyzing these themes; later we reflect on our personal experiences and examine our beliefs and assumptions about specific issues. The students therefore have a two-step entry into the concepts and ideas of the course, which also encourages them to consider different perspectives on the issues. In addition, this method had another benefit: it encourages students to think broadly about a range of problems and to seek new organization and methods to deal with them, something that Argyris and Schon had advocated for increasing professional effectiveness (1974).

We also draw on Argyris and Schon's idea that in the traditional approach to problem solving, tacit knowledge is important to a great professional who functions independently and who can organize a diagnosis and propose an elegant solution. They believe, however, that the criteria for diagnosis and solution should depend on information and knowledge gathered from all participants in a given situation. What they suggest is a more interactive group approach, where people collaborate in the diagnostic and problem-solving operations (1974). This philosophy have been integrated into Schon's work *The Reflective Practitioner* (1983).

Collaborative group processes are integral to promoting reflection. We organize small- and large-group work where everyone can share insights and experiences. In this context students are expected to reflect together on developmental and professional problems and construct diagnoses and solutions. We also want to incorporate what Mezirow has described as "communicative learning," where individuals not only reflect on their own assumptions and values, but are challenged to understand what others communicate about values, ideals, feelings, moral decisions, and concepts such as freedom, justice, love, labor, commitment, and democracy. In this type of discourse, students can evaluate critically their own beliefs through a group discussion in which many people's ideas are presented, analyzed, and challenged according to their validity and merit (1990).

We prefer a gender-balanced teaching team, believing that male and female instructors, preferably from different professional backgrounds, can speak from a broader range of experience and model respect for gender differences and multiple perspectives. My colleague and I take turns presenting various subject matter and co-lead large group discussions. Usually we begin each class by initiating a conversation about some significant themes from the day's readings. Later on, the students convene in regular small groups, where individual students, in rotation, take responsibility for sharing a reflective essay and then leading a discussion on additional themes from the readings. By this means we encourage the students to develop and refine their group leadership skills. After the small-group session, the large group reconvenes for a final analysis of the material, where we synthesize key ideas and prompt further reflection on critical issues. In the evening students write journal entries about provocative themes from the day's class or events in the class itself. The journal writing allows for reflective withdrawal and reentry with the material and abets the process of teaching reflective skills (Lukinsky, 1990). We read the journals periodically and participate in a written dialogue with the individual students. This exchange enables us to address some of the most private, sensitive issues of the students, and we are able to offer them highly individualized feedback to promote their personal development.

Creating a Positive Environment for Reflection

The first class session is always critical for establishing an atmosphere of honesty, openness, and caring. What is essential at this moment is that teachers model the reflective stance they are asking the learners to adopt (Brookfield, 1990). We begin by sharing with the class reflections on our own life's journeys. I often speak about my experience of losing a job in a state mental health system due to the Reagan cutbacks, the resulting pain and confusion this caused me, and how, after a great deal of reflection, I eventually pursued graduate work in educational psychology. This experience has been formative for me, solidifying my commitment to a self-reflective process and personal development, which I explain to the class. I want them to see how a personal crisis can be the impetus for a very positive transformation in one's adult life. My colleague often shares some similar reflections of her own.

Personal disclosures, carefully chosen and sincerely offered, have a very positive effect on the group. The members recognize that we are genuinely committed to the ideas and process of the course, that we are willing to share openly, and that we also want to hear about their formative experiences. Of all the conditions that are necessary for encouraging reflection on adult development, this initial modeling seems among the most critical because it sets a tone for the whole enterprise; it becomes a foundation for building the future sessions. It is therefore imperative that instructors consider deeply their own experiences with the course themes and share these in an authentic way. Also, the particular episodes one shares are crucial because the most significant adult learning occurs in connection with major life transitions, events such as divorce, retirement, returning to school or the work force, or a change in job status (Mezirow, 1990). Selecting experiences that touch upon these life transitions leads the group into a fertile area for future reflection and learning.

One other point should be made about the introductory session. The sharing of our life experiences initiated a fundamental process for the course, i.e., the process of storytelling. This activity, as it related to personal and professional themes, is instrumental for the learning task (Schon, 1988). In describing our experiences we share not only key facts but our perspectives on them, our values and feelings, and how we make sense of these experiences (Witherell, 1991). Through our storytelling we come to understand more clearly how we make meaning in our lives, and this becomes prime material for critical analysis and reflection. The voices in our carefully selected texts also assist us in this process: by hearing and analyzing these voices we are better able to recognize and experience our own voices, our own stories.

Examining Life Course Issues Using
Narratives from Anthropology

Narratives from anthropology offer an array of material for exploring central themes in adult development: the life histories of key subjects, accounts of cultural and community influences on people's lives, and descriptions of organizational and institutional life. We like to begin our study with Barbara Myerhoff's anthropological treatise, *Number Our Days,* an investigation of a Jewish center for the aged in Los Angeles. We identify critical developmental issues that emerge from this story of people in their seventies and eighties, issues relating to personal development, family life, and professional development, topics that engage everyone in the class.

The life histories become a springboard for very personal reflections on the themes that characters in this story have had to deal with.

For example, Shmuel, a tailor in the book, spoke with pride about his work, even though he had often spent long hours in tiresome and boring labor; yet he found great satisfaction in knowing that people wore his quality garments. This story has led to a discussion about personal motivation, job satisfaction, and work stress. The most satisfying work expresses our special talents and our personal values, but often we can only discern these after some practical experiences and serious reflection. Our class analyzes the process of discernment, where we get in touch with our deepest, most consistent feelings about our work, which can then inform our job selection and hopefully increase job satisfaction.

Anthropological accounts such as *Number Our Days* have encouraged us to engage in a discussion about power, leadership, and group dynamics in organizations. In this particular ethnographic study a man named Kominsky runs the center. Although many of his values are consistent with those of his constituency, he tends to make decisions in a unilateral, authoritarian way, which eventually leads to a popular uprising against him. We use this incident as a starting point for a discussion about authority and organizational life. For example, one student, a young woman who had been teaching for a year, told of the frustrations she had had with her principal. Fresh out of school and armed with many new ideas, she had had trouble in getting the principal to listen to her; she received the organizational message to keep her head down and her mouth shut. She had a lot of anger about this style of leadership and the school's organizational dynamics; she felt she was being treated this way because she was new, young, and a woman.

Things got a bit heated in the class when a couple of older men in the group, who were in positions of authority themselves, responded to her statements. When they tried to explain some other reasons for the principal's behavior, the conversation polarized. At that point another woman, who was in her forties, shared her experience of anger with a boss. She had done some reflection about why a particular boss's behavior had regularly made her so upset, even with regard to the smallest matters. She realized that he often behaved toward her in ways that her father had, acting condescendingly and insensitively. Anger toward her father transferred to the boss, making the situation even more difficult, until she understood the connection. She suggested that the younger woman try to differentiate some of the sources of her own intense anger.

Ultimately, we designed a role-play with the young woman and one of the men who acted as her principal. The objectives here were twofold: to practice communication skills that she could later use at the actual school site and to invite her to reflect critically on her own behavior in this situation. As Schon has pointed out, a part of teaching reflective skills is getting learners to see how their embedded strategies and assumptions mirror and reinforce the features of the organizational world that makes them cynical and frustrated (1988). At the conclusion of this role-play the entire class contributed analyses and interpretations, providing the young woman with numerous ideas to consider. This is a cogent example of the way that the group members collaborate in diagnosis and problem solving and how members assist one another in developing critical reflection skills.

A Psychological Theory for Adult Development

Robert Kegan's *The Evolving Self* provides us with a dialectical, constructivist view of human development (1982). Kegan posits that individuals construct meaning in different ways during the various phases of their lives and that their focus during these phases shifts back and forth between a primary concern for self and a primary concern for other. Using this conceptual framework, we are able to evaluate the process of meaning-making during childhood, adolescence, and adulthood. One application of Kegan's theory suggests that when people hold different perspectives on experiences and situations, due to their different developmental phases, conflict and misunderstanding can result. We often attribute this to poor communication, but Kegan argues that these are fundamental orientations that affect our ways of knowing, and to improve communication we need to gain a deeper understanding of how the other person is making meaning at his or her particular phase. My colleague once shared a poignant example from her own life when she described her efforts to infuse responsible adult values in her teenage son, who, despite her efforts, continued to act from a value system derived from his peer group, which promoted reckless behavior. She recognized how fused his identity was with his peer group and how his sense of self intertwined with his group role. Her efforts to separate him from some of his friends didn't relate well to his way of making meaning and met with tremendous resistance. Analyzing this, she adjusted her strategies with more positive results.—She and other parents organized more constructive peer-group activities where the adolescents could be together, but without high-risk behavior. Class members then added their own examples of this phenomenon, addressing communication issues within families, educational settings, and organizational contexts. This communication problem also applies to our class itself, where the students' ages run from the early twenties to the mid-forties. At times our communication is affected by differences in developmental perspective. For example, in the previously mentioned conflict between the young woman and the older male students, different developmental perspectives contributed to the intense class-room debate. According to Kegan's theory, she may have been moving through the phase where the individual focuses on self-definition and independence, and often takes a strong ideological stance. For her, the disagreement with the principal represented a sharp ideological clash, and she held on tightly to the values which defined her. For the male students, who may have been constructing meaning from a more connected phase, the problem demonstrated the need for interdependent self-definition, a partial self-surrender in order to create a positive interdependence between her and her boss. She defended her position according to her high principles, while the older students tried to point out that the situation wasn't as black and white as she thought. By applying Kegan's theory, we gained insights into these patterns of communication within our class.

Another way to understand developmental changes in our meaning systems is through fiction. Stories offer encapsulated versions of life experiences, which provide insights into how we differentiate ourselves from the world and from each other. Dorothy Canfield's short story, "Sex Education" (1945), richly balances the academic writing of Kegan, offering a tale of how we interpret life events differently depending on our developmental perspective, as our ways of meaning-making change due to growth and maturity. In this story a woman recounts a certain incident from her youth and tells it three different times. Each retelling takes place after a significant lapse in time, and the woman interprets the episode differently on each occasion, each time gaining greater insight. In the final retelling she recognizes more clearly her own role in what happened, affixing less blame to the other person and recognizing her own responsibility in the situation. Over time she has assumed a more adult perspective, eventually reaching Kegan's Interindividual Phase, where one recognizes one's interdependence with others and a shared responsibility for life events.

The short story has inspired us to reflect on the ways this process occurs within our own lives. We analyze the ways our own interpretations of personal events have changed over the years, from childhood, adolescence, and into adulthood. I recall one older student coura-geously speaking about the problems he had experienced in his childhood, related to his father's drinking and violent behavior. He had hated his father into his early twenties, but as time went on, he began to gain a new perspective. His father had been an Army combat veteran. The student, through conversations with his extended family, began to realize how traumatized his father had been by his wartime experiences. A sympathy in the student began to grow, and, as it did, he recognized his own responsibility for many family incidents—how his own anger and bitterness had caused him to provoke conflict. These revelations later led to a reconciliation between the two, as both accepted responsibility for their part in the hostilities. The student said their relationship had greatly improved.

This highly personal sharing is an example of how insights from the short story inform the analysis of our personal experiences. Students gain new sensitivity to the dynamics of psychological change and how we can nurture it in ourselves and others. A key element in this process is getting adult learners to accept greater personal responsibility for their life experiences instead of blaming others for the problems that have occurred. Even though there can be justification at times for blaming others, when individuals take responsibility for their own lives they are better able to promote constructive change, both within themselves and in their relationships with others. Often a change in perspective begins with a recognition of the forces that are causing another person's pain and struggle, which opens our eyes to the reasons for his or her suffering, and part of our suffering, too. This can become a vital stimulus for a reevaluation of our experiences. When this student shared his insights in this regard, it assisted all of us in reflecting on this process, helping us to see the need for taking personal responsibility for our lives, and the rewards that can come from such an effort.

An Autobiographical Narrative

An historical, autobiographical narrative, "Incidents in the Life of a Slave Girl" (1861), by Harriet Ann Jacobs, relates the experiences of a young woman who fled slavery in the old South, went through perilous adventures in her escape, and finally won her freedom. Her narrative not only illuminates her painful struggle to achieve freedom but also gives a class keen insights into the social conditions of her time. In articulating the experiences of a black woman from an earlier century, this piece has stirred some of the basic truths of the human heart, while providing a poignant view of the social injustices that have continued to infect our country. On the personal level, adults relate to the young woman's character and courage, pondering issues of self-sacrifice, love, and commitment. On the social level, we have considered the meaning of justice and democracy in our society. Students raise questions about justice, equality, and freedom for all people and how these ideals can influence our daily functioning, personally and professionally.

In these discussions, I found that it is essential to begin at the personal level, so we could relate, as individuals, to the young woman's struggle. This establishes a bond for us as human beings, and we can then explore the story with the feeling of a personal, caring relationship. This identification later permits a smoother entry into the critical reflection about current social issues. When members feel an individual connection with the narrator, it is easier for us to reflect on current interpersonal, interracial relations and for us to feel more of an investment as social change agents. This sequencing takes us away from social preaching; it helps us see the issues in an intimate way and recognize how we can play an important role in the reconstruction of society.

Gender and the Life Course

An examination of the life course naturally includes issues and questions of gender. We have addressed this subject through such texts as *Women's Ways of Knowing* (Belenky, et al., 1986) and *About Men* (Klein and Erickson, 1988). Issues of gender create some of the most contentious discussions for adults, which become, at times, somewhat explosive. Certain men become very defensive and resistant when confronted with women's ways of knowing, saying they feel excluded by the material. We have struggled as teachers to engage these men in considering how such feminist theory applies to their lives and to the women in their lives—their clients, their sisters, and their spouses. It is critical to help them see that the ways of knowing described in this volume could be applied to both men and women. We invite all students to share personal examples of the different stages, and, indeed, the topics of silence, received knowledge, and subjective knowledge do eventually elicit personal stories from both men and women, once common ground is established. I find it very useful to point out that constructed knowledge, the most developed stage of knowing in this theory, exemplifies development for all members of the class. In this stage a person integrates thinking and feeling, self and other in a wholistic way, a paradigm that brought together many of the issues we had been discussing throughout the course. When people realize the broad integrative nature of this stage, they are better able to appreciate the meaning and value of the theory itself and its general applicability to people's lives.

About Men, on the other hand, is a collection of short articles written for the New York Times column by that name. Many of the essays depict the evolving role of men in our society, demonstrating a movement away from a traditionally defined gender role toward one with a greater integration of male and female traits, a trend that is occurring for both men and women. For certain students who wish to hold on to the traditional roles, this is a threatening prospect. Yet it tied in with an important idea from Robert Kegan, which he derived from Carl Jung. Kegan's highest phase of development includes the awareness of the contrasexual element within, i.e., the female traits within the male and the male traits within the female. When one cultivates the contrasexual traits and creates a better balance within oneself, the person gains greater flexibility in responding to life situations, as well as an increased understanding of the opposite sex, which can improve interpersonal relations.

As instructors, however, we need to be sensitive to the differences people have in regard to these roles, and it becomes a challenge to help people retain their self-esteem when some of their basic assumptions are brought into question. While part of the intent of the class may be to raise people's consciousness about new possibilities for men and women in society, it is clear that these issues could become politically inflammatory, producing intense disagreements. When class members genuinely struggle with deeply held assumptions, heat occurs, but this can be part of a transformative process. What we as teachers need to do is demonstrate respect for each class member as an individual, appreciate the pain of his or her struggle, show diplomacy and understanding, and yet, at the same time, challenge the class members to consider deeply these issues. Obviously this is a very difficult task, which no one can do perfectly every time.

But when real flare-ups of fiery emotion do occur during our discussions, it is valuable to call "time out" and ask the class to step back and look at what is going on, to consider its own process. This procedure helps reestablish a more rational tone and a more productive exchange. When a class is able to bring to consciousness some of the forces underlying the intense debate, important learning takes place. The group also gains additional perspective on the reflective process in action. Ultimately, we try to make people more aware of the significance of these issues in their lives, so they could continue to reflect and work on them in the future.

A Jungian Perspective

Robert Bly's *A Little Book on the Human Shadow* (1988) has also given adults an opportunity to look at development from the viewpoint of Carl Jung's personality theory (Young-Eisendrath and Hall, 1991). In this approach, adults must get in touch with their "shadow," i.e., the part of their personalities that they repress and deny. Because we are hesitant to face this part of ourselves, it remains unconscious and fuels our compulsions and neuroses. The shadow concept helps us to think more objectively about the negative behaviors and experiences we have repressed during our development, the parts of ourselves connected with disappointment, failure, and frustration. By confronting this side of ourselves, reflecting on it, and accepting it, we can attain a greater level of integration and wholeness in our personalities.

In large group sessions, students have analyzed the kinds of messages we received when we were young about what a "good boy" or "good girl" should or shouldn't do. We were told: always be polite and considerate; don't get angry; don't be too assertive. Because of these messages, we tried to hide feelings and behaviors that weren't acceptable, pushing them into the shadow. This process went on in each stage of our development, influenced by familial, social, and cultural pressures. We have reflected on the fact that all of us, as human beings, possess a range of traits, some of which are viewed as good and others as bad, and we need to accept that in ourselves. When we do not, we tend to project the undesirable traits on other people, stereotype them, and then see ourselves as purer and better than we are.

During our discussions, we often make connections with other texts in the course, particularly with multicultural and gender-related themes. Our stereotyping of people, along ethnic, racial, and gender lines, is an attempt to avoid seeing certain qualities in ourselves, making it harder to relate to others as people and to integrate our own personalities. We have applied some of these ideas to our heated discussions about gender. Some of the resistances people show to certain ideas relate to this shadow effect: they do not want to see the opposite male or female traits in themselves, although those traits are there. Getting people to recognize and accept their shadow is a very touchy, difficult task. There are many awkward moments in discussions, when people are hesitant to acknowledge their behavior, which is the nature of the beast. But making people more aware of this phenomenon, and raising their consciousness about it, initiates an analytical and reflective process that can have many future benefits if they continue to work with it. As is often the case in exploring adult development, we do not see the immediate results of our work, but we initiate processes that will promote growth and learning after the course concludes. It is valuable to recognize and appreciate that dynamic in order to keep our efforts in perspective.

Group Work and Journal Writing

During the large-group discussions, a few people are often reluctant to share very personal experiences. But this resistance declines in the small groups, which are more private and intimate, and participation there increases. Small-group work is vital because it offers a personal forum for self-expression, and this suits many people's group preference. Also, the use of the large- and small-group sessions in combination provides greater opportunity for dialectical exchange, where ideas forged in the large group can be carried into the small group for further refinement and expansion. However, it is in the journals that ideas really blossom, as many students speak about the troubling experiences they have been contending with for some time. For example, a young woman referred to the sexual abuse she had experienced in her extended family. In that family there had been very strong messages about loyalty and keeping up the family's image in the community, which contributed to her repression of these painful episodes. This experience had negatively affected many aspects of her life.

I found myself in a very delicate position with regard to her journal writing because I felt myself moving away from a teacher's role into that of a counselor. In this situation I took a client-centered approach, as Carl Rogers advocated, helping her to reflect on her experience in a way that would enable her to make decisions for herself (1961). I began by asking questions that got her to share as fully as possible her feelings and concerns. Then I asked her to identify what she thought were her options and how she would prioritize them. We then reflected together on the potential consequences for taking various options, or not taking them, so she could determine what would be best for her to do. I believe an instructor must be very cautious about jumping in with advice, since one can have an inordinate amount of influence in such a situation. Rather, it can be opportunity to encourage further personal reflection and self-analysis. Whenever one is examining adult development, this type of sharing in the journals will occur and one should be prepared for it. The journal writing becomes a critical component in the course, not just for nurturing reflection but for the interpersonal exchange between instructor and student, which can promote healing and growth.

Conclusions

Texts, ideas, and concepts drawn from the liberal arts offer multiple perspectives on the themes of adult development. They reflect the real diversity of human experience and the varied approaches to understanding that experience, which can broaden people's thinking. In addition, the voices that speak through the various narratives assist class members in finding and comprehending their own voices—a vital element in the reflective-developmental process because as we develop a better sense of our own voices, we obtain a deeper understanding of ourselves. And by challenging students to respond to the ideas posed by these materials, they develop flexible, creative thinking, an asset for problem solving in both the personal and professional arenas.

Faculty and students can become fellow explorers who unearth more questions than answers as they mine the course content. This egalitarianism, based on mutual respect, puts people on an equal footing as adult learners and makes it easier for people to share very personal experiences during the class discussions. However, teachers still play an important role in modeling reflective processes for the students. As instructors, we need to consider deeply our own experiences and discuss these in a frank, authentic way. At times we have to share life events that are very painful and difficult, for these experiences have often been the most transformative. We also need to demonstrate an openness to the insights others may have about these experiences, a willingness to listen and consider perspectives different from our own. The students are then able to do the same—to share, listen, reflect, and consider various viewpoints—in order to sharpen their critical reflection.

Instructors should monitor the classroom dynamics so that students are able to maintain adequate self-esteem in the face of challenges to their personal assumptions. As I mentioned at the beginning, this process can be an explosive one, and the instructors need to demonstrate caring and sensitivity. When the subject matter deals with culture, gender, power, and authority issues, the discussions can, at times, become volatile. Similarly, when people are talking to each other from different developmental stages, communication can also break down. When things do become too intense in the classroom, it is useful to have the group step back and study its own process, a technique that reduces turmoil and promotes group reflection skills.

This approach to content and process has relevance for future professional training. It offers students an opportunity to view personal and professional challenges from several angles and inspires them to find creative ways to meet these challenges. But most importantly, it fosters the development of critical reflection, which balances traditional technical training. By encouraging adult learners to become more reflective, they connect with the deeper levels of their own experience, which enables them to discuss these issues with both colleagues and clients. Thus, they develop into professionals who are capable of refining their skills over time and who can promote growth in their own lives and those of others.

6

Digging, Daring, and Discovering: Sifting the Soil of Professional Life through Journal Writing

JOANNE E. COOPER

It is no accident that a recent text on liberal learning, *Continuing Liberal Education* by D. B. House (1991), begins with a discussion of two journals, Anne Frank's *The Diary of a Young Girl*, and Thomas Merton's *The Seven Story Mountain*. These texts, according to House (1991, p. x), "celebrate the human spirit and the aspiration to overcome adversity and affliction." In addition, the personal chronicles of Frank and Merton embody the major goals of liberal education today: "learning for the sake of learning," and "for the love of knowledge." House claims that "continuing one's liberal education beyond the traditional undergraduate years is becoming one of the most important phenomena in American education today" (1991, p. x). He suggests that educators infuse traditional graduate education with a liberal core. A powerful tool for the encouragement of liberal learning is the classroom journal, a place to explore the human spirit and the aspiration in all of us to overcome adversity.

Recent research underscores the importance of dialogue and journal writing as powerful, reflective practices that promote adult learning and context-embedded critical thinking (Cooper, 1991; Gannett, 1992). This chapter will describe adult learners' use of classroom journals as a way of examining organizational and professional life. The use of journal keeping in graduate, professional education demonstrates that the facilitation of personally relevant learning is essential if students are to reach some integration of personal and professional identity.

Students report that through their dialogue journals they are able to capture elusive insights and guide their own learning. This process provides documentation of epistemological growth and increases understanding of how the past influences the future. As one student stated, "It measures movement." A primary goal of this pedagogical process is that students begin to understand themselves as professionals who have both personal and public lives. Journals provide a process for the integration of both dimensions within students, between students and faculty and, perhaps ultimately, within education's organizational settings.

I will address three major themes in this chapter: students' fear of writing; their struggles to understand, integrate, or overcome the influence of past events; and their efforts to integrate their personal and professional lives, to find a sense of balance. Initial responses by students to the request that they keep journals both in and outside of class are surprisingly negative. Students have grown up with a deluge of comments about spelling, punctuation, and grammar, and, as a result, they fear writing. They see it as a way to be judged. They fail to see it as a valuable tool for reflection and for communicating with the self and others. Once they begin to trust the process and stop worrying about spelling and punctuation, students are able to address past critical incidents in their lives and to begin the complex task of integrating their personal and professional selves. They search honestly and touchingly for a sense of balance.

Description of
Class Journal Assignments

I ask students in my graduate-level courses to keep an individual journal throughout the course and to turn it in several times during the term. The aim of the journal is to help them think critically about the readings and class discussions and about their own personal and professional lives. Here is a sample assignment as it might be written in the course syllabus:

> You will be keeping a personal journal throughout the course. You will be writing in it both in class and on your own personal time. This text will function as a "learning log," a place for you to ask questions about the readings, work through individual questions you have posed for yourself, write reactions to the class assignments and events, and begin to compile writing you might use in your final project. According to Mezirow (1990), learning involves "making a new or revised interpretation of the meaning of an experience, which guides subsequent understanding, appreciation, and action." This is the main task

for your journal writing: to examine the meaning of your own experiences in the light of possible new or revised interpretations.

Responses to these journals are given in longhand in the margins or between sections of the journal or are typed and returned as a separate page. In either case the essential element is that the student knows the instructor will be reading and responding to the writing. Instructors should provide thought-provoking, nonjudgmental responses. The crippling past effects of editing and correction on the writing process clearly emerge when students write about their own fears and avoidance of writing.

With written responses to the content of the writing, the journal becomes a dialogue between student and faculty member, as well as a dialogue with the self. Students are routinely asked to extend the classroom assignments by writing further in their journals. For instance, metaphors for one's school or organization were generated in class and shared. Students were then invited to generate metaphors for the professional self in their individual journals. Critical incidents were identified and described through in-class writing. Later some students wrote unsent letters in their journals to individuals identified in those incidents: bosses, grandmothers, mentors, students, and so on.

In addition to the individual journals, one class kept a "class journal." This class met every Saturday and as students entered class each morning or throughout the day, during breaks, and so on, they were invited to contribute entries to the class journal. They enjoyed reading others' entries, as well as contributing their own. This journal became a collective record of events, feelings, discoveries, and questions as the course progressed. At one point, I selected a variety of responses from the class journal, wrote them up anonymously, ran them off as a handout, and asked students to pick one in class, write a response to it, and share their responses with the class. Individual journal responses can also be collected and used as a class exercise in this same manner.

I asked students to bring their journals to class and to add "freewrite" entries at the beginning and end of each class. Freewriting is essentially writing what flows from the connection between the responding mind and the page. This works well if the class lasts over several hours. The beginning entry serves to help students make the transition from home to class and grounds them in the course and classroom. It is an opportunity for them to anticipate what they might be learning. Final entries help students reflect upon the day's events and identify key learning experiences.

Fear of Writing

One of my most startling discoveries, as I began to encourage graduate students to keep learning logs or journals, was their fear of and resistance to the writing process. Many students carry only negative experiences with them involving writing. Their pasts are filled with memories of red ink marks all over their papers. The word "writing" brings to mind memories of thoughts that won't come or can't be articulated; the exhausting process of editing, reediting, and reediting; and feelings of being judged inadequate or humiliated. Very little in their past suggests that writing can be satisfying or enlightening. Most graduate students do not associate writing with its primary function: a vehicle for communication with the self and others, a way to think more clearly. I am not advocating that writing never be corrected or graded. I think there is a time and place for teaching students how to write well. However, writing is a powerful communicative process, a way for students to think on paper, to communicate with the self and others. This function is lost in the deluge of "red pen marks" most students have experienced.

Thus the first task I faced was to help students to move beyond these negative connotations and begin to experience writing in productive and helpful ways. One student wrote:

When I first heard you say that we were going to write and think in this class, I wanted to quit . . . . During our first break, I was trying to recopy our first exercise because I was afraid as to how it would appear. I am not confident or able to write and hand assignments in without much editing . . . . when I write a paper for a particular class, I usually start a month in advance . . . . Thank heaven for my computer. This year I destroyed a small forest . . . of paper . . . . in the editing process of my papers . . . . I decided to stay with the class when you said that spelling and grammar was [sic] not the objectives of the journal . . . . By the end of this course my personal goal is to write and not edit at all and be confident that the writing will be okay. Thank you for the opportunity.

The irony here is that this student, despite some errors, already writes clearly and is able to communicate his thoughts on paper without massive editing. What has our educational process done to students to give them such a skewed view of their own writing ability? How can we help students to overcome their fear and rediscover their own latent ability to write well? These were some of the questions I struggled with at the beginning of my classes. I wrote in my journal:

Reading students' journals, I realize that so far, the course is "more than I was afraid to hope that it might be." I had wanted to create a place where students were comfortable, safe, open, and willing to share both personal and professional concerns. But this takes courage and faith, courage to look at the negative as well as positive aspects of one's life, to share what one sees, to have faith that others won't judge your journey, ridicule your choices, and that they will hear your questions and respond in kind. Despite my fears, the course seems to be progressing well.

As one student put it, "I see the process at work. Each day, each hour, each activity moves me into more clarity about me and my life. I especially appreciate the forum and acceptance of my ideas and conclusions. I feel the sense of commonality growing among us while we also realize our differences. I value the collegiality of this setting. Thank you!"

By writing about their own fears and resistance, students were able to articulate questions that frequently arise in classes where journals have been assigned. After reading an excerpt from Baldwin's text *One to One,* (1977), this student wrote about the "right" way to keep a journal:

> I belong to the set of people who have an anxiety attack whenever they need to write. I don't especially care to write and I don't write with ease. I guess I am, as Christina Baldwin so aptly stated, in a state of rebellion to the writing process . . . . Ms. Baldwin suggests that what might be helpful to promote journal writing is 'actually writing successful journal entries which build our confidence in our ability to communicate, to reach in and find, to let ourselves hang out on paper.' But, what is a successful entry? Who judges whether it is successful? If the writer determines it for him/herself, what criteria does he/she use? Does it depend on where you judge yourself to be as a writer?

These are excellent and perceptive questions. Having been judged frequently, students expect more judgments and wonder about the criteria to be used. I try to collect and respond to student journals early in the course so they receive immediate encouragement and see the wide range of possible "correct" methods for keeping a learning log or journal.

As students write, insights about their own fear of writing emerge. One student wrote,

> I just had an insight that I fear judgment on my spelling or misspellings as a reflection of character or the lack of it. I guess I've avoided writing whenever possible. That has led to no improvement in my writing and spelling skills. I see now that I need to change what I do if I want to change the way I am.

As students begin to write more, they learn the value of writing as a communication process and discover their own ability to improve their writing through practice. Like the student above, they also uncover hidden assumptions about their self-esteem and its connection to writing, assumptions that drive the fear of writing many students feel. Graduate students in education can then move to an understanding of their own students' experiences and their role in the education process. This journal entry reflects that process:

> Lawrence Yep says that a good writer is 'like a necromancer' who must breathe life into the skeleton. . . . the writer 'wakens the dragon within . . . . The pool is stirred and that welling up of energy and life revitalizes the spirit and soul. Every teacher should have such a Taoist ceremony of 'waking the dragon.' It is only when we waken those things within, do we know how to waken them in the lives of others, and especially our students.

Sometimes, faculty with the best of intentions misuse or abuse writing in the classroom and abuse students in the process. One student used her journal to write/vent about another course she was taking that made use of "forced freewrites." This professor was asking for focused freewrites in the classroom and grading students on the results. The writing was so focused that it was more like an essay and required students to state the reasons for their arguments in the opening paragraph. The pressure simply paralyzed this student, leaving her unable to write at all: "I told myself, 'I can't do this. I know nothing about the topic . . . .' I tried to *map* the ideas. Nothing worked. I was frozen."

In her journal, this student goes on to describe her teacher and the effect of his teaching on her: "He paced the room, looked over our shoulders, and made comments about how the freewrite will help to organize our ideas quickly and resembles on-the-job writing experiences. Each time he made a point, I objected silently. The block grew thicker . . . . I was furious, but in my obedience I smiled, as if I were wrong, and tried to write—unsuccessfully. I stared. Nothing emerged. On the other hand, a voice inside desperately called, 'Write! You can do it. Your grade depends on this freewrite.' Freewrites count 15 percent of our grade."

This student was finally able to break through her writer's block and insomnia by telling herself to "write *nonsense* if nothing comes to mind. If anything, I'll fulfill the requirement and earn my 15 percent." But the experience left her angry and despairing:

> Is this the kind of *torture* we put our students through daily? If we don't create safe environments for learning, how can we help our students, teachers and staff live healthy lives?

The irony here is that the course was in public health and yet it created an unhealthy atmosphere in which students were too frightened to learn from what this student describes as "the superimposed, instructor-driven 'freewrite' and 'required sharing' of our writing."

The danger here is that students will learn to hate the writing process, to see it as a way to expose themselves to criticism rather than a way to think more clearly. Faculty must create a classroom atmosphere in which learners are safe to explore their own confusion and to share that confusion only when they wish to. This student writes:

> Again I am learning how to trust the process. Never thought I would have the opportunity to vent my personal feelings about how much I objected to someone *misusing* writing as a tool for imposing a grade—under the false assumption that it will make us better writers. *Hogwash!* Only if we construct our own meaning . . . will it improve our writing.

Only because the course I taught created a safe atmosphere for the expression of personal fears and feelings was I able to learn about how writing can be misused. I believe this student's experience is a caution to us all. There is sometimes a fine line between writing assignments that allow students to explore and construct their own meaning from course material and writing assignments that threaten and humiliate, blocking rather than facilitating learning.

As the course progressed, most students learned that writing and sharing what you've written with others facilitates the process of discovery and helps you to think more clearly.

One student wrote:

> I was just thinking what I have to resolve for myself in order to reap the benefits that should come from continuing to journal write after this course is over . . . when the external inspiration and motivation are gone. I have to overcome my reluctance to write as well as provide the *time* to write. As I read and listen to you and others in class I become "more" convinced that this technique is a very useful one. As I write, write, and write, I feel more comfortable about writing.

Thus students involved in liberal education can be invited to use journal writing as a way to examine the personal and professional issues in their lives. Their first barrier is fear of the writing process itself. A second barrier is fear of what they will uncover as they begin to examine previously uncharted territory.

Wrestling with the Past

The world moves so quickly for all of us that we have very little time to stop and reflect upon what just happened. Like sponges, we store up the events of our lives until we are in danger of leaking all over our fellow professionals. Graduate level course work can be a time to stuff in more information and more experiences or it can be a time to stop and reflect upon what is already stored there. Sometimes it can be both.

One of the most powerful experiences for students is the reflection upon and sharing of experience. One of my students quoted Winnie The Pooh (*The House at Pooh Corner*, 1970) in trying to capture the essence of this process:

> When you are a Bear of Very Little Brain and you think of things, you find sometimes that a thing which seemed very thingish inside you is quite different when it gets out into the open and has other people looking at it.

As this quote illustrates, students quickly begin to understand and appreciate the power of examining and sharing their reflections of past events. They also realize that the process is not an easy one. One student wrote, "I wonder if I will have the wisdom and perhaps courage to look at myself through my writing . . . for I have discovered, as I write and write, that there are certain 'things' that I don't want to write about." Students at this point in the process need three things: the privacy to examine difficult issues, permission to share whatever they wish, and a safe, nonjudgmental classroom atmosphere in which to share their thoughts.

One student asked me, "What if we don't want to look at some things?" My answer, "Then don't." I believe in the ultimate wisdom of individuals to know when they are ready to look at a particular "thing" inside and when they are not. Keeping a classroom safe for students means they are not only safe to explore whatever they wish but safe to leave particularly painful parts of their lives untouched. Swartzlander, Pace, and Stamler (1993) suggest important ways in which students should be protected from overly intrusive writing assignments. Students should never feel that they must "deal with" their emotional problems in writing in order to succeed in a course. They must be free to decide what they want to write about. An accepting classroom atmosphere means they are free to write about how upsetting missing the bus to class was, if that is what they choose. Students must know that they are not being pressured in any way to say or write anything that makes them feel uncomfortable and if they choose to do so, their privacy will be carefully protected. Their writing should not be shared with colleagues or other students, and only those who volunteer should be asked to read personal assignments aloud in class. I always try to tell students before they begin writing whether they will be sharing what they've written so that they can decide before they begin what subject they might feel safe exploring. Simply becoming aware that there are things you don't want to examine can be enlightening. As one student wrote, "Perhaps it is the "things" I avoid that will provide me with the most insight." Yet, as Swartzlander, Pace, and Stamler assert (1993, P. 32), students deserve both the respect and dignity of being free to choose what they will explore or reveal in class and free "to work on their own psychological issues in their own time and ways. We should be in the business of encouraging emotional development—*not* mandating it."

One student described her learning in the course as "creeping up on you like a sore throat." The metaphor reflects both the growing awareness she was experiencing and the fact that the process can be a painful one. She compared this learning to learning that "floods over you like a streetlamp." She states, "This class and the learning crept up on me rather than flooded over me. It was like a book that you read every night over a few months. You need it as a comfort—not racing through it, but rather savoring it." The sore throat metaphor is particularly appropriate because it describes the amount of pain a student can endure and still find learning "a comfort." Students should be encouraged to pace their own learning in ways that offer comfort and safety, not forced to race into areas than may leave them more humiliated and damaged than when they began the course.

One painful area for many professionals is unresolved relationships with others in the workplace. One student used her journal to write a letter to her former principal. She acknowledged her gratitude, "I know that I was very fortunate to have a mentor like you." Then she moved on to the hard part.

> I need to get this off my chest, so here goes . . . . Many times (1) You made me feel so speechless, (2) Gave me mixed messages. Sometimes your reasoning, "It's for the kids, so . . . " sounded more like avoiding the issue. You never embarrassed me in front of others, but in your office you started chipping away at my self-esteem. That I allowed you to do this makes me angry at myself.

Relations with other professionals are often complex, too complex for us to thoroughly investigate as we move rapidly through our workday. Journal writing allows students to examine both the benefits and frustrations of these relationships. In the case of mentors, students need to sort what they want to take with them and what they want to reject from the model they are presented with. In the unsent letter to her principal, this student wrote,

> You were not a political animal and did not play the game . . . . Will I be also able to stay away from this game? I hope so. What is this game? I see it as the 'you pat my back. I pat yours.' syndrome. The poser plays at the expense of services to students.

And then, having identified the game and its results, this student goes on to ask an ultimate question, "Is it that I can't or don't want to play?" These questions, even if left unanswered in the journal, bring working professionals closer to an understanding of organizational life and how their personal values are synthesized with the demands of that life.

It is easy to lose oneself in the demands of professional life. In reflecting upon the upcoming school year, one student wrote,

> When I finally get on campus, I want to be mentally prepared to be the type of administrator I can live with day to day. I want to leave this class with a direction in mind and goals for myself.

However, this student also realizes that the process is not easy. She writes, "This is a reflective time for me. It's reassuring and anxiety provoking at the same time. I like to do this kind of writing, but I haven't done it for a long, long, time." Here she acknowledges the dichotomy of safety and fear, her own rustiness in trying to use reflective writing and finally comes to an acknowledgement of the benefits: "This process brings me in touch with what's wrong and what's right."

The busy days of administrators barely allow them time to identify "what is." Beyond "what is" lies the realm of "what's right and what's wrong," which involves a synthesis of personal and professional values with the events of organizational life. Reflective writing and sharing allows students to use Pooh's process of getting a "thing" out into the open where both the individual and others can look at it and begin to decide "what's right and what's wrong."

Part of the process of reflection is the acceptance or rejection of the judgments of others. Without a chance to get it out into the open, an event can remain very "thingish" inside. One student had been carrying the negative assessment of her first principal around with her for years. She used the journal process and her final paper, which analyzed critical events in her life, to examine the impact of this man's judgment on her self-image. At the end of the class she wrote,

> I have learned the value of reflection, but I have also learned that I am not a failure . . . that year in Smith River, Kansas, happened - it's over and I'm moving on. If I fail in the future, it will be because of me—not because I'm fulfilling a prophecy of (her former principal).

Thus the reflective process can be a healing one, a chance to take out those "thingish" events from the past, examine them, decide what's wrong and what's right and move on. In the busy lives of professional educators this can be an invaluable opportunity and one that is central to liberal graduate education.

The Integration of Personal and Professional Lives

A final contribution of journal writing to liberal graduate education is its facilitation of the integration of personal and professional concerns. So much of graduate education involves only professional training. Very little attention is paid to the personal lives of working professionals. Yet, these individuals bring who they are to work and to graduate classrooms every day. A central concern of liberal education must be the integration of these issues, creating whole, balanced persons. The balance of the personal and the professional, the private and the public is a difficult, yet vital part of professional training.

The personal influences the professional in both positive and negative ways. Individual values and ethical standards impact the decisions professionals make, the ways in which they implement policy, deal with their colleagues and their clients. In addition, personal problems and past experiences influence professional action in the workplace. Professionals who are dealing with a death in the family, illness, divorce, alcohol or drug problems, or any number of other personal issues behave differently on the job as a result of these stresses. One student, in reflecting on the negative influences of personal life, writes about a former teacher:

> Separation of personal and professional...yes we cannot leave the personal at home when we step into our professional role. But as an administrator, when do we say the personal is dysfunctional and needs to be addressed by the individual . . . . Senior English, Mrs. B. She was an alcoholic, as students, we could smell the strong sweet/sour odor on her breath . . . . we got spelling tests and materials that seemed a hundred years old . . . . we would hope she wouldn't show up and looked forward to substitutes.

Here, the personal and professional should perhaps be separate, but they are not. Ultimately, we are all whole individuals who bring our personal experiences and needs to work each day. Only when administrators begin to acknowledge this fact, can they grapple with the problems they face. This problem is but one administrators face, and many would state that their most serious problems on the job are interpersonal, not fiscal, academic, or curricular. Simply denying that these problems exist, or asking individuals to do so, is not a viable solution.

Given these influences on professional life, both positive and negative, it is imperative that professionals begin to deal with, not deny, the influence of personal life on professional action. The bureaucratic pressures toward depersonalized, rational, objective, role-bound relations in the workplace create a kind of schizophrenia in professionals, which paralyzes them when the influences are negative and diminishes them when the influences are positive. Reflecting on this split and the need to find balance, a director of community services wrote:

> Sometimes I think I'm schizophrenic. I do relate when we discuss "women's ways of knowing," but I also have a very rational, logical side
> . . . . Sometimes our lives *force* us to be the rational, critical thinkers we are. There are not always situations in which we can fully examine feelings. It is also *easier*, in my opinion, to look at the rational. It is cold, and hard and real—no room for questions. When I am in a difficult situation, personally or professionally, I will often look at it rationally, solve the problem and go on—not really thinking about the emotional—I don't always like myself when that happens, but it does happen. It is sort of a betrayal of self when I let this happen. I tout all this flexibility, caring about others stuff, but at times, I have to admit, I just say *Yes* or *No*. It is a *very* hard balance and I don't always do well.

In her discussion of "Action Learning and Reflection in the Workplace," Victoria Marsick describes the work of facilitators who assist professionals in reevaluating or reformulating an identified problem. One such problem, identified by the company's CEO as a lack of planning and the need to make operations more rational, was eventually reframed in terms of the CEO's dysfunctional management style. Thus, problems that appear procedural often emerge as ultimately personal in nature. Marsick states that "In many such situations, as in the study by Kaplan, Drath, and Kofodimos (1985), those surrounding a chief executive officer do not dare to confront him or her with what are often open secrets." (in Mezirow, 1990, pp. 40-41). She advocates the use of learning journals, which can be discussed in groups to raise awareness levels and build theory:

Journals help managers keep track of reflections, feelings, reactions, responses, and personal beliefs. Journals also enable a group to build a documentary trail of how the group's understanding of a problem has changed and to track influences on this shift in understanding.

Students, such as the following, can become aware of the need for this forum and the benefits journal writing provide:

> This class has made me realize that I need to do more soul searching as I wrote my paper. I sometimes feel that I have lost myself—have lost who I am and what I was—what have I become or what am I working to become? The writing has uncovered more questions for me, not answers. Questions that perhaps we all face at times—but when/how do we address these questions?

This student has used the writing process as a vehicle for beginning to examine the personal/professional split many professionals discover at work in their lives as a result of bureaucratic pressures. Acknowledging this split and examining the results are first steps toward integration. Simply burying one's personal life only means that feelings may build and emerge in uncontrollable, inappropriate ways. In the meantime, professionals who attempt to bury half of who they are in the workplace feel lost, scattered, and directionless, as the above student attests. Journals can be a powerful tool in assisting professionals to reflect upon and build integrated, whole identities. These individuals can then bring the power of healthier, integrated lives to bear upon the complex problems today's professional life presents.

Conclusion

If, as House (1991, p. x) seems to imply, liberal education aims not only to foster lifelong learning, but to "celebrate the human spirit and the aspiration to overcome adversity," then journal keeping may be an ideal means to foster such learning. Journals have the capacity both to become lifelong tools in the learning process and to allow individuals to identify and overcome the adversities of life.

One of the first adversities many students face in the classroom is their fear of writing. To help students overcome this fear or resistance, faculty need to create safe classroom environments, both for the free expression of thoughts on paper without the dreaded red ink pen and for the exploration of areas adult learners may have avoided or left unexamined in the past. Beyond an examination of the past, lies the need to examine and integrate students' current personal and professional lives. Given these tasks, the most meaningful learning often requires courage, fortitude, and the caring support of others. Students learn best when that support comes from both their peers and their teachers.

It may sound like a trite oversimplification to say that faculty, even at the graduate level, must learn to value, care for, and even love their students better. Yet, this may be exactly what is needed. As Paul Browlee (1992, p. 6), President of the Association of American Colleges states:

> Love of learning is a phrase that slips easily off the tongue. It is harder to recognize the love that faculty bear for students when as teachers they struggle, year after year, to teach well, to grow with their field, to care even when students are sometimes indifferent.... In the final analysis, however, when a student knows that she or he is deeply valued, cared for, and yes, loved as a learner, then, and maybe only then, can a student become liberally educated.

Journal keeping in the classroom fosters dialogue with faculty and provides a basis for caring and supportive dialogues with others. Thus, this pedagogical tool can be a major factor in helping students to feel valued and cared for and in providing them with a liberal education.

This final note on laughter reflects the support and caring students can feel through the writing and sharing process. It was written by the same student who earlier stated that she has an extreme anxiety attack whenever she needs to write, doesn't care to write, and rebels against the process. This passage attests not only to the supportive classroom atmosphere necessary for liberal learning and the examination of professional life, but to the power of the writing process in moving students from resistance to eloquence:

> What does the class feel like—it's a place for laughter. Laughter that greets us each Saturday. Laughter to lighten the sometimes heart-wrenching, thought-provoking ideas. Once I felt afraid to laugh -to laugh at myself. There is something wrong if others laugh at you . . . but as the years have gone, one learns the laughter of binding. The laughter that makes an individual more human, more connected with others. It's good to share a laugh together. It brings us closer. . . . It binds us to each other. If we couldn't laugh together . . . we'd cry separately.

7

Self-interest and its Relation to an Ethic of Care

TERRENCE R. WHALEY

Making ethical decisions is at the heart of professional practice. It is the dilemmas of practice that students in the professions bring forward for consideration that enlarge the theoretical. The questions that students frame regarding the effects of gender on the construction of their ethical stance, for example, can become a source of significant development for the teachers' thinking as well.

Though the argument of this essay is theoretical, it arose out of practical considerations raised by graduate professional students. The questions that generated my own thinking grew out of a seminar in which students were considering whether the notion of an ethic of care and an ethic of principle, as elaborated by Carol Gilligan, Nona Lyons, and Nel Noddings, were gender-related, and if so, what implications it had for their own behavior as service professionals (1982; 1983; 1984): If men and women in service professions orient themselves in different ways to ethical issues, then how does this fact show itself in the decisions they make in their professional lives? Do men and women, on the average, actually make different decisions? Or do they merely analyze situations differently in order to arrive at the same decisions? As a preliminary step at an answer, the class considered a problem involving hiring practices typical of the service fields. Students imagined that they were part of an interviewing team to screen candidates for a counseling job in a public agency. Two women applied. Both were qualified. One, however, had a more impressive dossier and performed better in the interview than did the other. They were to imagine, too, that the husband of the less qualified person had recently died of cancer, causing the widow not only the emotional trauma but the financial burden attendant upon such a loss. The students were then asked to wonder about the effect this additional information would have on their decisions.

Their recommendations seemed to fall conveniently under the moral categories of care and principle. We claimed an orientation of principle for those students who either disqualified themselves from the team or excluded the additional information from consideration. Those students who hired the bereaved candidate were associated with an ethic of care. Thus it seemed that the different orientations did, in fact, obtain different results. Principle hired the better qualified and care the less. But within the category of care, the students were not aligned. Some responded out of sympathy, adjusting their feelings with the belief that the better qualified candidate would have little trouble finding a job in the future. But other students of care sought principle to justify their choice, arguing that the suffering itself outweighed a glib interview, at least for this particular position. A sufferer has greater capacity for empathy than a nonsufferer.

The discussion settled nothing, nor was it intended to, the hypothetical situation being too vague and ill-defined to obtain unequivocal results. But it did engage lively commentary and pointed to what interests me here: Can normative response be rigorously fixed to normative categories, such as care and principle, and what significance can be attached to the altruism implicit in this discussion? Whatever interest students had in the question, they showed a selflessness that cut across both orientations. None of the arguments from either side made reference to personal motive, and it was this omission that caused me to wonder about the relationship between self and motive within ethical situations.

A Theoretical Check on an Ethic of Care

Given the needs of today's students and those clients served by the social service professions, an ethic of care, consistently and rigorously applied, becomes nearly irrational without a theoretical check to caring. A radical or unconditional regard for the other with no theoretical means of ending that care risks the integrity and well-being of the caregiver. In what follows, I will attempt to provide such a theoretical check, one which preserves the integrity of the care-giver and which may, at the same time, leave undiminished the salutary effects of exclusive regard for other. I use the hackneyed and somewhat pejorative term "self-interest," to name the check to care. I hope, however, to give the term a technical and more rigorous formulation within my argument by associating it with reasons and motives to act within caregiving situations that are in contrast to the reasons and motives required by an ethic of care. I also take the view, along with many of the formulators of feminist ethics, including Nel Noddings and Carol Gilligan, that an ethic of care does not give full and adequate response in all situations of moral concern and that some principles of justice or equity or impartiality are necessary complements. With this assumption I don't entirely escape the debate between the advocates of a feminist ethics and those of a deontic or Kantian ethics, for at least one feature that joins these two moral orientations, I shall argue, is my idea of self-interest, a feature only apparently unrelated to these two ethical orientations.

It is difficult to keep the logic of opposition intact when marking rigorous distinction between an ethic of care and an ethic of principle. We can in a rhetorical sense appreciate the fact of separate and distinct orientations; but to secure the distinctions precisely or technically in a philosophical manner has so far, it seems to me, defied the attempts of even those thinkers most eminent in formulating or in having noticed the separate orientations in the first place. It may be that oppositional logic fails in this case because an ethic of care and an ethic of principle implicate each other in fundamental and inescapable ways. Though I believe this to be the case, I am not here prepared to defend such a claim, only to provide, rather, some evidence suggestive of how the two orientations are inextricably bound up with each other and to show how self-interest can involve both. Carol Gilligan's well-known Jake and Amy example is illustrative.

Jake and Amy, two eleven-year-olds, bright and articulate, and members of Gilligan's study of moral development recounted in *In a different voice* (1982, pp. 25-32), are given one of Lawrence Kohlberg's dilemmas to solve,—the Heinz dilemma. The dilemma places the respondent in the position of having to decide whether or not a penniless Heinz should steal a lifesaving drug for his dying wife from a callous pharmacist who refuses to give Heinz the drug. Applying moral principles as one applies theorems and definitions in school geometry, Jake has no trouble. "Steal the drug!" Amy struggles. In her attempt to satisfy all the persons involved in this dilemma, she is finally unable to come to any real decision, maintaining somewhat feebly that "stealing is wrong" and believing all along that if she had opportunity she could persuade the druggist to give up the drug. Gilligan comments on the two responses:

> Both children thus recognize the need for agreement but see it mediated in different ways—he impersonally through systems of logic and law, she personally through communication in relationship. Just

as he relies on the conventions of logic to deduce the solution to this dilemma, assuming these conventions to be shared, so she relies on a process of communication, assuming connection and believing that her voice will be heard (1982, p. 29).

Again we have the language of opposition to demarcate the differences in response, a language not quite adequate to master its own intention to separate decisively the two orientations. What undermines intention here is the problematic "personal/impersonal" distinction. That the personal intimately involves the impersonal is something Gilligan herself recognizes. To use a Gilligan figure, the one becomes the ground for the appearance of the other, and vice versa.

It is true that in one sense Jake behaves impersonally in relying on the "conventions of logic." The effects of his logic, the distribution of justice, are delivered impersonally by him. He favors none of the participants in this dilemma, all having equal status under his laws. But if we examine the case from the point of view of the moral agent himself, it is not at all clear whether or not Jake is behaving from impersonal motives. He may be, but Gilligan's account suggests otherwise:

> Yet as his self-description radiates the self-confidence of a child who has arrived, in Erikson's terms, at a favorable balance of industry over inferiority—competent, sure of himself, and knowing well the rules of the game—so his emergent capacity for formal thought, his ability to think about thinking and to reason things out in a logical way, frees him from dependence on authority and allows him to find solutions to problems by himself (p. 27).

Were we to infer from this description that Jake's motives are to show off his capacity to think clearly and logically or to affirm the strength of his autonomy, his newly won independence—and there seems nothing in the description to block this inference—then Jake's motives are not impersonal: they make "essential reference to himself as such" (Darwall, p. 130) for which reason they are personal and because they are so, disqualify him, in the Kantian sense, from being a moral agent at all. Jake seems no different from Kant's tradesman, who charges a fair and just price for goods to all his clients, savvy adults and innocent children alike, but not from a good will. He is too prudent for that, knowing that such honesty is just good business in the long run:

> Men are thus honestly served; but this is not enough to make us believe that the tradesman has so acted from duty and from principles of honesty: his own advantage required it; it is out of the question in this case to suppose that he might besides have a direct inclination in

favour of the buyers, so that, as it were, from love he should give no advantage to one over another. Accordingly the action was done neither from duty nor from direct inclination, but merely with a selfish view (Kant, 1963, p. 258).

We can't rule out from our limited description of Jake's reasoning that his will is good. But that is just the point—the description of his behavior is in accord with what a good will requires, but it does not entail that Jake actually possess such a will. But Amy does, and that she does is clear from her struggle with the dilemma. Here is Gilligan's characterization of that struggle:

> Seeing in the dilemma not a math problem with humans but a narrative of relationships that extends over time, Amy envisions the wife's continuing need for her husband and the husband's continuing concern for his wife and seeks to respond to the druggist's need in a way that would sustain rather than sever connection. Just as she ties the wife's survival to the preservation of relationships, so she considers the value of the wife's life in a context of relationships, saying that it would be wrong to let her die because, "if she died, it hurts a lot of people and it hurts her" (p. 28).

Gilligan is right. Amy is personally involved with the lives of these characters in a way that Jake is not. She seems genuinely concerned about their well-being, a genuineness that Kant's tradesman can claim only with some embarrassment since his interests are advanced with his concern for other. But Amy's motives, however, are not personal. Her reasons for wanting to compose the dilemma as she does make no essential reference to herself as such. She gains nothing from a solution. In fact, her method seems to threaten her own interests, the persistent probing of the questioner that she might gain a higher rating on Kohlberg's scale must diminish her self-esteem. And though it might, Amy persists in her attempt to find a settlement satisfactory for all. She sees things from an impersonal point of view, adjudicating the rival claims in a way that gets the approbation of Kant. She may have no concept of Kantian duty, but she does have what Kant claims to be the equivalent, a "direct inclination" to promote human flourishing out of a deep regard (Kant uses "love," but is that not a kind of "deep regard"?) for other. She possesses a good will.

I must, however, proceed carefully at this point, wishing not to suggest that feminist theorists have somehow been misled to position themselves in contrast to Kantian ethics and that Kant's morality is somehow a disguised version of their own. Such is clearly not the case, but the *Grundlegung* — what can be claimed, I think, with some confidence — of all Kant's corpus shows this contrast in its weakest form. A much stronger warrant is found in other places and especially in his Lectures on Ethics where he argues that the connectedness and cordiality of human association is as much a response of fear and suspicion as it is of care and regard.

> "Friendship is not of heaven but of the earth; the complete moral perfection of heaven must be universal; but friendship is not universal; it is a peculiar association of specific persons; it is man's refuge in this world from his distrust of his fellows, in which he can reveal his disposition to another and enter into communion with him" (Ethics, 206-7).

Friendship built on a Hobbsean communion of exclusivity, Kant finds it hardly an adequate ground upon which to construct a morality. Within the circle of friendship, the rights and privileges of cordiality are extended justly and equitably to members, but outside the circle hostility and discrimination affront the nonmembers (Held, pp. 114-15).

The Place for Self-interest in an Ethic of Care

Nonetheless with this Kantian analysis of the Amy-Jake example, I'm in a position to give the concept of "self-interest" some formal definition. I wish to term Amy's motives for acting "objective" and oppose them to Jake's motives, at least as I have characterized them, which I will term "subjective." The subjective/objective distinction as a means of separating certain reasons or motives for acting from others has become well-established within moral discourse (Darwall, pp. 130-147, Parfit, p. 143). As I stated earlier, Amy's train of reasoning in trying to resolve the dilemma makes no essential reference to herself as such. Apart from her "direct inclination" to be concerned for others, the many other personal interests that she must have seem to bear not at all on how she deals with the dilemma. Her view is impersonal and her reasons for acting objective. Jake, on the other hand, if his motives are as we have characterized them, has a personal view and reasons for acting that are subjective. Jake may not be opposed to seeing Heinz, his dying wife, and the pharmacist all doing well under the circumstances. He's probably not indifferent to their careers, but, as Gilligan points out, he has other interests that bear directly on the dilemma. He receives personal satisfaction from solving math or logical problems of which the Heinz dilemma is representative. Such an attitude may pose problems for Jake as a moral agent. This interpretation conflicts with the way many commentators on the Heinz dilemma have interpreted Jake's behavior, seeing his logical, impersonal response to the characters as just what impartiality requires. And they are right so long as they confine their perspective to his treatment of the characters themselves. But from the perspective of his motivation, at least some of his reasons for acting are subjective, a condition which, I shall contend, interferes with his ability to remain impartial. It is not Amy's impartiality that is suspect, but Jake's.

To see how Jake's subjective reasons interfere with his chances of acting impartially, we can again avail ourselves of a Gilligan example:

> A group of industrious, prudent moles have spent the summer digging a burrow where they will spend the winter. A lazy, improvident porcupine who has not prepared a winter shelter approaches the moles and pleads to share their burrow. The moles take pity on the porcupine and agree to let him in. Unfortunately, the moles did not anticipate the problem the porcupine's sharp quills would pose in close quarters. Once the porcupine has moved in, the moles are constantly being stabbed. The question is, what should the moles do (Meyers, 1987 p. 141)?

The responses to this question tended to fall into a pattern related to gender. Many of the women (one-third, Meyers reports) found ways of accommodating the porcupine, softening, for example, the sharpness of the quills with a blanket as a possible solution, while none of the men inclined to show any concern for the porcupine. Most thought that throwing him out was appropriate, and the rest were willing to see even worse happen to him. Thus the fable shows the existence of two moral orientations and that one is favored more by women than by men. But does Meyers go too far with her admonition that "it is important to recognize not only that the solutions proposed by exponents of the rights perspective differ from those proposed by exponents of the care perspective but also that the reasoning leading to these divergent solutions differs" (p. 141)? As an empirical finding, Meyer's statement is fine as long as the exponents of care (however they are identified) in this particular instance did in fact reason differently and to divergent solutions from the exponents of an ethic of principle. But if Meyers is proposing the general conclusion that the two moral orientations, when fully and consistently employed, get different moral results, then we have a conclusion truly surprising. I shall argue later that egoism, as distinct an orientation as it is from an ethic of care, may be indistinguishable from care in its results (Sidgwick, 1966). It may be possible to draw such a conclusion from the story of the moles and porcupine, but it is not the only one. The story admits of enough interpretive possibility to accommodate my characterization of the motivation of Amy and Jake.

We have no reason to believe that Jake would have felt any more sympathy for the porcupine than did the male subjects of Gilligan's study. He would have been in accord, we are sure, with the decision to bar the porcupine from the burrow. We feel just as certain that had Amy been a subject in the study she would have sided with the group of females willing to find some way to provide for the porcupine. But does this necessarily evidence a different method of reasoning about moral situations? We notice that the blanket and the use to which it can be put are not a part of the original problem. The blanket becomes the solution to the problem and just the sort of solution we believe Amy capable of discovering. Would transforming the original problem to include this additional data have any influence on Jake's decision to oust the porcupine? He would be unable to dismiss this information as irrelevant, for Gilligan tells us that he places high value on life within his moral hierarchy — "constructing the dilemma [Heinz], as Kohlberg did, as a conflict between the values of property and life, he discerns the logical priority of life" (1982, p. 26).

Given a second chance, Jake might reason this way: The porcupine's life has an intrinsic value that outweighs the value of punishing him for his improvidence. The punishment is too severe, since the chances are good that he would perish without food for the winter. The chronic suffering, however, that the moles would inevitably experience from the quills is a disutility, especially if life threatening, which, again, argues for his ouster. But with the blanket this objection is obviated so that all can now live together, if not in complete serenity, with little inconvenience from each other. Thus Jake's principles without inconsistency, whether Kantian or utilitarian, might lead him to abandon his initial decision and allow, instead, the porcupine to stay for the winter, a reversal that puts him in agreement with the exponents of an ethic of care. What Jake concedes — and this is the point — is not any weakness in his method but a narrowness in his perspective. Thus we wonder not about his method but how to account for the narrowness of his perspective and, at the same time, for the expansiveness of Amy's. Jake himself would probably locate whatever failure might be attributed to him in the design of the problem itself, which omits, he would say, relevant and essential information.

Subjective and Objective Reasons

Such is the explanatory role I'm assigning to subjective and objective reasons. Because Jake's reasons are subjective and satisfied only after they have touched on his own interests, he has no reason to delay his decision. He is not interested in changing the contours of the problem or its conditions or how it might be transformed into one less destructive to the people involved. This is the work of the imagination. He is interested in demonstrating his independence of mind and his skill as a logician, interests that narrow his vision and tend naturally to harden his sympathies for others. Logic requires us to abstract from the situation what is human, all those qualities that engage our sentiments. Amy, because her reasons are objective and make no reference to herself as such, has no way of receiving satisfaction from any solution which fails to please all members of the dilemma. And if I'm right about their motives, then Amy may have and probably does have a greater claim to impartiality than does Jake. Jake's subjective reasons inhibit him from assuming the moral posture expected of a moral agent.

> A rational and impartial sympathetic spectator is a person who takes up a general perspective: he assumes a position where his own interests are not at stake and he possesses all the requisite information and powers of reasoning. So situated he is equally responsive and sympathetic to the desires and satisfactions of everyone affected by the social system. His own interests do not thwart his natural sympathy for the aspirations of others and he has perfect knowledge of these endeavors and what they mean for those who have them. Responding to the interest of each person in the same way, an impartial spectator gives free reign to his capacity for sympathetic identification by viewing each person's situation as it affects that person (Rawls, p. 186).

Neither Amy nor Jake measures up to this ideal completely. But Amy's attitude represents the better fit. Because she responds to the content of the moral situation, Amy identifies sympathetically, seeks relevant knowledge, and suppresses her own interests. Because Jake responds to the form of the moral situation, he has trouble doing any of these things.

Although subjective reasons may not be those reasons most promotive of adequate moral response, there is nothing necessarily wrong with them, and they can have an appropriate role to play in the schools and public service professions. In what follows, I shall delineate that role and show how subjective reasons might be profitably aligned with the objective reasons of an ethic of care. Artificial as it may be, the Heinz dilemma, together with Amy's response to it, has a pertinence immediately recognizable to those of us in the professions. Such situations are not uncommon and are just the kind of situations that either drive people out of the professions altogether or exact such a toll as to render them incapable of effective practice (Bolman and Deal, 1991).

Application to Dilemmas of Practice

Many of the situations arising within our troubled institutions contain all of the conditions of the Heinz dilemma as seen from Amy's point of view, in which there is a problem involving a set of competing human relationships and interests so confounded as to resist a hopeful or satisfactory resolution for any of the persons involved. The frustration Amy feels for the futility of her effort is the same frustration countless people feel in the professions every day. Because these professions are defined by the services they provide, they can hardly abandon their primary goal of the care of others or relegate it to a position of secondary importance. The principal satisfactions of their members must derive from how well they discharge their primary goal. This doesn't mean, however, that we need to forego other satisfactions, just those that bear directly on our own self-interest, the kind of subjective motive I've attributed to Jake. If self-interest can buoy our spirits and sustain us in our primary aim, then reconstituting our institutions and attitudes about our work to include subjective, self-interested motivation seems in order. We surely would not wish to disqualify Jake from employment in a public service profession because he enjoys solving tough, interpersonal problems for the subjective reasons I've outlined. As long as his reasons and the behaviors issuing from them are concordant with the requirements of an ethic of care, he makes an important and valuable contribution.

The problem of exhausting the care-giver has not gone unnoticed by advocates of the ethic of care. Nel Noddings has given much thought to how the response of the cared-for might be improved as a means to revive flagging spirit and effort on the part of the care-giver. And she makes reference to how subjective, self-interested motive might play a part in such a revival.

A mathematics teacher might, for example, take on a group of students when they enter high school and guide them through their entire high school mathematics curriculum. The advantages in such a scheme are obvious and multiple: First, a setting may be established in which moral education is possible —teacher and students can develop a relation that makes confirmation possible. Second, academic and professional benefits may be realized—the teacher may enjoy the stimulation of a variety of mathematical subjects and avoid the deadly boredom of teaching five classes of Algebra 1; the teacher may come to understand the whole math curriculum and not just a tiny part of it (1988, p. 225).

The thematic movement of this passage is in the direction of enhancing connectedness and regard for students by altering "instructional arrangements" in more suitable ways. Noddings' is an argument directed against those instructional arrangements found in many schools that seem designed for the convenience of the teacher, the administration, or the community at the unmistakable inconvenience of the student. But Noddings within her thematization includes the self-interest of the practitioner in just the way I want here to characterize its efficacy in relation to an ethics of care. We notice that the second group of "obvious advantages" bear directly on the teacher's interests—Noddings terms them "academic and professional," to which I would add "personal" —and Noddings's point is that these advantages are not in conflict with the first set, merely coincident with it. But I would like to suggest a stronger connection and one that Noddings's description seems to permit.

If a mathematics teacher knows, for example, that one of her students, Rose, is talented in art and wants more than anything to be an artist, the teacher may properly lower her expectations for Rose in math. Indeed, she and Rose may consciously work together to construct a mathematical experience for Rose that will honestly satisfy the institution, take as little of Rose's effort as possible, and preserve the teacher's integrity as a mathematics teacher. Teacher and student may chat about art, and the teacher may learn something. They will surely talk about requirements for the art schools to which Rose intends to apply—their GPA demands, how much math they require, and the like. Teacher and student become partners in fostering the student's growth. The student accepts responsibility for both completion of the work negotiated and the mutually constructed decision to do just this much mathematics (p. 225).

This story tells of a teacher subordinating her own interests in the process of discharging her primary obligation to minister to the needs of her students, only to discover that such unexpected benefits as quiet conversation and an appreciation of art may occur as well. The practice of care motivated from purely objective reasons may as a result engender self-interested, subjective reasons in the process. But the converse can be just as true. We surely can imagine a teacher, whose ethical orientation is, let us say, a kind of moral egoism, deciding classroom policy and arrangements based on what promotes her own interests only to discover in time that she has come to possess a genuine regard for her students.

A practical ethic

Let me illustrate by contrasting this hypothetical story of Rose with the true story of Mario. A number of years ago a colleague of mine at a city high school in Seattle—we'll call her Lucinda Matlock to keep anonymity—taught American literature to juniors, and Mario happened to be a student in one of Lucinda's classes. In those days it was departmental policy to have a memorization assignment of some kind in each literature class, a minimum of ten to fifteen lines of some poet covered in the course that each student was to memorize. This was true of this particular course. At the end of one class period and before all of the other students had completely filed out of the room, Mario launched into a tirade about how unfair this assignment was and that Lucinda should know that he did drugs and couldn't possibly summon the concentration necessary to memorize anything. The few students still hanging around the desk concurred that it would be indeed difficult for Mario to satisfy the requirement.

Lucinda didn't in fact know that Mario did drugs, but when she brought this up with the head counselor he confirmed the fact and mentioned also that Mario was one of the school's providers of drugs as well. Part of Mario's charm was his ability to improvise defiance and injured pride within the same gesture. Mario couldn't have been over five feet tall, usually wore a floor-length leather trench coat with the belt tied at the waist, and when in a funk, which he often was, chose to strut, stopping occasionally to throw a sharp chop with his arm at the air and to glower. He almost never smiled and usually wore a sneer. Lucinda found this complaint of his, and that he thought it a perfectly legitimate one, so felicitous that she immediately warmed to this sullen little drug dealer. She claimed to have even apologized to him for her insensitivity; anyway, she persuaded him that memorizing fifteen lines wasn't so difficult and that she would help him. The two spent several lunch periods together, she amused to witness the sullenness drain from his face replaced by bewilderment at the poetry and he constrained with furrowed brow to recite line by enigmatic line:

> There was a child went forth every day,
> And the first object he look'd upon, that object he became,

And that object became part of him for the day or certain part of the day,
Or for many years or stretching cycles of years.

Mario managed to memorize fifteen lines of Whitman to pass the class and to graduate from high school. And this represents a confirmation of sorts no different in its effects from Rose's. Mario took some satisfaction in accomplishing a feat he believed himself incapable of and even showed some insight into the poetry, remarking that Whitman must have done drugs himself. But this teacher's motives were subjective. They were located neither in ethics nor in a deep regard for other. That Mario was able to "recruit" Lucinda had much more to do with her trained responsiveness to ethnography or to story (Kegan, pp. 19-20). Mario himself and the novelty of his attitude to schoolwork must have struck such a chord, reminding her of other such misfits familiar from her reading of fiction.

But the story doesn't end here. What makes subjective motives robust is their ability to turn into objective ones. And although Lucinda's reasons for personally assisting Mario in completing this task were not pure according to the dictates of an ethics of care, we sense that she must have found the experience affirming to some extent and received from it the unexpected satisfaction of Mario's success and her participation in it and of the guarded friendship the two developed afterward. It became her custom to admonish us, her colleagues, new teachers and student teachers alike, to get to know our students on a personal level, to take an interest in their lives irrespective of how well they do in school, especially those students we find difficult to manage or who show personal animus toward us. Theirs are not only the more interesting stories, she would claim, but our interest in them weakens their resistance, making life in the classroom less stressful and more enjoyable. It was an exhortation appealing to our self-interest, providing us with subjective reasons to feign a posture of care for strictly personal or professional gain. But even this attitude we later came to suspect was Lucinda's public posture, for whatever reasons, adopted as a persona to conceal a genuine regard for her students. We were never sure whether or not Lucinda's public declarations matched her true sentiments, she being particularly wary of showing any kind of sentimentality.

But were her public posture a deceit betraying a true regard for her students, it was a posture offering us an insight sustaining in its own right, offering us a means of acquiring personal satisfactions not directly related to our primary obligation of providing for the educational needs of our clients. Lucinda's admonition invited us to become anthropologists or ethnographers (Witherell and Noddings, Part III especially, 1991). Our clients were interesting case studies, and sometimes the more recalcitrant the client, the more interesting the study, as in Mario's case. Just what to do with Mario from the perspective of an ethic of care is an open question. Could the caregiver behave just as Lucinda did without any violation to the spirit of an ethic of care? Perhaps. She might have, without violation, sought to remove him from her classroom, arguing for a more "appropriate" setting for Mario where he might be less of a nuisance to his fellows and where he could receive counseling for his drug habit and antisocial behavior. But from an anthropological point of view, it was necessary for Lucinda to keep Mario in class; he nourishing her ethnographic interest in narrative. She took steps to make sure that he was receiving what the school system had to offer in terms of such help—she apprized the counseling staff of Mario's behavior at least—so that she could without misgivings indulge this personal interest of hers. The ethic of care provided a check to the legitimacy of this particular subjective motivation.

Conclusions

What subjective motivation does for the service professions is to broaden the reasons for joining them and to increase the possibility of finding enjoyment and satisfaction once employed. The Mario incident tells of one such motive. It is a motive noticed many times before. And although Robert Coles, for example, may argue for our listening to the stories of our clients in order to improve practice, storytelling is more than an instrumentum for him (1988). We sense that the narratives he listened to in his practice and related to us in his books provide satisfactions independently of their help in diagnosing and treating the patients under his care.

In providing fellowships for teachers in various subject matters, The National Endowment for the Humanities recognizes the importance of subjective motive by its insistence on the stipulation that none of the fellows are to develop curriculum for students, that their time and energy must be devoted exclusively to the texts to be examined, that is, to the subject matters engaging to their personal interests (1986). Eisner's description of the various roles teachers assume in the performance of their work is grounded on a kind of self-interest (1979). Connoisseurship may or may not have any relationship to an ethic of care, but teaching offers a connoisseur an excellent arena in which to display his taste, or a fool or a clown to crave a kind of wit.

Apart from the somewhat disconcerting result that a teacher systematically practicing an ethic of care may make decisions and behave in ways indistinguishable from a teacher practicing a kind of ethical egoism, it is a result that underscores the importance of self-interest even within an ethic of care by removing some of the austerity attaching to a profession whose sole concern is proffered as the care of other. To allow self-interest to play a major and acceptable role in ethical models of public-service is to widen our perspective of what it means to be in a public service profession and the possible motives for taking up such a profession. Moreover, these two orientations become interactive, each keeping the other in check. Professionals working in the service of others (caregivers) seek to understand how to survive and maintain their sense of self and their fundamental orientation to provide for the needs of others. Self-interest, so long as it gets satisfied, sustains the caregiver in his task, while ethical caring sees to it that self-interest is not satisfied to the detriment of the cared-for. Both are dimensions for reflection on action within professional contexts.

8

Liberation, Multiculturalism, and Professional Education

ZAHER WAHAB

We live in an increasingly diverse, pluralistic, and heterogeneous society and world. Let us review the demographics. According
to the 1990 census, there were 248.7 million people in the United
States, up by about 10 percent from 1980. Of this total, about 109
million were Anglo-European-white, 30 million African-American, 22
million Latino-Hispanic, 7 million Asian- and Pacific Islander-Ameri-
can, 2 million Native American, and the rest called "other" (U.S.
Census, 1990). About 14 percent of adults and 20 percent of children
under 17 are what Euroamericans call "minorities." Currently, 32
percent of school pupils are children of color; their number will
increase to 42 percent by the year 2000.

By the turn of the century an estimated 22 million of the 140
million workers in this country will be members of minority groups.
Minorities in U.S. society are reproducing themselves at such a rapid
pace that by the year 2050, Euroamericans will become "the minority"
(Quality Education for Minorities Project, 1990). In the twenty-five
largest cities in the country, more than half of school children are
members of minority groups (The Commission on Minority Participation in Education and American Life, 1988). Yet academic discourse
about "minority" and "majority" issues has been timid and inadequate, treating people of color either as problems to be dealt with or
avoiding the issue entirely. Controversy over the meaning and significance of multiculturalism and pluralism points to an inherent weakness in comprehending what really constitutes the United States.

In this chapter I challenge those of us in higher education to
reassess our role, function, and responsibility in society, rethink what
we have been doing thus far, and recast and restructure the way we
have been preparing professionals for human services. I maintain

Zaher Wahab

that American higher education has pursued approaches to diversity
and multiculturalism that have seriously inhibited the professionals'
fundamental understanding of race, power, and culture, thus doing
disservice to society by reinscribing existing paradigms. I present a
vision for education and society and an outline of how we might go
about educating people for the gradual realization of that vision.

The Impact of Racism on the Discourse
of Multiculturalism

Eurocentric academics have seized the initiative and shaped the
discourse around multiculturalism at all levels of education; hence
racism in society is reflected and reinforced by the policies, practices,
and structures of educational institutions. There are numerous and
unmistakable signs all around us indicating a resurgence of old and
new forms of racism in our society.

According to the *Chronicle of Higher Education* (January 22,
1992), the proportion of students of color in institutions of higher
learning has increased to 20 percent. This indicates progress except
when we consider that the increase is partly attributed to minority
increase in the population at large. More minorities graduate from
high school and do better on the SAT and/or ACT tests, but fewer of
them actually proceed to postsecondary institutions. Well over half of
all minorities in higher education study part-time and at two-year
community colleges; of these, only one in four transfers to four-year
institutions. Most minorities study either vocational training or the
"soft sciences." Many attend largely or exclusively minority colleges
and/or universities. A majority are in public, not private intellectual
institutions. And due partly to resurgent racism and cultural academic tensions in the academy, many drop out before finishing.
Minorities, women, and poor students made progress in higher education until the mid-1970s, but for minorities and low-income students that progress stalled after 1975. Blacks and Hispanics ages 25-
29 are half as likely as whites to graduate from four-year colleges. The
situation is very much the same for students from low-income families
(The *Chronicle*, December 4, 1991). Obviously higher education needs
to do more in educating minorities and distributing cultural capital
more equitably.

When people of color attempt to improve their situation in
education and life or when they try to make education culturally
inclusive, indeed when they attempt to promote interethnic-interra-

cial-intercultural understanding, harmony, and cooperation, they incur Eurocentric rejection and wrath. Thus presidents, journalists, academics, politicians, and public figures have gone on the offensive charging proponents of multiculturalism with the crime of "political correctness," the politicization of the academy, propaganda, brainwashing, intimidation, disunity, disloyalty, anti-Americanism, and heresy against Judeo-Christian Western civilization. Bush, Bennett, Buchanan, Levin, Jensen, Bloom, Hirsch, Cheney, and Schlafly, the most prominent cultural "freedom fighters," led the white supremacist assault on pluralism to new heights.

William Bennett, the self-styled culture czar, played a prominent role during the debate and struggle to modify the "Western Civilization" program at Stanford University to incorporate work by and about non-Europeans and women. He argued vehemently for the continuation of the Western Civilization curricular requirement and against the inclusion of race, class, and gender. First, he said, "because it is ours." Western civilization "is the culture in which we all live." Second, "because it is good" and the West has set moral, political, economic, and social standards for the rest of the world." Third, "the West is a source of incomparable intellectual complexity and diversity and depth, and because the classics of Western philosophy and literature amount to a great debate on the perennial questions." And fourth, "we must protect the West because it is under attack, from both without and within, by charges of racism, imperialism, sexism, capitalism, ethnocentrism, elitism, and a host of other isms." Bennett asserted that the "common American culture including the elements of the democratic ethic, work ethic, and Judeo-Christian ethic, was indeed alive, well, thriving, supported by *all* Americans and the envy of much of the world" [Bennett and other cultural mercenaries are richly rewarded and underwritten by corporate America and the bourgeois academic-political-cultural establishment] (*The Stanford Observer,* April-May 1988; November-December, 1990).

Adhering to the "divide and conquer" dictum, the ruling elite, with much help from its cultural-ideological messengers, has carefully orchestrated the politics of resentment among white Americans in order to continue the undeclared war on people of color. As part of a massive distortion, affirmative action is now called "reverse discrimination," school integration called "forced busing," minorities and women referred to as "special interest groups," the poor (whites and nonwhites) called "welfare queens, bums, and parasites," proportional representation and fair share labeled as "quotas", and third world national liberationists as liars, fundamentalists and "terrorists" who are a threat to 'our' national security. The studies of race, class, and gender are referred to as 'special interest and advocacy' programs, and multiculturalism and cultural democracy as threats to unity and the very fabric of American life. Thus we are surrounded by an ecology of old, new, structural, scientific, institutional, individual, and collective racism—all in the service of a Eurocentric worldview that disdains true social, economic, political, and cultural democracy.

Limits and Possibilities of Multicultural Education

Genuine multicultural education should begin first with the solid commitment of school faculty, staff, and administrators. Professors and/or teachers cannot be expected to implement multicultural programs appropriately without the opportunity to explore and to appreciate the necessity for such changes. Educators need the challenge, opportunity, and support to examine their own culture and identify attitudes and conduct. The importance of multicultural education must be explored with staff, faculty, administrators, and the community. This must include the direct examination of racism as a social construct and its maintenance through the "culture of power" and "the power of culture" within the United States.

Most educators and professionals believe that they are not prejudiced and that they are removed from the issue of racism. Such beliefs allow them to ignore schools' institutionalized racism. This illusion must be challenged in order to engage full participation in creating change. Similarly, teachers are proud of being "color-blind," ignoring the realities of racism in the daily functioning of educational institutions and the lives of people of color and thus implicitly establishing the dominant cultural experience as the norm. Whites need to be challenged to comprehend institutional as well as individual racism (Darder, 1991) and to address their participation in the continuation of systemic and "scientific" racism.

Educators and other professionals think and feel that white students are unaffected by diversity issues. Instructors do not appreciate the need for a human rights–oriented program in professional schools with predominantly white populations. Perhaps one of the greatest lessons to be gained through investigating multiple perspectives is the recognition of our own ethnoracial construction and its impact that we carry through life. This awareness is the first step in untangling racism and antiracism in our lives and our institutions. As Darder writes: "White educators who are working with bicultural students must first come to acknowledge their own limitations, prejudices, and biases, and must be willing to enter into dialogue with their students in a spirit of humility and with respect for the knowledge that students bring to the classroom" (1991, p. 70)

Education should always be a reciprocal process in which the educator is open to all that the students feel, think, dream, and live. Students, in turn, should be open to the opportunities teachers can provide to develop their voice and critical thinking skills, examine their histories, reflect on the world, and engage the dominant educational discourse as free agents who are able to influence and transform their world. The educator and student, the professional and client are involved in collaborative illumination and empowerment. This process is more difficult than it would first appear, for it requires letting go of the control and power associated with being privileged and with knowing and holding official authority. It requires the student/client to teach the teacher/professional risk, faith, courage, respect, trust, and love (Freire, 1970). As difficult as this process is, the outcome opens up real possibilities for everyone involved to develop an understanding of multiculturalism that challenges racism and classism.

Another reason for our failure to achieve true multicultural education has to do with the routine daily functioning of institutions such as graduate schools. The language, organizational culture, power relations, institutional norms, rules and regulations, ethos, reward and punishment structures, professionalism, illusions of scientific objectivity, and professional detachment all serve to legitimate, perpetuate, and obscure systemic institutional racism. Language, power, culture, and the authority of science and professionalism converge to reflect, maintain, and reinscribe interethnic-interracial hierarchies. This process is so subtle and pervasive that many members of both dominant and subordinate groups are oblivious to and deformed by it. Thus they internalize racism, sexism, and classism, and it all appears natural, rational, universal, and inevitable. There is an ominous silence about this subterranean racism.

Mandates and Imperatives: A Redefinition of the Liberal Arts for Professionals

The academy, including graduate professional programs, has failed to respond effectively to the crisis and opportunity of pluralism. As Giroux, (1988, 1992) observes, we need to be seriously concerned about how we educate future professionals in the language and practice of ethics, compassion, struggle, solidarity, and creative imagination. We need a new education for leadership with vision, ethics, language, and a public philosophy strongly committed to social, educational, economic, political, *and* cultural democracy. We want professional educators and human-service people who promote critical literacy and pedagogy, substantive democracy, and inclusivity and who function as change agents. This requires that academic and public discourse itself must confront the "logic" of instrumentalism, technicism, market forces, global competition, militarism, consumerism, monoculturalism, homogenization, individualism, and nationalism. Academics must understand and teach how language, culture, and power are interrelated in society.

Graduate schools can and must become centers for new social, moral, and intellectual leadership. Discourse in this emerging leadership must include the language of critique and possibility. In our academic exchanges, we must speak about diversity, community, solidarity, compassion, justice, social transformation, struggle, and the common good. The new language must expose white-collar crime, racism, sexism, classism, corporate-government collusion, ecocide, and the betrayal of democracy. The new professional education must inspire, impart, and apply what it means to live in a diverse and troubled world. It must confront inequalities and expose the system of domination and the structures of oppression (Hooks, 1990). We must view oppression as a social construction that can be changed through collective action. Professional leadership should enable educators to provide witness and testimony to the subjugated, the forgotten, the oppressed, and the victimized. The heart of professional education should be commitment to teaching intellectual, moral, and civic courage and responsible citizenship.

Future professionals must learn to judge situations, policies, and practices according to their impact on the most vulnerable and oppressed in society (Bloch, 1986). They must also address the issue of language as social construction and the use, abuse, and misuse of academic and public discourse. Professionals need to be able to demystify the language of education in both professional and public discourse by being dialectical and dialogical (Freire and Shor, 1987). We must assist them to collectively revitalize and build a democratic sociocultural order that is inclusive, humane, open, flexible, dynamic, supportive, pluralistic, just, and liberating. We must take responsibility for constructing an education that makes our students and colleagues agents in their lives, not objects.

I suggest a redefinition and reconceptualization of the liberal arts within professional education, one that has at its heart developing professionals who are responsible and critical citizens, militant activists, and visionaries, who get involved in improving the human condition (Arnowitz and Giroux, 1985). Professional education must teach students to make connections between their private and public lives, between various disciplines, and among professional work, ethics, and citizenship. It must make it clear to all how individuals are socially constructed and are thus deeply raced, classed, and gendered (Apple, 1986). It must help people to know what this fact means for their careers and private lives. To paraphrase Galeano and Fuentes (Simonson and Walker, 1988), we are what we think, read, and believe in, and we are what we are trying to do and to be.

The liberal arts should direct the inquiry in graduate professional studies programs to develop what Giroux calls emancipatory theories of leadership and a language that is critical, rigorous, accessible, ethical, inspiring, and visionary. We need a new language, new questions, and new answers to educational, ethnoracial, political, economic and sociocultural problems and challenges. We must reject or modify much of the discourse in our fields of endeavor. In short we must decenter Eurocentrism in its entirety. We need an interdisciplinary language that synthesizes theory, practice, and politics into praxis (Freire and Shor, 1987), realizing that these are all forms of social construction reflecting certain power relationships. These are temporary 'regimes of truth' (Foucault, 1977) and by no means natural, permanent, universal, or inevitable (Rosaldo, 1990).

We need a new language that conceives of classrooms as democratic public spheres where meanings are constructed, negotiated, contested, deconstructed, and reconstructed (Giroux, 1988). We must renegotiate the dynamics of race, culture, and power in education and society. We must realize, in this era of postmodernism, poststructuralism, and deconstruction, everything must be interrogated honestly, courageously, and vigorously and altered when necessary and desirable (Norris, 1991). And we must defend educational settings as public arenas that perform vital public services (Giroux, 1988). We cannot achieve democracy without understanding and confronting power, what it is, who has it, and how it is exercised (Chomsky, 1987; Foucault, 1977). In educational dialogue we must discern who decides, who gains, and who wins in society and the world at large (Domhoff, 1986).

Educators must develop a full understanding of the fact that they are indeed, cultural symbolic workers, having much in common with all other workers. Professionals must know how this country came to be, who did what to whom, the various forces at work, and the necessity to reconstruct American history and society (Means, 1992).

We must impart a sense of futurity very different from the past and the present. We need a different education for a new world.

We can teach future professionals how to think critically and dialectically. We must teach them how to challenge the "regimes of truth" in their fields, work, and public life. And we must teach them to struggle for the redistribution, redirection, and different use of the human, financial, natural, productive, and cultural resources of the country. We must inspire them with love, hope, vision, compassion, solidarity, and a strong commitment to improving life for all living creatures. We must inspire reverence for nature and the mysteries of life. We must model and teach respect, acceptance, tolerance, coexistence, humility, and moderation. We must teach Americans to need, want, consume, desire, and waste less.

We need to educate future professionals in how to behave as autonomous, transformative, and organic intellectuals (Gramsci, 1971), not as technicians, civil servants, clerks, managers, hegemonic or accommodationist intellectuals, and managers or ruling-class sharpshooters (Aronowitz and Giroux, 1985). We must teach them how to empower themselves, their colleagues and their communities, how to build activist coalitions, and how to lead the struggle for fundamental social transformation.

We must teach students how to analyze, critique, confront, expose, and deconstruct the vulgarities in the popular mass culture in print, television, radio, and daily language (Parenti, 1991). We must insist on complete academic and intellectual freedom. We must repossess our airways. We must teach teachers to exercise sound judgment about what to include or exclude in the curriculum and texts and how to undermine 'official knowledge' they work with (Apple, 1993). In short, we must teach them how to decolonize their own minds and consciousness and those of their associates, clients, students, and fellow humans (Freire and Shor, 1987, Memmi, 1967). We can do all this by teaching critical literacy and the ability to conduct multiple discourses with a wide variety of people. Our students need the awareness, skills, knowledge, values, and commitment to deterritorialize (Gomez-Pena, 1988), take risks, and cross boundaries because they have to be able to clarify, problematize, contextualize, connect, create, and recreate.

Furthermore, we must explore with our students the following: when, why, and how did Eurocentrism, capitalism, Christianity, Westernism/modernism, the standard culture, and the classics as the canon come to occupy privileged positions? What mechanisms legitimate, disseminate, defend, and preserve these in this country and globally? Can we speak in terms of a monoculture in a multicultural world? Is there, or should there be, just one text imposed on very diverse students? Where did the demarcation between "high" and "low" cultures originate and why? Why such hierarchies? Current and future academics, intellectuals, and professionals must come to terms with these questions with honesty, clarity, courage, and intelligence (Amin, 1989; Gless and Smith, 1992).

Educators and professionals must confront and resolve this essential contradiction in their lives. Instead of perpetuating the manufactured and imposed consensus from above, they must build on the principles of unity based on diversity from below (Chomsky, 1987, 88, 89). We must start from where we are as national and world communities, even though this is chaotic and contentious. We must pursue these dialectics to their logical and natural conclusions. This will indeed require courage, clarity, honesty, and some sacrifice from us, but liberal arts and professional education programs must place this at the very center of their inquiry. Otherwise, they too remain captives in and instruments of what Michele Wallace calls "cultural detention centers."

Connecting Culture and Power in Bicultural Education

Darder (1991) states that we must understand the close relation between education, culture and power in society at large if we are to understand where and how the subjugation of bicultural students takes place. We can build the foundations of a genuine bicultural education in a multicultural society. We must understand how power within and between groups mediates cultural and pedagogical relationships. Most social science, especially anthropology, focuses on culture excluding power. But power works on and through people, institutions, and symbols. An educational theory of cultural democracy must confront how meaning is imposed and perpetuated in school through dialectics prevalent in the larger society. School is in many ways a microcosm of the sociocultural system at large. We must recognize culture in its material and nonmaterial forms, culture as process, product, and ideology (in schools), and the dynamics of relationships between dominant and subordinate cultures.

Human Rights Education as a Step Toward
Multicultural Education

Critical pedagogy is a crucial means by which professionals can disrupt the perpetuation of racism, sexism, and classism. To be effective in preparing students to live, learn, and work in a genuinely pluralistic, interdependent world, schools must adopt a multifaceted approach that involves faculty, staff, and students in critical thinking dialogue about their lives, the world, and social institutions. To achieve this involves both an appreciation of differences and an understanding of common humanness and respect for one another. Toward this end, current multicultural education programs are necessary but grossly insufficient in their most common forms in today's institutions.

It is imperative that we create professional educational programs with a strong component on broad human rights for all students and people. This would require close examination of the way we interact with students, each other, and the community and how we conduct our classrooms, as well as the inclusion of diverse perspectives throughout educational curricula. While we must make strenuous efforts to honor cultural paradigms in the interest of making a difference in the education and well-being of students from subjugated cultures, we must prepare *all* students to think critically about their world and challenge them to be informed, ethical, and active citizens prepared to make a difference.

Lynch suggests that "human rights education is . . . a moral education about the way that human beings behave towards each other in the family, in groups, in their community, in their nation and globally." (1989, p. 77). The goals, content, and objectives of such education are broad and include helping students to develop a strong sense of social responsibility that leads to the observance of equality in everyday conduct. Human rights education is not an alternative to multicultural education but a crucial dimension of and adjunct to it. Garcia suggests that there are four instructional dimensions within multicultural education: (1) cultural education that builds cognitive understanding about groups; (2) language education that builds literacy in a modern foreign language; (3) intergroup education that builds positive relations between students who differ by class, gender, race, handicap, or religion; and (4) human rights education that builds ethical responsibility among students (1991).

These models emphasize process over content and focus on personal/professional relationships. But in order to actively combat racism and address the needs and experiences of bicultural students, all of these aspects of multicultural education must be employed. Stronger emphasis on expanded human rights education should be included in the liberal arts component of professional education programs.

Toward a New Vision

The United States has reached a historical crossroads. Ethnoracial and cultural heterogeneity has created unprecedented challenges and opportunities. The motto, "E Pluribus Unum" (out of many, one) now acquires a special significance in the nation's history. Pluribus does not just say "everyone for himself/herself" and "Unum" does not mean "we are all the same." The fact is that U.S. society has evolved to a point where either isolationalist multiculturalism or oppressive monoculturalism are unthinkable. Neither invasive assimilationism nor rejectionist separatism will do. A quick glance at recent events in the country and the world makes this abundantly clear. Therefore, the choice is not among chauvinistic, ethnocentric, xenophobic, antagonistic, and atomized, cultural relativism/pluralism; Eurocentric, oppressive, imperialistic monoculturalism; or a kind of benign, tokenistic, hierarchical, exotic 'pluralism' and 'diversity' with a clear Eurocentric white-supremacist culture as standard-model at the top. We need a different kind of sociocultural organization, a new design, and restructuring, a new paradigm.

We must develop a multiculturation in which the mutual acculturation of people, groups, and institutions is based on the quest for positive commonalties and the nourishing of enriching differences (Cortes, 1990). We must conceptualize, cultivate, and perfect a new vision of American society based on the principles of universal humanism and humanist universalism. This model of society is to be participatory democratic, intercommunalist, interethnic-intercultural-interracial socialist, decentralized, and sustainable. It must be founded on solidarity, variety, trust, respect, natural justice, and collective self-management. Such a society is to be guided by the principles of tolerance, peace, harmony, justice, equity, material and psychosocial well-being for all, fair distribution of cultural capital, and on humane values. We must work on replacing competition, possessive individualism, aggression, acquisitiveness, and endless consumption with cooperation, harmony, generosity, and sharing. We must think of sustainable development instead of mindless destructive growth. We must stop denaturizing nature and learn to cooperate with and accommodate to it.

We must scale down gigantic bureaucracies, organizations, multinational corporations, and educational institutions. We must restore the idea and reality of community. We must redefine and reorganize work not as an alienating dangerous evil, but as a pleasant, dignified, fulfilling vocation. We must ensure high quality, equal, universal education as a right and necessity, not as a privilege or commodity. We must infuse ethics into every aspect of our individual, collective, private, and public lives. We must stop exploiting, destabilizing, or waging wars on other countries and live in harmony, cooperation, and mutuality with them. We must think and live relationally.

Multicultural Democracy

A monumental shift is underway in U.S. society with the emerging majority being people of color. To paraphrase DuBois (1975) we can no longer consider the North Atlantic community as the center of world civilization or the universe nor should we look upon Eurocentrism as the norm against which all others are judged. We must view and deal with this society and the world at large in their true proportions and dimensions. The numerical majority must be accorded its due and rightful place in the scheme of things. All policies, institutions, and practices must reflect this essential truth. The domestic and global pyramidal structures of power, privilege, oppression, domination, exploitation, and exclusion must be replaced with new egalitarian humane, and democratic forms. If this reversal is not done deliberately, peacefully, and justly, it will be forced from below. For as Paulo Freire states, "oppressed people cannot remain oppressed forever." And, as DuBois observed, we are planning for war. Actually, the war is being waged now, albeit undeclared and in a nonspectacular fashion.

A philosophy of cultural democracy was articulated by Manual Ramirez and Alfredo Castenada (1974) as the principle whereby "every individual has the right to maintain bicultural identity." Biculturalism refers to the phenomenon where individuals learn to function in two divergent cultural systems—their primary culture and the dominant mainstream culture surrounding them. It refers also to the way in which the dominated resolve and mediate the tensions, contradictions, and differences between two cultures, the home and school cultures, and the way in which people of color deal with Eurocentrism and racism in U.S. society. This can be done if we commit our intelligence, will, courage, and resources to it. We can therefore create a new definition of multiculturalism, one that is worthy of the traditions of the liberal arts, which liberates those who embrace the quest and who seek a new world order. The challenge is to invest professionals with this ethic and vision at its core, taking charge of the liberal arts within its domain. We will, indeed, "rise or fall together."

9

Citizens and the Conduct of Ecological Science: A Response to the "Tragedy of the Commons"

CHARLES R. AULT, JR.

In a democracy, citizens, differing in training and interests, share responsibility for determining the uses of science. Acknowledgment of this shared responsibility is the impetus behind a core course for teachers, principals, psychologists, and public administrators entitled, "Ecological Knowledge for Environmental Problem-Solving." Three themes weave through the course: the challenge of sustainable exploitation of natural resources, the role of ecological understanding in policy and life-style choices, and the anchoring of values about people and their relation to nature in literature. To link these three themes, the class examines a case about local development, regulation, and management of a natural resource. Our goal in studying this case is to promote among citizens a sense of "place" as both a feeling of significance about local ecology and a personal role in the conduct of science. This chapter invites the reader to consider the vitality of these questions for the interdisciplinary education of professionals as informed citizens.

What aspects of scientific reasoning are of value to a socially responsible, scientifically literate citizenry, which collectively has no choice but to seek ways of promoting the habitability of the Earth? Real problems of environmental degradation and resource utilization are embedded in complicated social contexts as well as complex scientific ones. These problems defy simple, unambiguous solutions, reflecting both the intractable nature of the problem, the diverse cognitive styles of problem solvers, and the disparity among value systems held by those who share concerns for solutions.

Naive notions of the nature of science tend to disenfranchise both lay people and experts. When common people believe that "when *all* of the facts are known, the issue will be resolved" and "that only the properly trained experts can discover the facts," they absolve themselves of responsibility. On the other hand, when they believe that "facts can be found to support any position" and "scientists only reach conclusions that support their self-interests," they deny themselves knowledge essential to their well-being.

When experts disparage lay understanding of technical matters, they ignore the public's right to shape the context and direction for the conduct of science. Distrust by experts of public understanding of scientific matters reinforces—even legitimates—the naive "fact" and "self-interest" notions. Citizens need to realize that much of science is concerned with judgments about likelihood and probability, rather than producing immutable rules, and that controversy in science is as much about the relevant context for findings as over their validity.

Environmental Problems

Often scientific solutions to problems ignore the interaction between separate components (biological and hydrological, for example, in obtaining hydropower), with dire consequences for large-scale systems. Salmon, for example, return nutrients from the sea to forest floor soil via predator and scavenger excrement and carcass decomposition. In an effort to engineer "inexpensive" sources of electrical power, fish-killing turbines may impact soil fertility.

Real environmental problems have physical, psychological, social, ethical, and philosophical components, acknowledged or not. "Not only are they complex, ill-defined, and difficult to bound, but the available information is commonly incomplete and ambiguous" (Miller, 1985, p. 24). People respond to these problems all too often by simplifying them to isolated subcomponents and solving these with analytical skills. However, simplification can misidentify the problem and underestimate (or ignore) complex interactions. Oversimplification may obscure how exploration of different interpretations of a problem might provide contributions toward an adequate solution.

To err in the interpretation of catastrophic suffering by solely blaming "natural disaster" is, of course, as misguided as to err by failing to understand human interactions with natural systems. Apple (1992) cogently argues how interpreting human tragedies as a consequence of "natural disasters" masks the role of economic and political structures. In many parts of the world, "natural disasters" make headlines when hundreds, if not thousands, of poor people perish due to storms, drought, and flooding. Apple uses an example from South America in which the "natural disaster" of massive mudslides induced by torrential rainfall killed large numbers of people. He claims, "A closer examination of this case reveals nothing natural about the catastrophe at all" (p. 779). This conclusion rests upon examination of economic structures that allow a wealthy minority of the population to control land in the valleys—where annual rainfall patterns do not cause the kinds of death and destruction experienced by poor people living, not by choice but by economic necessity, on unstable slopes. In brief, poverty and history crowd poor people onto dangerous land. In many such cases, lifting the veil of the "natural disaster" label opens to inspection the interaction of our social systems with processes beyond our control. In this inspection, value and science matter equally.

A Course in Environmental Problem Solving

Our course on ecological knowledge for environmental problem solving challenges students to conceptualize the interactive nature of their surroundings. The ecological framework they study in so doing is presented on three levels of sophistication. The book by Orians (1986a) that inspired the title of the course addresses concepts of population ecology at a level that stretches the understanding of secondary science teachers and natural resource policymakers. It includes case histories of environmental problems interpreted through the lens of population ecology. Miller's (1991) textbook on environmental science provides a comprehensive overview of the "ecosystem" concept and its relation to energy, resource, and pollution issues. Lastly, students learn to apply a framework of ecology concepts developed for the Seaside, Oregon, public school curriculum. This framework—adapted from a number of resources (e.g., Murphy, 1979; Darnnell, 1976) has proven of value not only to school students but also to interpretive centers and land use planners.

During the summer of 1992, the case was the Tualatin River, a waterway impacted by forestry, feedlots, nurseries, auto salvage yards, industry, recreational and flood control dams, city park development, beavers and herons, headwater diversion projects, invasive reed canary grass, agricultural runoff, real estate promotion, canoeists, wetlands preservation laws, and sewage treatment. In particular, students examined a proposal to establish a 3,000-acre National Wildlife Refuge along the river adjacent to the urban growth boundary of Portland, Oregon (Harrison, 1992). Students were invited to participate in the process of defining the educational purposes this refuge might serve for the region.

From the Concept of a "Commons" to Student Proposals

This chapter begins with a discussion of the concept of a "commons," as does the "Ecological Knowledge" course, and ends with excerpts from student proposals for engaging public interest in ecological thinking through the educational functions of a wildlife refuge. The notion of a commons tragedy stems from the tendency of the rational pursuit of individual gain to result in collective decline in the quality of a resource (Ostrom, 1991). Communication about future consequences of trends in our economic behavior is the path out of this dilemma, and the knowledge most appropriate for understanding where such trends may be leading is often found through ecological science (see the July/August 1992, special issue of *The Ecologist,* "Whose Common Future?" for an up-to-date, comprehensive examination of the centrality of the commons idea to ecological interpretations of economic development). Hence, the second part of this chapter dwells on ecological perspectives of environmental problems and the role of science in adjudicating disputes, especially as espoused by Orians (1986a, 1986b). My conclusions draw upon examples of natural history literature where systems of values find expression in ways that may ultimately prompt people to care about ecological science and commons-caused environmental problems.

Educators (especially science teachers), counseling psychologists, and public administrators all have much to contribute to defining multiple perspectives toward complex environmental problems and much to gain from each other's ways of interpreting them. In their professional lives, they all share a commitment to helping people avoid catastrophe and deal with tragedy, increasingly so in regard to natural resources and natural disasters. A most useful concept from economic theory for engaging diverse professionals in study consistent with this social imperative is that of a "commons."

The Concept of the Commons

Humanist Perspectives and Economic Models

Perhaps John McPhee is today's most expressive witness to natural phenomena from the perspective of human purpose. His writings reflect a humanist's journey into the interaction of human sensibilities and frailties with primordial nature and, in many respects, its monumental indifference to human cares. In McPhee's *The Control of Nature* (1989), we find an account of "Los Angeles Against the Mountains" (pp. 181-272). Told from the point of view of a family in terror, McPhee describes a mudslide—more properly, a debris flow—in the San Gabriel Mountains. The narrative winds back and forth between human interest and basic geology, all in keeping with the theme of "Los Angeles against the San Gabriel Mountains" (p. 183). McPhee writes:

> Most people along the mountain front are about as mindful of debris flows as those corpses were. Here today, gone tomorrow. Those who worry build barricades. They build things called deflection walls—a practice that raises legal antennae and, when the caroming debris breaks into the home of a neighbor, probes the wisdom of Robert Frost. At least one family has experienced so many debris flows coming through their back yard that they long ago installed overhead doors in the rear end of their built-in garage. To guide the flows, they put deflection walls in their back yard. Now when the boulders come they open both ends of their garage, and the debris goes through to the street. (p. 189)

The chapter continues to explain the engineering structures throughout the Los Angeles basin designed to trap, store, carry, and distribute water—and, when caroming down steep slopes, debris as well. This engineering is L.A.'s attempt to "control nature"—"a web of engineering that does not so much reinforce as replace the natural river systems" (p. 192). On the steep slopes of the San Gabriel Mountains, concrete barriers ("cribs") "convert plunging streams into boulder staircases, and hypothetically cause erosion to work against itself" (p. 193).

McPhee has used humanism and literary style to place the engineering sciences squarely within the interdisciplinary stew served up by earth and environmental problems. Continuing with the theme of the L.A. basin, another discipline has much to offer: economics. In particular, water—wanted and unwanted—is a "commons" problem for its residents. Science and environmental educators generally trace their grasp of "commons dilemmas" to the 1968 paper by Garrett Hardin titled, "The Tragedy of the Commons." L.A.'s water is an ideal example of a commons problem (Ostrom, 1987).

The Tragedy of the Commons

Hardin states the commons's dilemma as a conflict between moral principle and self-interest arising when positive effects of an action accrue to an individual while negative ones are shared widely among members of the group. His example is an open pasture. All goes well for the rational herdsman until the population of livestock begins to degrade the quality of the common range. By adding more animals, the herdsman realizes a direct benefit; he shares the cost of deterioration with the other people of the village. Pursuing his interests leads to tragedy, but not to do so endangers his ability to support his family. Hardin concludes:

> Therein is the tragedy. Each man is locked into a system that compels him to increase his herd without limit—in a world that is limited. Ruin is the destination toward which all men rush, each pursuing his own best interest in a society that believes in the freedom of the commons. (Hardin, cited in Ostrom, p. 2)

Any case of concentrated benefits and dispersed costs is a candidate for the commons schema: fisheries, air quality, sewage disposal, landfill, natural resources, grazing lands, forests—and, in the original Hardin paper, the most strikingly troublesome commons of all, "freedom to breed" (Hardin believed that overpopulation was the consequence of the same logic degrading the herdman's commons). Hardin's article has emerged as ". . . the dominant framework within which social scientists portray environmental resource issues" (Godwin and Shepard, cited in Ostrom, 1987, p. 1). Noting that Hardin was "not the first to notice the tragedy of the commons" (p. 1), Ostrom quotes from Aristotle's Politics, Book II, chapter 3: "What is common to the greatest number has the least care bestowed upon it. Everyone thinks chiefly of his own, hardly at all the common interest" (pp. 2-3).

After reviewing classical papers on the tragedy of the commons preceding Hardin's essay, Ostrom concludes that examination of the "stark features of the formal representation" of the problem conform to the structure of a class of decision problems labeled "The Prisoner's Dilemma" (e.g., as discussed in Campbell and Sowden, 1985). In such a dilemma, best decisions for individuals are not the best joint outcomes. Individual rational choice leads to collectively considered irrational results. The dilemma poses the question, "Can rational creatures cooperate?"

Governing the Commons

Limits to the commons model. What the tragedy of the commons and the prisoner's dilemma predicate are (a) a mathematical model or scoring scheme to keep track of human interaction and (b) a matrix of outcomes that cannot be changed. Inevitable "ruination" and distrust of rational cooperation suggest the need for distasteful, coercive political arrangements. However, Ostrom points out the tragedy exists in the model by mathematical necessity; in the real world, by analogy only. The real world has factors at work that the model ignores. Foremost among these are communication and the ability to change outcomes. In some situations, people can not only choose actions but also act to change structures, and in contexts encouraging open exchange of accurate information, they may decide to do so. "Ruination" is the prediction based upon a model of logic and assignment of payoff values; for Ostrom it is an empirical question. She has studied cases of successful escape from the tragedy of the commons, acknowledging that these solved cases may be rare, yet claiming theoretical value in understanding the "escapes." Argues Ostrom, "These success stories are particularly interesting because none of them relies on central control nor market mechanisms as its primary mode of management." Resolution does depend, in her selected cases, upon institutional arrangements characteristic of self-governing, democratic societies.

   The example of West Basin. The first case addressed by Ostrom is that of West Basin, California—the groundwater resource for the Los Angeles metropolitan area. This case is a clear example of an earth science/environmental science issue embedded in a sociopolitical context. It demonstrates how the economic construct of a "commons" connects to the need for good information from science, yet how the science alone cannot resolve the dilemma.

   In West Basin, annual overdraft of groundwater by mid-century had lowered water levels to such an extent that saltwater had begun to intrude. The incentive to pump water in order to secure and maintain water rights was leading to disaster. For hundreds of water producers, "no mechanism existed for them to come to agreement concerning joint strategies" (Ostrom, p. 11). Yet today, "West Basin is in better condition than it was forty years ago" (p. 11). Users established a forum for discussion about common problems, sought the best information about the conditions of the basin, and agreed to consider joint production alternatives. With equity court procedures to assist their efforts, the users negotiated contracts among themselves limiting production. They had, in effect, changed the structure of the choices. Each water producer agreed to limit production if, and only if, 80 percent of all producers in West Basin so agreed.

   Clearly, the groundwater of West Basin is but one component of the complex water needs of arid Southern California. Los Angeles reaches across the state and back to the Rocky Mountains in its thirst and may have an eye on the soggy Northwest as well. A commons solution is seldom permanent and another level of commons dilemma almost always awaits citizen attention.

The tragedy of the commons is, perhaps, the most central message to grasp in an education for lives as environmentally responsible citizens, for the principle of individual benefit/shared costs is endemic to the impact of industrial, commercial society on the long-term habitability of the globe. What the example illustrates is how a logico-mathematical model helps to frame the problem but, at the same time, obscures alternative solutions. In complex, intractable problem-solving contexts, alternative solutions are a must. As revealed by Ostrom's work, thinking can consider changing the choices, not just how to decide among them. Information may be sought from a variety of sources, with no predetermined formula as to what information to exclude or include. Some of the best and most essential information for resolving commons dilemmas is found in the science of ecology. We turn next to the ecological framework as taught in our environmental problem-solving course.

A Framework for Ecological Interpretation

A Brief Epistemological Introduction to Science:
Events and Concepts

Neal Maine, as the science specialist for the Seaside, Oregon, school district and an advocate of ecology as *the* "citizen science" (Maine, 1992), teaches the "complete symmetry" of interactive processes in the environment, with wonder being as much an objective of learning as knowledge. Yet he underscores the point that all ecosystem interactions are value-free; there are no good or bad interactions, only living organisms reacting or responding to events according to the chemical and physical limits by which they are bound. Perhaps two statements best capture the kind of understanding promoted by Maine's approach: (1) The environment has no "away" (matter is always present somewhere and usually cycles). (2) "Growth" is a conceptual illusion (life reorganizes matter; matter gained is matter lost elsewhere).

These two statements suggest an understanding encompassing both an "event-sense" of the subject—the "what really happens" that we care about—as well as an "invented-concept" approach to knowledge—the "freedom to conceive" that both constrains and liberates thinking. Epistemologically, Maine's thinking holds that the business of choosing ways to conceive of events is as important to making discoveries about events as is conducting empirical work.

Our discussion has dealt at length with the merits of choosing to conceive of events using the concept of a "commons." Throughout this discussion the definition of "concept" remained informal. The demands of mastering a framework of ecological concepts calls for an explicit definition of "concept." A concept is a sign or symbol, shared socially, signifying a pattern or regularity in events or objects (Gowin, 1981). Note that this definition has three parts: sign, events, and pattern. The idea of a pattern in events means imposing some boundary on our experience of them—boundaries we share with each other by virtue of the symbolic power of concepts. For example, when visiting a rose garden, the boundary of the "leaf" concept is chosen so that we can distinguish "twigs" and "petals." Nature admits to no fixed boundary between leaf and petal—the latter evolved from the former over eons. We impose the boundary in order to make sense of our experience of roses for our purposes, thorns included. If we succeed in communicating the boundaries we have imposed upon events—and the purpose for doing so—we can achieve shared meaning of concepts. This shared meaning permits us to have a common experience (or interpretation) of events and objects in the rose garden—on at least one level of conceptualization.

If we fail to achieve shared meaning for our concepts, then the heritage of human thinking assembled through our social nature over time is inaccessible. If you cannot crack the code—grasp the meaning—then the knowledge held by others cannot be shared with you. In communicating concepts, we help each other along with the process of conceiving patterns among events.

Reference, relation, and purpose characterize the meaning of a concept. Concepts are invented in light of purposes we value, and articulated as classes and relations in intelligible ways in order to enhance the achievement of these purposes. Because these purposes in science are to make sense of and predictions about a world not of our making, the concepts we find plausible are neither arbitrary nor idiosyncratic. They are judged worthy, at the very least, on the basis of their utility—a notion that links "what we value" with "what we trust" about our knowledge of events.

Keep in mind that persons lacking any substantial background in science predominate in the core course, "Ecological Knowledge for Environmental Problem-Solving." Typically, however, 20 percent of the students in the class hold degrees in biological science. Ideally, this epistemological introduction to concepts is a way of leveling the playing field for making progress in understanding science, regard-less of background.

Ecosystems, Ecology, and Environmentalism

An ecological framework uses concepts to impose boundaries on our experience of events, elevating to attention and concern patterns and regularities of an interactive, biological world. The events-of-interest become those of ecosystem functioning; the concepts, those of ecological science. Through this science we obtain records of the events-of-interest and guidance in making generalizations and claims about ecosystems given the records. Valuing accompanies the inter-pretation of these claims and leads to actions chosen in light of these "ecological findings." This valuing elevates knowledge from the realm of ecological science to that of environmentalism.

Ecosystems. Ecosystems, whether considered as one large Earth System or countless, smaller unique ecosystems, are defined by humans. However, the interactions of matter and energy that go on within them are independent of our thinking. We attempt to commu-nicate our understanding of these interactions according to human purpose, using "systems concepts" (i.e., inputs, interactions, sub-systems, outputs) and methods we agree upon. These concepts shape our thinking, our aims for inquiry, and the quality of our conversa-tions with each other about how the living world works. An "ecosys-tem-sense" of how our surroundings operate is the event focus of our ecological framework.

Ecology. From concepts about events, we build statements. Some are claims. They make statements about the world as we conclude it to be. Some are principles. They act as rules to guide our thinking. Our trusted statements about ecosystems and the methods for improving upon this knowledge are the science of ecology. In ecology, there are many claims about how ecosystems respond to perturbations such as logging practices. There are rules to guide thinking such as the operation of a food chain and how it concentrates fat-soluble com-pounds. These claims and rules exist within a context of inquiry dedicated to holistic understanding of biological processes—in keep-ing with an aim of predicting the effects of perturbing the system. Still, this inquiry remains basically unlinked to issues of social value.

Environmentalism. To work toward such linkage is to engage in "environmentalism," to embed thoughtful consideration of ecology within human systems of interaction and valuing. Environmentalism focuses primarily on human behavior, on the cultural arrangements that mediate human activity and ecosystem functioning. Ecology informs this mediation, the tool of the timber harvester as much as the wilderness preservationist. It is a human science intended to help us know what we are doing. Ecology does not tell us what we ought to do, only what reactions and responses living organisms might likely make to perturbations of their surroundings. What we do with ecological understanding is environmentalism.

Summary

To summarize this epistemologically oriented introduction to ecology: concepts are freely invented, mental constructions, brought into existence according to our human-centered purposes. We do not discover concepts. We make discoveries by using concepts to make sense of the world—for our purposes, from our frame of reference in it. The first step, or perhaps the ultimate last step, in understanding a concept is to know what purpose it serves; prediction, for example. "Prediction" is the forge of scientific concepts, and it tempers the designs our thinking might usefully construct.

Science tends to construe the universe as "space, time, energy, matter." Nothing else. Finding only matter and energy, changing through space and time, is not simply a fruit of scientific method but an assumption about how to construe the world in the first place in order to make sense of it for our purpose of prediction. Ecological science, as a humanly valued, predictive enterprise, inherits this conceptual pedigree of space, time, energy, matter.

In terms of ecological concepts, we phrase ecological questions. A good ecological question focuses our minds on what activity we might engage in to answer the question. It alerts our thinking to the categories needed to apprehend patterns among interactive, biological events. These categories, as learned from prior experience, are about the interactions through time and in limited space of the matter and energy entities we call organisms.

Avoiding Intimidation by Science Concepts

Interest, Skills, and "Tom Sawyer" Science

As stated above, an epistemologically oriented approach to science concepts may level the playing field for the science-trained and nonscientist alike. This leveling is one of two crucial steps necessary to fostering mutual respect and cooperation among diverse learners.

The second step is to validate the frameworks people bring to interpretive tasks independent of instruction about ecological concepts. This process begins with a task-centered experience intended to awaken interest in nature.

For example, students assemble on the edge of a forest. Given minimal information, they are asked to "map the boundaries of lichens on tree trunks." The instructor provides large pieces of clear plastic to wrap around tree trunks and marker pens of different colors to use in outlining the margins of lichens. Students are given virtually no information about lichens (an algal-fungi partnership) except that they can be found by looking for color variation on the trunks of trees. One last instruction is to mark the north side of the plastic once it is wrapped around the tree.

After mapping lichens on the trunks of several red alders (and given *minimal information* about lichens), students reassemble at the edge of the forest. They inspect each others' lichen maps informally for a few minutes. Soon the instructor poses key questions such as, "What interpretive framework did you bring to the task? What meaning did lichen-looking have for you? What feelings did lichen-looking evoke? ("Oh, gross!" or "I don't get it" or "They're amazing.") Through discussion, previous experience and prior knowledge about the natural world comes to light. There is a deliberate attempt to validate whatever framework was used in making sense of lichen-looking. The emphasis on this phase of the lesson is encouragement of interest by directing attention and then encouraging personal reflection.

More is done with the maps as students seek more information about lichens and make increasingly purposeful comparisons of their maps. Some begin to wonder whether any portion of a red alder trunk is free of lichens. Others distinguish between mosses and lichens; some between different types of lichens. The "north" label on the maps opens questions about the relative abundance of one or another type of organism depending on direction faced. Ways of comparing abundance, percent covered, and diversity, permit hypothesizing about lichen growth at the edge versus the interior of the forest, on youthful versus older trees, on broadleafed versus conifer trees, and so on. The questions become more telling as they begin to incorporate more purpose. Lichen-looking becomes a way of finding out what is happening in the forest and an invitation to engage in ecological science.

This model of encouraging personal involvement begins with (1) crafting an encounter, prompting an experience. The purpose of this phase is to foster interest and validate personal reflection. The encounter included the (2) introduction of tools and skills that made processes of investigation simple and available. From this combination of interest and skill (along with trust in one's prior knowledge) came (3) questions that called for more experience and study.

"Science" gets going with step 3. An expert investigator can reverse the sequence—be engaged in the science and invite participation by citizens who end with a personal encounter with nature. Starting with step 3 means having a good question in mind and some competence with the skills needed to study it. Busy with the "science," the investigator attracts curious onlookers. They are lured into participation by an interesting encounter with the phenomena under study—making lichen maps or inventories of streambank vegetation, for example. At this stage citizens have joined in the conduct of a style of science aptly termed "biological monitoring." I like to call this approach "Tom Sawyer Science." The scientist, in the role of Tom Sawyer, has the arduous task of whitewashing a very long fence. As each passerby asks, "What are you doing?" the scientist replies with an invitation to help out. Just as in whitewashing a fence, many hands (and minds) may usefully contribute to monitoring the surroundings, whether forest, stream, schoolyard, industrial corridor, or park.

Point one in the lesson is that everyone brings to bear on lichen-looking some previous experience and knowledge. Point number two is the potential value of having a *common interpretive framework* that extends personal reflection in the direction of intelligent functioning of a democratic citizenry. The common framework should lead to a reorganization, not a preemption, of personal knowledge. To grasp the significance of their participation in "Tom Sawyer Science," citizens need to understand the value of biological monitoring to solving ecological problems.

Of course, in this class, the common framework is an introductory version of ecological science. Based upon course readings, students make short lists of what they believe to be concepts essential to an ecological framework. They are asked, "What statements of relationship between pairs of concepts on your list hold meaning for you?" and "Which one concept appears to be most centrally organizing to your understanding?"

In summary, to lessen the potential for science to intimidate, our course encourages reflection on personal experience and prompts interest before stressing concepts and objectives. The aim is to lure students into the conduct of science using simple skills and readily available materials, setting the stage for deliberate study and additional experiences. Ecology—framed as interactions among organisms and their habitats—becomes a set of tools for reorganizing personal experience in order to participate in biological monitoring.

Organisms and Habitats

Space, Energy, Matter

The measure of a good conceptual framework is its generation of productive questions, given the aim of making sense of the phenomenon of interest. In introducing the common citizen to ecology, such a framework must achieve simplicity without simple-mindedness. In other words, the entry point for citizen grasp of ecology ought to be a procedure for framing questions whose answers might genuinely inform science. In the simplest sense, ecology raises questions about what happens to matter in a finite space. Study proceeds to track energy as it moves through this system. Interesting "effects" are cast as changes over time in the interactions among elements of the system.

Of course these questions are not about all matter in just any space and over time scales of undefined extent, but about space, matter, energy, and time of concern to biological beings, ourselves included. These biological beings are called "organisms," the root of this term connoting persistent patterns of organization—"turtleness" or "mapledom," to be whimsical. Of concern to organism survival is habitat—the space, matter, and energy needs they have through time.

Biological interest in this system, therefore, centers upon the lives of organisms. Schoolbook science, regrettably, convinces most citizens that the appropriate path to knowledge about organisms is to be found in nomenclature. There are classes and orders, families and species, vertebrates and invertebrates, mollusks and cnidarians, sea slugs and carpenter ants to keep well-sorted, to burden memory. Ecologists defer to no one in their penchant for systematic nomenclature, but from a citizen perspective the first organism question to ask is not "What is it?" but rather, "What is it doing?"

Individuals, Populations, Communities, Ecosystems

The "doing" question gets at interest in interaction, and it rightfully begins with focus on individual organisms. One very approachable source of information about individual organisms comes from the tradition of natural history writings. Natural history combines interest, appreciation, science, and folklore—all in the service of making sense of what an organism might be doing. However, constrained by the criterion of prediction, ecology is less eclectic than natural history.

Ecology is still in the on-deck circle with questions about individual organisms, about who eats whom, or how escapes are made. It steps to the plate with concern for populations of organisms—fluctuations, migrations, reproductive rates, and environmental tolerances. Populations, by virtue of their genetic inheritance are, in effect, repositories of information about habitat predictability. The instruction set held by the population for how to make more individuals capable of surviving and making still more individuals is a kind of habitat gambling figured according to historical successes. No habitat, however, has a guaranteed future.

Populations do not play out their life histories in isolation. Within a finite space, many populations—or at least several individuals from different populations—exchange matter and energy. They consume and decompose each other—beginning this chain with "photon predation" (a phrase referring to photosynthesis coined by Orians, 1986a) and ending it with "heat waste." As Neal Maine points out, an osprey feasting on a trout is not only equipped with the instructions for turning trout-matter into osprey, but also with directions for using the energy of the trout to do so. "What a deal!"

Populations, like organisms, are relatively amenable to study and can be characterized in terms of variables measuring, for example, environmental tolerances, reproductive rates, or predator-prey fluctuations. Difficulty arises in taking the next step back and perceiving, then conceiving, of regularities in communities of populations. "How's the community doing?" becomes the key question at this level. The categories for framing meaningful answers, however, are troublesome, conceptually and empirically.

Abstractions such as "stress" and "stability," build upon notions of organism "tolerances" for physical "limiting factors." In our course on ecological knowledge for environmental problem solving we have reached, at this point, a science saturation level for many students. Students are invited to use the text resources of the course to bring preliminary closure to their interpretive framework of ecology concepts. More importantly, they are told to visit the reflecting pond on the college campus and test the question-generating capacity of the framework they have studied. They are prompted with questions such as, "What are the finite boundaries to the system? What is the source of energy? What are the organisms? What are they doing? Who enters, who leaves? Which populations are rising and which are falling? How is matter reorganized, energy transferred? How is space shared?"

The Orians Model

To Perturb and Predict

Orians (1986a, 1986b) introduced the students of "Ecological Knowledge for Environmental Problem-Solving" to some novel ways of construing nature. For example: all organisms are predators when conceived as energy-eaters. Plants are simply "photon predators." Agriculture is as much an ecosystem as any other. Ecologically it is an example of our deliberate actions to prolong "early succession stages" in plant communities. Agriculture perturbs nature by halting succession. Humans depend on the profligate production of nature at early successional stages.

What Orians seeks through ecological science is prediction of the effects of specific perturbations of ecosystems. Some of these are deliberate human commercial, agricultural, and industrial enterprises. Others are accidents. What effects are unlikely are as important to predict as ones that are.

Unfundable Experiments

Perturbations to ecosystems, large and small, happen all the time: off-coast oil spills, pesticide spraying to control for gypsy moths, release of domestic animals to the wild, invasion of non-native plant species, changes in discharge from reservoirs, prolonged drought, mild winters, changes in sewage treatment plants, and so on. Orians notes that these perturbations in effect surround us with ecological experiments that no one would ever fund as a research project.

Of course, as natural experiments, they come with the extraordinary complexity presented by interactions among large numbers of uncontrolled variables. The irony for ecology, as the "citizen science," is that this most complex of experimental designs may actually be the one most amenable to participation. Simply monitoring for outcomes on a wide scale may provide scientists with data otherwise unobtainable yet needed for building predictive models.

Below I outline seven steps Orians advocates for the incorporation of ecological science into environmental problem solving. Note the prominence of values in step one and "significant change" in step six. "Biological Monitoring" is featured as step seven but also alluded to as "baseline data" in step five. Citizens, both those trained in science and those not, have vital stakes in deciding what science to do.

Step one: Define Goals.

(1) What components of the environment are perceived as valuable?

(2) What degree of protection, exploitation, control is desired?

(3) What are the costs environmentally, financially?

Step two: Scope the Problem. (Seek input from all interested parties.)

Step three: Build a Conceptual Model.

(1) What are the relationships between actions and environmental effects?

(2) What are the physical and biological pathways of ecological effects?

(3) Hypothetically, what effects should not occur?

(4) Can the relationships be quantified?

Step four: Establish Boundaries.

(1) What are the boundaries in space, time and ecology?

(2) What are the systems?

(3) What are the subtle pathways?

Step five: Develop and Test Hypotheses.

(1) What is the relationship between an action (independent variable) and an ecosystem component effect (dependent variable)?

(2) Can a "perturbation study" be done on a pilot scale?

(3) Has "baseline data" been collected before a project begins?

Step six: Specify Predictions.

(1) The change and the period of change.

(2) The degree of uncertainty about the change.

(3) The biological importance of the change.

(4) "Significant change is a judgment that transcends science."

Step seven: Biological Monitoring.

(1) What effects signal degradation or improvement?

(2) May citizens do any part of the science?

(3) Are hypotheses tested in the context of baseline information?

Conclusion

Natural History and Felt Significance

Having come to the end of the Orians model, the statement, "Significant change is a judgment that transcends science," stands out. Judgment is a decision based upon valuing. The third component of the "Ecological Knowledge" course turns to natural history writings in order to anchor the concept of value. This valuing begins with the question, "What features of nature evoke feelings for you, positive or negative?" This question asks about "features of nature" associated with particular feelings—such as enjoying the hum of a bug and observing what it does to make the sound. Reflecting on this correspondence yields an appreciative sense of nature and the knowledge of how to make appreciative events recur (Pepi, 1985).

Earlier, I presented a brief epistemology drawn primarily from the work of D. Bob Gowin's *Educating* (1981). David Pepi (1985) used Gowin's philosophy to construct a theory of "Nature Appreciation" or, as Pepi characterizes his theory, "Thoreau's Method." The theory begins with the concept of "felt significance." The event of interest in the theory is one of appreciating—being actively engaged in appreciating nature. For this event to occur, feeling and meaning must merge. This merger is felt significance. Feelings can exist apart from meaning—"the pond is creepy." Meaning can exist without feeling—"I know about the pond, but I don't know whether I like it or not." The relation between feeling and meaning is contingent. Gowin continues to elaborate upon the concept of "felt significance:"

> Most of the time, human beings respond not to raw events but to the meaning of events. We judge events for their import, for what is likely to follow from them. Import suggests importance, a test of further connections in experience. Some of these meanings undoubtedly refer to such qualities as enjoyment, suffering, liking, prizing, shunning, fearing, hating, loving. As we sort through these various ordinary human experiences, we generally determine what they mean for us by relating them to their source, their direct experience, and to their upshot—that is, to antecedents, consummations, and their consequences. Out of the ground of meanings such as these, value as felt significance emerges.
>
> Felt significance is a magnifying glass of focusing meanings, making them intense to the point of recognizable significance. As we grasp meanings, we may feel significance. The feeling of the significance—the connection-making—is the basis of value in experience. When we are listening to a teacher or reading a book or writing or paying attention to a conversation, we are grasping meanings. When we also feel the significance, we are making another connection: we are adding value. Meaning is both a prior condition and an ingredient in events which have value. . .
>
> Educating is significant when it generates connections in experience, when it overcomes separation and creates human harmony. What are we connecting? For the individual person we are bringing together thinking and feeling and acting. For persons in a social

setting we are bringing together purposes which can be shared, a sense of mutuality and mutual accommodation. Love and work are productive values for human beings. I would add education, for the acts of educating and their products endow us with the ability to connect things, to separate things, and to see why such conncetions are significant. . .

The flourishing integration of thinking and feeling and acting is a mark of an educated person. (Gowin, 1981, pp. 43-46)

Drawing upon Gowin, Pepi uses the same sense of valuing as "connecting." The focus is on the connection of features of nature to feelings, then feelings to meanings about objects and events in nature. The increase in meaningful connections in experience is the feeling of significance. This felt significance is the primary determinant of "judgments of significance," what Orians notes that science cannot decide. It is the basis for making decisions to act.

Inquiry about valuing depends upon idealization. Value concepts point to regularities in our experience of feelings. Instances of felt significance become the events of interest for the inquiry. Felt significance leads us to attend to valuing, to connecting things up. We proceed to make judgments using idealizations to inspect our experiences of significance. Inquiry about valuing leads to ordinal judgments. We ask, in value inquiry, "What is lacking? What is abundant? What would be better? Useful? Right? Ideal?" These are precisely the questions found in natural history writings, where, from Thoreau forward, moralizing and judgment accompany dispassionate observation of nature.

What's a Refuge For?

On the last day of "Ecological Knowledge," students canoe a section of the Tualatin River. The trip is primarily designed to foster appreciative events. It is the third of three trips to the Tualatin. On one outing, they explore its headwaters and transition to agricultural environs. On another, they work upstream from its mouth at the Willamette River to the region proposed as a National Wildlife Refuge.

Speakers from government agencies (city manager, sewerage engineer) address the class on environmental problems in the Tualatin watershed, both now and in the past. Through these individuals, students learn of the ongoing political process of securing lands for a National Wildlife Refuge. Based upon what they have learned in "Ecological Knowledge," they make their contribution to this process through suggesting a list of opportunities presented by the refuge to the community.

At the top of the list is citizen involvement in biological monitoring of the restoration effort for refuge lands. As the Fish and Wildlife Service works to change agricultural systems in wildlife habitats, much will be done to alter the hydrology of the area. There will be effects on water quality, invertebrate populations, and succession of wetland plants. Visitors could be trained, by interpretive signs, to watch for certain "indicator" or "keystone" species and report their observations to a data bank. School groups could be brought onto the site not simply for interpretive talks but for the purpose of conducting inventory work—to secure some of the "baseline data" Orians calls for. At the same time, students expressed concern over human impact on wildlife habitat. Plans would have to recognize the value of restricting human access.

Farming itself might continue to have some role within the refuge, in part as an interpretive tool for understanding human perturbations of ecological systems. The issue of what to do to restore the region to "pristine" conditions is troublesome: the entire regime is altered in irreversible ways. "Refuge," in a fundamental sense, is simply the latest stage in a series of human alterations of the Tualatin basin.

The dependence the community has on the Tualatin as a commons deserves emphasis in how the refuge is presented to the public educationally. Historically, it was a conveyor belt for logs. Currently, as much as half of its discharge during summer is effluent from sewage treatment plants. The Tualatin is a source of drinking water and serves a number of recreational uses. As a greenbelt preserve, it enhances real estate values. Any educational development of a refuge or environmental center at the Tualatin, students insisted, must bring together the full array of players on the commons: dairy farmers, onion growers, wildlife biologists, homeowners, soil scientists, industrial developers, timber harvesters, sewerage engineers, land use planners, and schools.

In summary, the class departed from conventional notions of environmental education: design an interpretive center, bring groups to it, conduct natural history lessons. Instead, they supported the idea of making what is good for the purposes of the refuge an outcome of educational activities. Citizens, school-age or adult, should participate in restructuring the commons, studying the effects of change, and communicating to each other the significance of these changes.

In "How Inexorable is the Tragedy of the Commons?" Ostrom asks, "Do participants have control over the structure of the situation in which they find themselves?" In the case of the Tualatin River, it appears they do. In recognition of a common history and future, they are acting to restructure the situation. At the mouth of the river and midway along its course two new parks are planned. At its headwaters, engineers are constructing a diversion of the stream through a natural filtration levee. Cooperation among rational human beings appears possible, contrary to the tragic dilemma Hardin accepts. The National Science Foundation has awarded a grant entitled "Student Watershed Research Project" to the Saturday Academy at the Oregon Graduate Institute. On the evening news in October 1992, a Beaverton High School teacher and several students working under the auspices of this grant were interviewed. They were conducting inventories of plant and animal species in a wetlands that drains to the Tualatin. The biological monitoring data they obtain will be shared directly with government agencies. The promise of this example is the fact that it is far from an isolated case. Tom Sawyer science is catching on. As it does, the values citizens hold about how to structure their communities will increasingly respond to ecological interpretations of environmental problems.

10

The Internationalization of Professional Education

JACK CORBETT

In the introduction to this volume Wallace and Brody take note of conservative critiques of American education, specifically of demands for curriculum reform and for perspectives affirming what the critics contend to be the traditional values of American society. Unmentioned in their commentary, but also noteworthy, are the increasingly insistent calls from business, government, and intellectual leaders for the internationalization of American education. Internationalization or globalization is seen as necessary to: (1) enhance the country's ability to compete in global markets; (2) develop the capacity to recognize and respond to international problems such as hunger, poverty, and environmental deterioration; (3) understand and interpret political developments in countries as diverse as Korea, Iran, Bulgaria, or Nicaragua; and (4) address the implications of new waves of immigrants and refugees arriving in the United States. Whereas the conservative critics assume education best serves the nation by defining and inculcating their views on what it means to be an educated American, proponents of internationalization assert the importance of new knowledge and new ways of thinking about an irreversible global interdependence.

While it may sound like a poor pun to suggest there is a world of difference between general statements favoring the internationalization of education and actually doing so, we can identify three questions complicating the transition from theory to practice: (1) What is internationalization? (2) Whose interests should it serve? (3) How might it be implemented?

This chapter addresses these questions, putting emphasis on the third, in the context of professional education for public service. While some of the observations may be applicable elsewhere, there are

169

constraints that complicate professional education for the in-service, mid-career student increasingly prominent in graduate programs around the nation. For example, most public institutions and non-profit agencies employing public service professionals have limited staff development budgets. The criteria governing use of these budgets, e.g., the priority of practical skills training, immediate applicability in the workplace, or maximum staff access and the need to avoid spending funds in ways likely to evoke external criticism, make financial support for international courses or activities more problematic than in settings where it is less visible or seen as an investment in human resources.

Internationalization: What is it?

One widespread interpretation of internationalization attaches it to *language and area studies*. This interpretation places substantial weight on the capacity to use a foreign language, to display cultural sensitivity, and to serve as a broker between American and other societies. The language and area studies focus reflects both traditional undergraduate study abroad and graduate education in the social sciences and humanities. It also reflects evaluation and funding criteria of the National Defense Education Act, which encourage higher education to group programs of study around languages and regions. Some recent support for this approach flows from the view that lack of foreign language skills handicaps Americans in the international marketplace; the media routinely report enrollments in foreign language courses in the United States are but a small fraction of enrollments in English abroad. As most public service practitioners neither work in the international arena nor engage in scholarship that requires the depth of knowledge most university language and area studies programs provide, it is not clear how applicable this model might be.

A second interpretation emphasizes *subject and disciplinary competency*. Rather than begin with language and region as building blocks, this links internationalization more specifically with the needs, concerns, theories, and practices of subject area and discipline, e.g., education or psychology. Language and broad cultural skills give way to a treatment of internationalization as bounded by the central questions and interests of the discipline. For example, many master of public administration programs have a "comparative administration" course that aggregates discussions of processes, institutions, policies, and challenges in countries outside the United States. Course content, however, is driven by the perspectives and needs of American faculty and students, and these in turn are driven by the canons of their respective professions or disciplines. The subject or disciplinary emphasis bonds the international component more directly to the professional interest of the practitioner than does the area studies emphasis but often by removing it from the context that clarifies and amplifies meaning.

The third interpretation of internationalization stresses *interdisciplinary concerns,* such as the environment, peace, or basic human needs. These concerns transcend both geographic and disciplinary boundaries and may have an intrinsic appeal to those who find themselves searching for ways around barriers to creative thinking. The personal, national, or professional identity of participants in efforts to address interdisciplinary concerns matter less than their sense of a common purpose. One might address immigration from the standpoint of its implications for education, employment, social relations, mental health, housing, or another theme, a logical approach to public service professionals accustomed to working across organizational boundaries in complex agencies.

One drawback to this thematic interpretation of internationalization is its distance from the conceptual and disciplinary frameworks that undergird professional education. Interdisciplinary concerns may provide arenas for the exploration of internationalization, but even strong personal and institutional commitments must compete with established disciplinary and professional boundaries.

The central point is that our response to calls for internationalization of professional education reflects our presumption of what this entails, e.g., investing in knowledge of other cultures, isolated courses regarding professional practice abroad, or thematic explorations requiring integration of many bits and pieces of information. Those of us with a background in area studies may find it difficult to imagine how to abstract discussions of organizational leadership or family counseling from a broader, deeper social context, while colleagues working from a specific disciplinary base may have less interest in context except as it contributes to the theory and practice of the discipline. The dilemma is to work through and make explicit the significance of different meanings of internationalization as we make decisions about curricular resource allocation, personnel, or other aspects of professional education.

Internationalization: In Whose Interest?

In higher education the interests of central administrators, academic units, individual faculty members, and students rarely overlap perfectly. While there may be nominal agreement about the value of "excellence" or "creativity," as we move to operationalize excellence or creativity we engage in processes of boundary definition and priority-setting, which may give rise to legitimate differences of view. Not only do we interpret internationalization in different ways, but the interests we expect it to serve may shift as points of reference change within the institution. Unless these interests are delineated clearly we once again run the risk of ready agreement on abstractions and conflicts or misunderstandings on practice.

Central administrators bear the responsibility for institutional development and maintenance in the broadest sense, so it is not surprising to find proposals to internationalize higher education at a given institution that carry the imprint of this charge. Conversely, interest in internationalization elsewhere in the institution may draw little support from central administrators if they believe it might somehow complicate their roles. Many years ago, before internationalizing education came into vogue, a senior administrator labeled me an "Afghanistanist" because he assumed I had more interest in distant places than in the region the institution served. While that has changed across time, the important external reference groups for central administrators, e.g., their peers elsewhere or prospective donors, continue to exercise substantial influence over priorities. In the Pacific Northwest the international trade implications of the Pacific Rim and hopes of financial support from prosperous Asian business elites encourage presidents to give prominence to institutional plans featuring Asia and business as key components. Each institution hopes to position itself in a way to compete for external support, even though aggregate expectations probably far outstrip prospective donations. The net effect is to operationalize internationalization in a way that is compatible with central administrators' views of their roles, perhaps without regard for other institutional interests.

Academic units, e.g., departments, schools, or institutes, are apt to see their international interests as aligned with disciplinary, regional, or other emphases most central to their mission. A law school will be likely to address matters of international law, while an institute of Middle East studies will define its interests geographically. This may appear self-evident, yet it underscores the likelihood that differences will emerge between central administrators and academic units over the most appropriate thrust for internationalization. In turn there may be differences between academic units, particularly as the units respond to their external peers and constituencies. Teacher education departments may define certification criteria and approved curricula as more important influences on their internationalization than the preferences of their own institution. The net result is that both vertically and horizontally within the institution units compete to protect key interests related to internationalization, and this competition becomes more complex as external participants, whether prospective donors or licensing boards, influence the contexts and priorities of the units involved.

Still a third set of interests involved spring from the *faculty*. Some faculty members look upon the internationalization of professional education as opportunities to sustain preexisting international interests or to draw upon experience to advance personal or unit priorities. Others see internationalization as an opportunity to emulate their colleagues who have studied or worked abroad, i.e., it becomes bound up with notions of personal travel opportunity. This is hardly to be disparaged, as during an era of declining real incomes and limited resources it may permit exactly that, but it is indicative of the way interest becomes personalized. And it may be difficult not to feel envy of those friends and colleagues who appear to take off on all-expenses-paid journeys to exotic places, accompanied by students ready to be dazzled by one's knowledge or to contribute to research. How these visions square with those articulated by central administrators may be unclear and, frankly, unimportant to the faculty concerned, but they open another arena for conflict over whose interests will be served in what order.

Lest it appear the primary faculty interest in internationalization is deciding who gets to go where and when, it should be clear that some faculty see efforts to internationalize professional education as at best a fad, at worst a misguided movement that drains scarce resources and energies from more critical concerns. It is easy for those favoring internationalization to overlook or downplay the degree of faculty resistance, but it merits serious consideration. Most professional education curricula are already loaded with essential course materials, requirements mandated by licensing and certification boards, practica, and other demands, and faculty may resent pressures to add to the burden by incorporating international components as well. This is even more of an issue when finding and integrating new information may be made difficult by limitations on its availability. The incentive structures of most institutions generally discourage faculty from making the front-end investment in skills and knowledge necessary to participate in such internationalization, and to the extent those who already have them enjoyed competitive advantage, those who do not may believe it preferable to fight the general concept. And it is difficult to allay concerns that such courses are "soft," that credit for travel or study abroad is not as demanding as credit for rigorous courses taught on campus, and that internationalization takes away from the real work of the discipline or profession.

Finally, the *students* themselves may have some specific interests in internationalization as it relates to their professional development. Language and cultural skills may facilitate work with clients or students, a comparative perspective may enhance sensitivity to policies and practices affecting one's professional performance, and contacts with peers from other countries may be stimulating and challenging. Students, therefore, are inclined to approach internationalization on the basis of what it might contribute to them personally, not what it does for higher education in general. To the extent internationalization of professional education threatens to add to the cost and difficulty of attaining a degree, reduces attention to technical competence and professional practice, or appears driven by agendas that do not consider them, student response is likely to be resistance rather than acceptance. This is particularly true in situations where employers pay part of the cost of relevant courses, as it may be difficult to convince someone a course titled "Buddhism through Film" has much application to elementary school administration or urban planning. And sometimes feeding student resistance to internationalization one finds a deep-seated belief that American policies and practices are superior to those of other countries, rendering it a waste of time to learn what others do, or that the United States is such a distinctive society that lessons from abroad are not applicable here.

Again, it should not come as a surprise that different participants in professional education see internationalization from different points of view; higher education is hardly homogeneous. One should not expect, therefore, that interest in internationalization arising at one point in the institution to draw automatic acceptance elsewhere, that everyone accepts internationalization as a normative "good," or that all agree on the ground rules and criteria by which decisions should be made. Faculty accustomed to spending a department's limited research budget on student assistants for computer data entry may find it difficult to accept as legitimate its use for plane tickets abroad or international telephone calls. Students who see their performance enhanced by learning to work with an immi-grant, Spanish-speaking clientele are unimpressed by announce-ments of an Asian studies initiative. The challenge is to recognize and resolve differences in interest, not to pretend they do not exist.

Internationalization: How Might it be Implemented?

In institutions where the issues raised regarding what and in whose interest have been addressed or, more commonly, skirted in the hopes they will work out in practice and with experience, attention quickly shifts to implementation. What is to be done? As in many other areas of educational change, internationalization takes form through bold design and muddling along, committee efforts and individual entrepreneurship, enthusiasm on the part of some and skepticism on the part of others. Pushing forward in public service education is particularly demanding because of the difficulties in implementing internationalization from the top down; students and external con-stituencies must be convinced of its value, faculty need to adjust the curriculum and take on other responsibilities, and committees must address a host of operational issues. The most visible component, travel abroad, is only one aspect of internationalization, albeit the aspect that may stimulate faculty interest. In practice we can distin-guish at least four components to implementation.

The Curriculum

An obvious, yet potentially contentious place to begin, the curriculum is the repository of public mandates and private interests, of disciplinary consensus and hard-fought duels, of legislated require-ments and carefully-crafted flexibility. Efforts to internationalize the curriculum take place in a complex context, one made more so in the public services by the demands of certification and licensure in fields such as education, social work, and psychology. While each institution and profession has specific needs and histories affecting internation-alization of the curriculum, common areas of debate include format, cost, and support materials.

Perhaps the central issue in terms of format is whether interna-tionalization means the preparation of a separate, free-standing course or courses clearly identified as "international" in content, or whether that content is best distributed through the existing curricu-lum to bring it as close as possible to corresponding courses. Does one develop "everything you have wanted to know about education abroad" and package it as a discrete course taught by a prepared, enthusiastic faculty member? Will a survey course, thin in terms of substance and a departmental elective, draw students when scheduled against courses more directly related to a student's professional needs? A specific course provides clear evidence the academic unit is responding to calls to internationalize the curriculum, but it also suggests to students its content has the same kind of conceptual differentiation among courses that one finds elsewhere in the unit, e.g., human resources management, budgeting, research methods, comparative administration. If the message to students is that one can shift the focus of course content from a national to international arena, then isolating the international content of an entire discipline or field would appear self-defeating.

Cost refers less to financing, although this is by no means irrelevant, than it does to potential opportunity cost. Does the separate course cited above replace something else in the curriculum— what is being dropped and why?—or is it in addition to existing courses? If it is in addition to existing courses, does it affect their enrollments, reduce the number of elective courses, or increase the total number of credits required and in the process increase the cost of the degree? Integration of international content into a number of existing courses raises the same problems of deletion or compression of course content. Nor can we assume that all faculty share the enthusiasm for revising courses in order to include content that they regard as having lesser priority or which they feel unprepared to teach. And students in professional programs may doubt the value of cameo appearances of international examples or cases, particularly if making sense of these requires background information on culture and society not readily available. One of the most significant opportunity costs, therefore, may be the time and energy spent in faculty consultation and coordination trying to make these pieces add up into something meaningful.

Support materials, such as textbooks, library resources, videos, and other information sources that enrich teaching, are frequently in scarce supply. In fact, they may not exist; research abroad that approximates education in the public services as they are known in the United States may be quite limited. Traditional social science research is more readily accessible but generally has limited application to the public service professions. Also, Americans may not be prepared to work within conceptual frameworks, such as Marxism, which influence scholarship elsewhere. And, language and distribution barriers may keep Americans from drawing on important sources.

How many professors of science education in the United States read Japanese, Russian, or even German? How many graduate students? Distributors, seeing small, low-profit markets have no motivation to distribute materials from abroad or open new channels. Even Canadian publications are not easy to identify and often are slow to arrive. To the extent internationalization assumes access to research and learning materials in support of curriculum revision, it creates an additional set of challenges for administrators, faculty, and students.

Hosting

By hosting I refer to increasing the number of international students and/or faculty on campus. Students in the professions are able to contribute insights and knowledge based on education and work experience in their home countries. Faculty can do the same and may also serve as consultants on internationalization, facilitate outreach and networking, and provide useful contacts for host institution students and faculty who travel abroad. By recruiting international students and faculty, institutions may gain access to varying levels of expertise for extended periods without heavy local investment. The various Fulbright programs bringing students and faculty from abroad are perhaps the best-known mechanisms for facilitating an international presence on campus, but there are a wide array of possibilities, including the use of institutional funds as scholarships or salaries.

In practice there are some serious constraints to hosting as a means of internationalizing professional education. The first concern of international students is to succeed academically and earn a degree, not to serve as an institutional resource. It may be difficult for American faculty to assess the depth or accuracy of their knowledge about their own systems. Recruitment may be a major challenge, as many international students are attracted by the reputation of a Stanford, University of Wisconsin, or Cornell, and have their doubts about the educational or status value of attending a lesser-known institution. Among institutions in the early stages of internationalization there is a tendency to underestimate the human resource costs of socializing and supporting international students, leaving students feeling bewildered, hurt, or resentful or sympathetic faculty members feeling burdened by a social and academic responsibility they did not seek. Some of the same concerns relate to visiting faculty. Local faculty time devoted to facilitating entry and accommodation in the academic and general communities is time that cannot be invested in some other way. Faculty may come with professional and personal agendas inconsistent with the priorities of the host institution. And the policies and procedures that make up professional practice in another country may be of limited interest to students whose careers depend on their effective exercise of local policy and procedures. Hosting international students and faculty may be a rewarding experience, but as a strategy for internationalizing education it has clear limitations.

Exchanges

Exchanges are formalized, two-way movements of faculty and students. Exchanges do not need to be tightly coupled, i.e., "you come, I go," but over time there is an expectation of a flow in both directions between paired institutions in the United States and abroad or perhaps among consortia. The primary value of exchange agreements is that they facilitate the development of working relationships across time, infusing continuity and stability in the process. Exchanges require a considerable investment of time and energy to minimize misunderstandings and assure all parties are clear on responsibilities as well as opportunities. Some exchanges spring from prior collaboration, e.g., research between American and foreign colleagues. Others emerge on an *ad hoc* basis, and a few are negotiated from the very start. Over time they enable participating institutions to build pools of expertise and to reduce the socialization costs associated with the arrival of students or faculty from abroad, or in preparing their own participants for departure. Institutional learning about managing such relationships tends to be cumulative, there is a clearer logic guiding the acquisition of library resources and support materials, and U.S. faculty and students alike find it easier to rationalize integrating discussion of comparative examples from the partner society in the curriculum.

But there are some drawbacks, particularly for smaller institutions or those just beginning internationalization. One is the front-end cost of time and energy mentioned above. A second is the reality that exchanges begin to focus institutional attention on a single partner, and the emergence of that partner may have less to do with some clear rationale than with opportunity or the initiative of a single academic department or faculty member. If exchanges are very active it may be difficult to sustain more than one or two simply because of limits on resources or the number of students and faculty able to participate. If exchanges are not active they deteriorate into sporadic events, losing much of the value that motivated their creation. This in turn may create tacit pressures to allocate resources to sustain a relationship because it is there rather than because it yields value to both partners.

Field Experience

This is an umbrella term for sending students or faculty abroad. It includes study in foreign institutions, research, intensive seminars, teaching, or other activities that provide international experience. For some faculty, e.g., faculty with a strong comparative or area studies interest, research or teaching in international settings may be an integral aspect of their careers. For others it may be a rare event, one which is exciting, challenging, or frustrating. And for others the prospect or the belief that the organizational culture requires it can be distinctly unappealing and even threatening. Ongoing professional interests, family obligations, a distaste for travel, or other reasons may dissuade some from participation.

For students some of the same concerns hold true. For some the idea of observing professional practice, opportunities to learn about another culture and society (particularly if such learning is employment-related), and the challenge of dealing with a new environment stimulates participation. Yet for most in-service, mid-career students the traditional study-abroad programs are unsuitable because they demand time and financial commitments that are impossible to make, or because they are geared to broad surveys of history and society that do not meet the needs of students in a specific profession. Other constraints also affect student participation, e.g., schoolteachers cannot interrupt the school year to go abroad, and others in the public may be affected by work or budget cycles.

For both students and faculty the central challenge is to develop field experiences that fit their career, personal, and financial constraints and that also make sense from the standpoint of the institution. For those with strong international credentials and interests this is rarely a problem, but for most there is a need to develop models of field experience that fall outside the traditional long-term study or research abroad. Such models need, ideally, both internal integration (e.g., orientation-experience-reflection) and integration with other aspects of the internationalization effort on campus. As the field experience commonly reflects individual initiative, such as the student seeking opportunities for study abroad or faculty members pursuing research or other professional interests, internal integration is largely a solitary process, and integration on a larger sense is problematic, perhaps even disadvantageous. For academic units and the institution as a whole the central challenge is to find ways to facilitate, legitimize, and integrate the field experience with professional education on campus, as this treats such experience as a contribution to rather than a distraction from unit or institutional mission.

There are some caveats to all this. One is that notions of field experience vary. The traditional research or teaching Fulbright award is widely understood and usually carries a modest degree of prestige and institutional blessing. In many of the public service professions independent or funded research abroad is uncommon; therefore what one is doing may be less clear to colleagues, and its relationship to on-campus activities uncertain. Unlike on-campus research or teaching, which is part of a regular flow of activity, international field experiences by their nature require blocks of time when one is away, and without clear indicators of legitimacy being "away" is read as "being on vacation," as would more normally be the case with campus-bound colleagues. This creates the very real problem that colleagues on campus are tapped for committee meetings, advising, and other system maintenance chores while more fortunate (or opportunistic) faculty are in far-away places escaping the drudgery. Students, too, may think of field experiences as equivalent to vacations, particularly if they are familiar with "study tours," which place more emphasis on touring than on studying, or tales of professional seminars in exotic locations, which provide tax-deductible pretexts for fine vacations. Spouses, personnel development officers, and accrediting bodies may find it difficult to accept such experience as equivalent to education in the conventional campus setting. Thus while field experience may capture the qualities that we associate with proposals to internationalize education, it also raises the prospects of mythology, misunderstanding, and tension.

Internationalization of Professional Education at Lewis & Clark College

What is the point of this lengthy exegesis? It serves to frame and interpret the ongoing efforts of the graduate school of professional studies to clarify the internationalization of professional education. While some of the lessons we have learned may be unique to this institution, experience and conversations with colleagues elsewhere suggest that many of the themes, issues, and debates mentioned above reflect commonalties rather than a parochial history.

Lewis & Clark College enjoys a national reputation for the quality of its international programming for undergraduate students. In recent years approximately 60 percent of each graduating class has studied abroad, usually on faculty-led programs to countries as diverse as Hungary, Senegal, Indonesia, Nepal, and Nicaragua. It is a major factor in student decisions to enroll at Lewis & Clark and has long received explicit mention in the institution's mission statement. International studies have a strong influence on departmental curricula, campus events, and day-to-day activities.

The graduate school of professional studies, with its population consisting predominantly of in-service, place-bound students, some from fields with limited liberal arts exposure, did not have an international focus. By the late 1980s there was increasing concern among some GSPS faculty that the students in our programs were increasingly faced with demands of an international character, e.g., meeting the public service needs of a growing immigrant population or implementing global studies curricula, without the information or perspectives necessary to do so effectively. In addition, a self-study revealed more than 50 percent of the faculty had significant international experience gained through residence, work, or study abroad, and a number were eager to use this experience to strengthen the School's capacity to serve student and community needs. Initiative and resources had to be internally generated, as central administrators are most concerned with international programs for undergraduates and with the status of Asian studies, a reflection of the college's geographic location and faculty strength.

As discussions of internationalization unfolded, the primary participants proved to be the graduate school as an academic unit, primarily through the graduate core, and individual faculty. At the program (equivalent to departments elsewhere) level, there were, and are, varying degrees of interest, a reflection of variations in student composition, degree requirements, other priorities, and faculty initiative. Some programs tend or need to be more entrepreneurial than others, and some have preexisting skills that make certain approaches to internationalization easier to handle internally. Students enter discussions of internationalization in several ways, the most important of which are their perceptions of the utility of internationalization, i.e., what benefits do courses bring and their willingness/ability to pay. Some of these decisions are influenced, in turn, by such considerations as scheduling. Courses scheduled during vacations, thereby enabling students to accelerate progress toward their degrees, may be attractive even if the subject matter is not quite as central to them.

Discussions of internationalization have moved forward in a variety of venues. Relatively early the GSPS named an international planning committee, but its role was essentially information-gathering and advisory. As the graduate core committee considered modifications to the original core curriculum to make it more attractive to students and faculty, it opted to provide opportunities for internationalization through greater flexibility of course content. But perhaps most important have been the individual, informal discussions possible among a relatively small, cohesive faculty. For example, an early concern had to do with the interpretation we attached to internationalization. There was a recognition that with limited resources a specific focus could be an asset in helping to make our commitment visible and perhaps to serve as a basis for external funding. It was evident, however, that significant differences among programs precluded taking a subject or disciplinary approach, as excluded programs would have little motivation to support this. There was some sentiment to follow the central administration's tilt toward Asia, but few of our students have a great deal to do with Asia in professional practice. If an area focus made sense it would be Latin America, as many students find themselves in contact with the region's rapidly growing Hispanic population. And faculty expertise ranges from Canada and Latin America to Southeast Asia, Russia, and the Middle East.

To date there has been no resolution of this nor has it proven to be a concern of great importance. The graduate core has taken an interdisciplinary approach, searching for themes that cut across programs to use the critical issues seminars that form part of the core curriculum. Its flexibility on course content has encouraged individual faculty to experiment with different topics and treatments. The critical issues seminars provide a setting for dialogue among students and faculty around themes of common concern, and in the past two years some of the most successful have taken international themes. A very different approach has been a combined graduate core/public administration intensive language and cultural skills course in Mexico, an on-site effort to help public service professionals respond more effectively to a Spanish-speaking clientele. While the clarity of a single focus has not been realized, it may be that this has been more than offset by the diversity of faculty-generated explorations.

A second major area of concern has been the distinction between those faculty with an active interest in internationalization and those concerned that it could intrude into all areas of programming, curricula, and professional life. Some have research, teaching, and service interests remote from the international arena and voiced uneasiness that: (1) they might be expected to modify courses, (2) would be expected to surrender resources, and (3) might see personnel decisions, including salary review and hiring, influenced by whether one or not one participated in internationalization. In an institution suffering from significant resource scarcities and largely driven by tuition revenues, changing resource allocation patterns not only affect individual faculty interests but possibly program viability. To date these differences have remained muted. As it became clear that internationalization did not mean wholesale curriculum revision, altered expectations of faculty performance, or more limited resources, some of the anxiety died down. The on-campus courses and seminars have been self-financing, as have intensive off-campus programs in Mexico, Canada, and the United Kingdom. No particular accolades have accumulated to those who have taken the lead in internationalizing professional education, and there has been no advantage in salary review or promotion. As with the concern of a single focus versus a decentralized approach, operational decisions have devolved upon individual faculty, removing academic units from anything more active than an oversight and monitoring role.

One consequence of leaving initiative in the hands of individual faculty has been a tendency to see internationalization cluster in two of the four components mentioned earlier, curriculum and field experience. As noted above the curriculum component depends heavily on the existence of the graduate core, as the obligation to take a certain number of core hours generates a market for international courses. We have little reason to anticipate that students would sign up for these in the absence of requirements, as most would prefer to take courses more directly related to their professional development, a stance frequently seconded by licensing and certification boards, personnel officers, and faculty who believe students are losing something through participation in general core rather than program-specific courses. Given the core requirement, the courses with a significant international component are sometimes attractive because of their exotic content. As these courses are faculty-generated the requirement and market provide an outlet for faculty who wish to contribute to the international thrust but who have neither opportunity nor students within their professional programs.

A field experience built around an intensive seminar offered abroad also flows from faculty initiative. Such seminars are usually for a maximum of two weeks, include no more than twenty students, and provide either the language and cultural skills development mentioned earlier or an in-depth look at a specific topic of professional interest, such as the management of nonprofit organizations in the United Kingdom or the performance of the Canadian health—care system. For students such courses offer new experiences and insider perspectives they could not acquire on campus. The cost of travel and uncertainties as to how such courses might integrate with the rest of their requirements dissuade some students, although credit through the graduate core helps. The public administration program has made the most extensive use of such field experiences for students, largely because it builds a portion of its degree and training activities around live case analysis, and an intensive seminar abroad fits this style very nicely. Faculty organizing these comment on the labor-intensive character of such courses, but that has yet to be a deterrent.

On the other hand, there has been little faculty interest in pursuing research and teaching abroad. Collaborative research ventures are under way by faculty in counseling psychology and public administration, but these reflect individual faculty interests. In the last four years one faculty member has held a Fulbright to the Middle East and one teaches on a regular basis for a Mexican university, but there has been no great rush to head overseas. In part this reflects the weight of other interests and program needs, in part the graying of a professoriat with multiple obligations to family and community. It also reflects an institutional incentive system geared to publication and teaching, not to international activities (except as these might filter, indirectly, through research and teaching), and the realities of programs more dependent for their survival on productive interaction with local clienteles than with scholars and students abroad.

For this reason there has been little energy invested in hosting international students and scholars or in pursuing exchange relationships. High tuition costs and low visibility dissuade most international students from applying for graduate study. Those who do come find little institutional support, primarily because no one has given serious thought to what such students need or expect (there are support services for international students at the undergraduate level or in special English courses). Low visibility and few international contacts also limit the likelihood foreign faculty will seek out the graduate school. Its emphasis on practice rather than theory also make it relatively unattractive for many foreign scholars, as the professional practice of teacher education or counseling psychology in Oregon may appear to have limited relevance abroad. Those who are interested in practice tend to gravitate to better-known institutions. An exchange relationship suggests the resource base, human and financial, to sustain interaction across time. Given limited numbers of students and faculty interested and prepared to make such a commitment, exchanges are difficult to mount. One exception is a recent exchange of graduate students between the public administration program at the University of Victoria in British Columbia. This exchange, building on prior interest in Canada on the part of the public administration program, may expand to include faculty and other forms of collaboration in the future. At present, however, it stands alone.

Conclusion

In assessing the theory of internationalizing the education and its practice in the graduate school at Lewis & Clark, several points stand out as noteworthy.

(1) Despite an institutional environment that is fairly favorable by the standards of higher education, the degree and extent of internationalization is rather modest. Differing notions of what internationalization means, its place at Lewis & Clark, and strategies for implementation mean that the costs of coordination are high.

(2) Measured by the standards of where the graduate school stood in 1987, its accomplishments five years later are noteworthy. Several new courses have been created and integrated into the graduate core. More important, a mechanism now exists to facilitate such courses in the future, and the precedent of core flexibility accommodates that. Several intensive seminars geared to the needs and limitations of students have been offered abroad, and more are in the planning stages. One exchange agreement is in place. Several special training seminars for federal agencies have been offered in Canada, and the public administration program's assistance has been solicited by others for other international locations. Perhaps most significant, the cadre of faculty with international interests have been invigorated and encouraged to do more.

(3) While some elements in the institution may look upon international activity as a definite plus, others see it as a distraction, frivolity, or threat. The small size and generally tight-knit personal relations of the faculty have enabled potential conflicts to be managed through a process of mutual accommodation. The fundamental possibility of such conflicts has not been eliminated, however, and could be triggered by anything from personnel and policy changes to a rapid expansion or reduction in the number of students enrolled.

(4) To the extent internationalization of professional education has advanced at Lewis & Clark it has done so because of a willingness to give primacy to process rather than structure. No model was imposed from above,

no standardized expectations established. The graduate core and public administration modified the ways they do business in a fashion that accommodated and encouraged experimentation. The graduate school and the program directors monitor quality, performance, and satisfaction but lack the resources and sense of priority to intervene more aggressively to pursue a specific vision. Entrepreneurs experiment to see what works and how to raise the quality and variety of offerings.

What is less clear is whether this decentralized form of internationalization can survive across time. It is highly dependent on individual faculty initiative, and there is no guarantee that when those faculty cease to push this interest that others will display the same enthusiasm. Nor are there clear guidelines on what represents the limits of internationalization and how those limits are to be defined and maintained. There is an increasing interest in offering intensive field seminars, and at some point it may be necessary to limit or regulate them in some way. Some programs may find faculty are so involved with the international component of their responsibilities other key tasks have been left undone. As we respond both to our sense of community need and the challenge involved in trying the unknown, the question remains whether we can establish a legacy worth passing through time and across space.

Part III

Reflections on a Graduate Core Program

"Reflective thought," John Dewey tells us, is the "active, persistent, and careful consideration of any belief or supposed form of knowledge in the light of the grounds that support it, and the further conclusions to which it tends" (1910, p. 6). In the earlier sections of this book we have explored connections and tensions between professional knowledge and its use in practice, program goals grounded in the centrality of ethical inquiry in professional education, and the responsibility of faculty to struggle with those issues common to the professions. Now, consistent with Dewey's insight, we will consider some of "the further conclusions" to which this leads.

Implicit in all this are our beliefs in the power of reflective action for connecting the personal with the professional, legitimate self-interest within a communal ethical commitment, question-posing as well as answer-seeking, and faculty renewal as part of organizational revitalization. There are unanticipated issues of faculty and organizational development that emerge during the implementation of programs that challenge prevailing epistemologies and methodologies. The chapters presented here build a case for reflective thought that emerges out of dialogue and that seeks to develop personal meaning amidst organizational evolution. The authors understand that we are all teachers and learners and that as the educators of professionals we have a responsibility to make our concerns public to each other and to our students and to invite openness and reflection as models for our practice.

In chapter 11, "The Feminine in Public Service Professions: Implications for Graduate Instruction," Mary Henning-Stout considers the training and practice of professionals in terms of interpersonal skills required in public service. These skills are often designated as "feminine," and she invites inquiry into the extent to which masculine and feminine perspectives and voices are encouraged in the training process and in the professions themselves—the ways the two influence each other in a "dance of cultural construction." She reflects on the pedagogical challenges of raising these questions in a patriarchical culture.

On the other hand, a liberal arts program assumes that students of both sexes, various ages, and different career lines can learn from one another as well as from faculty, and that instructors can change and grow along with their students. In chapter 12, "Gender and Professional/Liberal Knowledge: Men's Perspectives," James Wallace considers how gender studies, which are central to this program, can be both liberalizing and professionalizing experiences for male faculty. Drawing on interviews with male colleagues, Wallace describes how various themes related to gender have promoted modified and meaningful ways of thinking and teaching.

Gordon Lindbloom, in chapter 13, "Learning about Organizational Cultures and Professional Competence," discusses successes and failures encountered while implementing a curriculum dealing with organizational life. He outlines some of the challenges facing professionals in organizations, reporting how graduate students gain insight into the way their organizations function. He shares the evolution of his thinking as he struggles with the connections between theory and practice and with the new expectations of an interdisciplinary curriculum.

In chapter 14, "The Evolution of a Graduate School: The Effects of Developing a Liberal Arts Core," Carolyn Bullard describes some of the unexpected outcomes of creating a core program. As former dean of the graduate school at Lewis & Clark, she assesses the outcomes of faculty working together on the core: increased understanding of the similarity of challenges faced by professionals in varied public service occupations, a broadening of our definitions of knowledge, the evolution of a shared language, the acknowledgment of the integration of personal and professional lives, and the growth of a sense of mutual responsibility for improving the organizational culture of professional programs.

Ken Kempner argues that the lessons of this case study of professional education are particularly significant when they are placed within the larger cultural context of defining knowledge and professional self. In his afterword, "The Search for Personal and Professional Meaning," Kempner considers the authors' commitments to challenge the parochialism of positivism in connection with the purposes of professional education and practice. He returns the reader to the original purpose of professional education—to create community as a model for life, to continually look for meaning, and to maintain the search as the essence of the journey of education, for faculty and teachers together.

11

The Feminine in Public Service Professions: Implications for Graduate Instruction

MARY HENNING-STOUT

My friend Mike is a school psychologist. He spends most of every day building and drawing upon relationships to gain information and develop collaborative ideas for responding to problems interfering with children's learning. He relies on his relationships with administrators, teachers, parents, and the children themselves to provide the service of his profession.

Mike is a big, white, educated, heterosexual, middle-class man. He is athletic. He likes to work on his car when it needs attention. He subscribes to *Sports Illustrated.* He is thirty-two and unmarried. Mike is also nurturing. He provides comfort and care to the children and adults with whom he works. Mike can be moved to tears when speaking about the trouble facing a child he is working to help. He listens carefully to the people in his personal and professional lives. He speaks with conviction about the importance of building and nurturing relationships—about the need for community.

Mike is a person who lives in ways that have been associated in our culture with being masculine or feminine. Because he is described as heterosexual and there is evidence of his interests in sports and auto mechanics (interests associated with masculinity), we are likely to be accepting of his more feminine characteristics. Most of us will read about Mike and his work and feel a sense of admiration for his integrity as a professional. If Mike were Judy, we would likely feel positively toward her as well. It would be interesting to know a woman who is a sports enthusiast, has skill in auto mechanics (again, interests associated with masculinity), and is an active public service professional.

As Margaret Mead (1972) noted, the activities associated with men in a culture are those most valued[1]. If I had not clarified Mike's heterosexuality and had described him as someone who liked to cook,

189

grow flowers, and enter crafts in local craft shows, the associations with him would likely have been less immediately positive. In general, the value ascribed in United States's culture to feminine behaviors and characteristics is low. At the same time, the value ascribed to a man's heterosexual masculinity is so high that any person who does not fit that mold is devalued, and, if the misfit is a man, he is likely feared and aggressively rejected. I use this example to demonstrate that the low status of the feminine in our culture has implications well beyond the status of people and professions. Recognizing the serious and pervasive effects of gendered cultural practices is fundamental to initiating any examination of these issues within the social service professions. Clear understanding of the magnitude of these issues provides the context within which the facts of professional life can best be interpreted.

The facts illustrating the differential treatment of activities associated with masculinity and femininity abound. For example, Mike's profession, school psychology, is the area of psychology most directly associated with service to children. The care and nurturing of children has been women's work in our culture. School psychologists earn less than any other group of psychologists (Meyers, 1988). As the number of women in school psychology (currently 60 percent) increases, this discrepancy in earnings is also increasing (Alpert and Conoley, 1988). Women's work, or work that is taken on by women, is less valued, and professions based in service to children and women are of lower status and lower pay.

At the same time, the value placed on interpersonal warmth and responsiveness (characteristics associated with femininity) within Mike's profession is high, regardless of the sex of the professional (Harris, Ingraham, and Lam, in press). Public service professions, like school psychology, vary somewhat in their social status, but all of them require human interaction—all of them are based in relationship. To teach, to counsel, to provide health care, to administer public policy— to be engaged in any of these practices is to spend the majority of time relating to people as individuals and in groups. Human connection is at the very center of these professions. The work of developing and nurturing those connections has, in our culture, been largely accomplished by women (Aptheker, 1989); and, thus culturally constructed as "feminine."

In this chapter, I take the position that this "women's work" is fundamental to the delivery of social services and must, therefore, be central to the graduate preparation of social service professionals. From this position, I consider traditions of philosophy and science for their influence on current social valuations of feminine activity and, in turn, upon the status of social service professions. Issues relevant to graduate instruction emerge immediately from this survey. Primary among them is the question of how feminine skills and behaviors can be given greater attention and enhanced status in the graduate preparation process itself. In response to this question, I describe the academic content as well as the pedagogical and experiential processes of a graduate course offered as part of the liberal arts core-course sequence of the graduate school of professional studies at Lewis & Clark College. Finally, I outline the implications for graduate faculty responsible for preparing social service professionals.

The Inverse Relationship of Femininity and Status

Rousseau, in his description of the education of Emile, explored the related educational implications for Sophie, Emile's wife. According to Rousseau, Sophie, and all women, were naturally intended to live in service of men:

> To oblige us to do us service, to gain our love and esteem, to rear us when young, to attend us when growing up, to advise, to console us, to soothe our pains, and to soften life with every kind of blandishment; these are the duties of the sex at all times and what they ought to learn from their infancy (Rousseau quoted by Kersey, 1981, p. 133).

Implicit in this eighteenth-century philosophy, one which remains a cornerstone of the Western philosophical canon, is permission for deeply institutionalized sexism. In this philosophy, the activities (and very existence) of women are valued and understood only insofar as they meet the needs of men. In addition, by restricting the duties assigned to women within the domestic sphere, there is no need to grant those activities any overt public (that is, economic) value. In this construction, women's activities and women themselves are staples, like air and water, available to support the people—the men.

Although a thorough review of the canon of Western philosophical thought is well beyond my intentions, I take Rousseau's philosophy as representative of the epistemological roots of contemporary constructions on work and relationship. Since the industrial revolution, many of the activities of women have moved into the public sphere as the demand for educating and caring for the citizenry has no longer been as readily met by the extended family (Aptheker, 1989). Even with this movement, the tenets of Rousseau's theory remained evident in the awarding of social status to professions in contemporary Western culture.

Among contemporary professionsals, people who work with money, business, and engineering (traditional male spheres of public activity) are paid at substantially higher rates than people who work in the social sphere with children, aging people, people with disabilities, or with other people who do not fit the dominant culture standard of the successfully educated male. In our capitalistic economy, the level of pay for work is the best indicator of the value placed on that work by the dominant culture. Given this relationship, the status of service professions—those grounded in activities historically assigned to women, is low.

This relationship has profound implications for the service professions, as we struggle for credibility and funding while resisting the press of culture to de-emphasize the relational nature (the integrity) of our work. The forces are great that push service professionals toward less relational orientations. Psychologists want to pinpoint the source of psychopathology and not be bogged down in the nuance of social and cultural context. Educators embrace medical explanations based in human systems (in relationships) as subjective and imprecise. We are easily attracted to judging success in terms of dollars spent or saved, scores on standardized tests, or numbers of bodies passing through our doors regardless of service outcome. In our daily practice if not in our stated philosophies, we act as if the forms and the numbers on those forms _are_ the job. The people, minimally reflected in triplicate, fall lower on the daily list of priorities.

The appeal of the impersonal is perpetuated in large part by the research underlying social service. Positivism has been the dominant paradigm for scientific research applied in the social disciplines. Positivism is a paradigm authored and sustained by educated people (predominantly men) and reflects the authors' understandings of the world (Harding, 1991). Positivism rests on the premise that pure knowledge is accessible through the reductive analysis of an object of study. Extended to the social sciences, this epistemology requires the researcher to act as if it were possible to be a separate, dispassionate, value-neutral observer of social phenomena (Hoshmand and Polkinghorne, 1992). Such an epistemology applied to understanding social events and behaviors restricts our perspective. Positivism can aid in the comparison of discrete and quantifiable phenomena but is inadequate to reflecting the complexity of the social relationships defining social events. Because the academic disciplines comprising the social sciences have embraced positivism, research has provided, for the most part, only the limited perspectives available within this paradigm.

The objectivity, impersonality, and asserted definitiveness of positivism are consistent with characteristics associated in our culture with masculinity. The authority granted positivism rests, in part, in this association. The education of current social service professionals *and* professors was steeped in allegiance to the positivist epistemology as the most, and perhaps only, credible way of knowing. Given these forces, the emphasis on the quantifiable and objective in contemporary social service practices is certainly understandable. As long as positivism remains the most valued way of knowing, activities reflecting that epistemology will be the ones most likely to be acknowledged and supported by the culture.

The influences of recorded philosophy and history and of a science based in positivism are immediately evident in the gendered valuations placed on human activities in Western culture. The status of a profession determines the resources made available by the culture for pursuing its goals. The social service professions depend upon skills that have been associated with femininity. These professions are also granted lower status in contemporary society. Because social service professions are most responsive when their feminine aspects are developed and practiced, there is an urgent necessity for establishing the central importance of feminine characteristics and activities to furthering any social service agenda.

Graduate Instruction: A Case Example

Over my time as a faculty member with the graduate school of professional studies at Lewis & Clark College, I have had the opportunity to teach eleven courses in the graduate core program (a program described in detail in Chapter 2) of which eight represented three distinct course offerings: Individual Ethical, and Organizational Development; Ways of Seeing, Ways of Knowing; and Gender and Education. Students in these courses were preparing to become (or were already) counselors, educators, or public administrators. In each of these courses we worked to identify explicit connections between the feminine in service professions and the more global professional contexts the courses address.

My focus here will be on Ways of Seeing, Ways of Knowing, a course I co-taught on two occasions with Joanne Mulcahy, a faculty person affiliated with the graduate school's Northwest Writing Institute and the College of Arts and Sciences. I do not intend this description as prescriptive, but rather as an example of ways these issues can be presented in graduate courses. In the syllabus we listed questions guiding our inquiry: How do we know what we know? How is meaning constructed? How does culture shape and reflect our realities?

We established our rationale for pursuing these questions with particular attention to the relevance of our topic for professional preparation:

> ... They are questions of philosophy, psychology, sociology, religion, anthropology, art—and they are also questions directly relevant to our professional activity as providers of social services. The way we make sense of the world determines the way we act within it. Our action affects the people and organizations we serve.

We also stated our goal for the course:

> To invite participants to think critically about the ways in which we construct and express meaning, individually and collectively. We will explore literary and scholarly narrative as a focus of theory in the human sciences. We will use writing, in and out of class, as a tool for creating our own stories and thereby understanding our cultures.

The content of this course allowed participants to approach the goals of the core program (see Chapter 2) through the door of culture, considering, in particular, the ways in which social service professionals shape and are shaped by their cultures. Entering the inquiry in this way, we focused particularly on identifying the ways we all can be restricted by our enculturation from complete understanding of people of other cultural groups. The multicultural focus of this course recognized the diversity of cultures in our world—a diversity everywhere evident in the work of social service professionals. This focus included ethnic, racial, economic class, and gender considerations. We sustained each of these considerations throughout the course as we identified and explored their similarities and divergences.

The format we developed for the class involved brief presentations by one or both of us. We used these primarily for introducing topics, readings, or authors and followed them with focused in-class writing and large-group discussions. Our intention with the writing and discussion was to provide structured opportunities for developing insights and ideas, integrating the content of the course, and generating new questions to be pursued in subsequent inquiry. Participants often used small-group work for processing in more depth insights or questions generated in individual writing and larger discussions. Working in smaller groups allowed individual students who were unlikely to speak up in large-group discussions greater opportunity to voice their thoughts and engage actively in the group's constructed understandings (Belenky, et al., 1986; Gilligan, Lyons, and Hanmer, 1990). Implicit and explicit in our course format was the high value we place as educators upon what can be learned from relationship that cannot be learned in isolation.

At the beginning of each class, we outlined the session on the board. We were clear that we would be prepared to cover the agenda, but would be attentive to the direction discussion was moving and the topics that emerged as most salient and engaging. We established as our priority students' gaining useful knowledge from the course and consistently strayed from class outlines in order to pursue issues (often quite controversial) that drew the liveliest interest and, in our opinion, led to the greatest learning.

This instructional format is based on understandings about the way many women come to know and has been referred to as connected teaching (Belenky et al., 1986; Clinchy, 1988). Connected teaching draws on the life experiences of the learners, viewing those experiences as immediately relevant and fundamental to the extension of knowledge. Recent research indicates that this approach to teaching is effective for both women and men (Clinchy, 1990). Yet, because of its relational emphasis, connected teaching can be classified, within contemporary constructions on gender, as feminine.

The format of the course was atypical when compared with more traditional didactic and content-based lecture formats for graduate instruction. The format itself provided several opportunities for discussing different ways of knowing, specifically the more masculine orientation toward authoritative truth and the more feminine orientation toward dynamic and relational understanding. We made overt the distinction between our approach and more traditional approaches and invited students to talk about their criteria for legitimate academic experiences. This afforded the opportunity for discussing the absence of relational experiences in most graduate courses and the irrationality of excluding such experiences from the curriculum for preparing social service professionals.

The discussion of course format was among the first in which we introduced gender issues in the structure of professional preparation and practice. Throughout the course, the inclusion of women's perspectives and the emphasis on the issues related to the feminine characteristics of social service professions drew the largest reaction, discussion, discomfort, and resistance. Although only one of several course foci, issues of gender were, for this group, the most intensely personal and essential of all those discussed. Of the twenty-eight participants in our class, well over half were women, all were European-American. As is typical for our graduate school, no one in the group was publicly of a minority sexual orientation. Because of this homogeneity, discussions of issues of race, ethnicity, and sexual orientation could remain academic. In spite of our attempts to push these issues, the personal discomfort demanded when facing people directly who have been oppressed by our culture could, for the most part, be avoided[2].

In contrast, the personal impact of issues of gender could not be avoided and became part of the text of the class. As such, they were engaged as instructive by some participants and resisted as unfair by others. The resistance to exploring gender issues helps illustrate some of the barriers to incorporating attention to feminine characteristics and women's experiences into graduate courses. We also found these points of resistance as thresholds for entry into discussions of the status and centrality of feminine characteristics to responsive social service delivery.

Comments by some participants early in the course illustrated their resistance. One theme evident in the early writings of a few students was disenchantment with our addressing issues of gender. One woman stated that she was tired of excuses—that being female did not make her more vulnerable. Her comment, among others, reflected the belief that women and men have equal opportunity. Students sharing this opinion read as outdated and whiny the course's attention to gender as a cultural construct worthy of consideration in professional training. In what had become a familiar manifestation of resistance, these students attached the label "feminist" to the course in order to justify rejection of its content.

We responded generally to this theme by focusing initial class discussions on inquiry into the origins and assumptions of contemporary cultural practices as evident in students' professional experiences. This kind of inquiry allowed acknowledgment of some students' boredom with what they identified as feminism: women complaining about being treated unfairly and expecting undue compensation on the part of dominant-culture men for this supposed inequity. This position was incorporated into the discussion of who decides what is and is not important (or boring) in the culture which, in turn, led to questions of who has access to that which the culture values. By incorporating rather than rejecting or deflecting this resistance, students moved along this path to a discussion of the assumptions underlying the status assigned to their professions.

A second and related theme in this class was anger with what some students interpreted as being led unaware into a course with a hidden feminist agenda. One man wrote of his unhappiness with being in what he saw as a feminist course, indicating he would not have registered had the content been clear in the course description. This man went on to suggest that we were discounting the experiences of men in the class by emphasizing the experiences of the women. Earlier that day, during class, he had made his first verbal contribution to class discussion describing the constraints of the rigid but unwritten dress code of corporate life, a life he had recently left to pursue a career as a counselor. I had noticed his contribution especially, because as he spoke, the bodies of all of the people in the room opened up toward him. Everyone seemed eager to ask questions and encourage his talking. Several other men had contributed in earlier discussions, and their contributions had tended to be longer than those of the women in the group. However, there seemed to be a shared sense of this man's resistance and a willingness to work to recruit him into the group with active listening and validating demonstrations of interest in his point of view.

This dynamic occurred early in the term, before we had established sufficient rapport within the class to use it as a point of inquiry and discussion. However, dynamics like the one occurring around this man's contribution to the discussion can be pointed out as illustrations of research on distribution of voice, attention, and interruptions (e.g., Fishman, 1983; Sadker, Sadker, and Kline, 1991; Tannen, 1991). These kinds of in-class phenomena served as powerful moments for noting the influence of gender in routine (i.e., unreflective) interaction.

Another man took issue with the reading list. He pointed out that the three required texts were authored by women and that twelve of the authors of the supplementary readings were women and ten were men. His interpretation of our reading list was familiar and consistent with responses to other core courses. When women authors represent half or more of the authors for required readings, both women and men students are likely to comment on their discomfort with the feminist slant of the course content. Such comments provide the opportunity to compare these reading lists with those of the other classes, which, though not overtly described as "masculinist," were mostly texts authored by men.

The feminist label is also readily attached to courses in which men are not allowed or encouraged to dominate class discussions. In these situations, men students sometimes perceive the class and professors' conduct of it as discriminating against them. In the class I am describing, men contributed as much as 40 percent of the comments in whole-class discussions, but represented only 21 percent of the participants.

The intensity and immediacy of issues of gender were illustrated by the responses of several men who were convinced they had become the dominated group in what they described as a feminist classroom.

This was particularly illustrated in choices some students made relative to the assignments of the course. For example, the final project for the class required participants to apply ethnographic methods to exploring a culture other than their own. To meet this requirements, one man chose to inquire into the culture of the class itself. His inquiry centered on asking whether this culture, like other larger cultures, had dominant and marginalized groups within it. He chose to explore his question and assumptions by interviewing another man in the class who had also been resistant throughout. He based his choice of interviewee on his understanding of standpoint theory (Harding, 1991), a theory we had discussed in class. His interviewee represented for him the best informant on the classroom's culture—a member of the group (men) he saw as most marginalized by the dominant culture (women).

During the interview he asked questions he later recognized as ones that lead the witness. For example, after the interviewee was asked on several occasions to identify the dominant culture of the class, he eventually came to attribute his discomfort in the classroom to his oppression by the dominant feminist group. The interview led the informant to this new interpretation and to his conclusion that he now understood the experience of marginalized people in contemporary U.S. culture.

The informant based his conclusion, in part, on his having felt uncomfortable speaking in class. He indicated that men were able to talk in class but did not feel like they were part of the dominant group. From his newly achieved vantage point, white women were in charge, and this prevented men from speaking. Frequency data from the large-group discussions reflect the actual extent to which males participated—contributing almost half of the comments and representing slightly less than one-fourth of the class participants. However, for the informant and for several other men in the class, more equal voice felt like censorship. One man shared his sense of this situation as silencing European-American men just because they had been dominant for centuries. He described the silencing of people like him as un-American.

Because these strong responses were not articulated until the end of the term, the issues could not be brought back for class discussion. One of the primary questions emerging is the meaning of the term, "dominant culture." In the class we used this term to indicate the members of any larger cultural group who controlled access to the most valued commodities of the culture. Those commodities could be tangible, emotional, economic, or spiritual. Access could be open or restricted to various degrees. A discussion of the dominant culture in our group would have been powerfully instructive because of the opportunity we would have for exploring the influence of a larger culture, such as that of the United States, on a smaller temporary culture of participants in a class. The discussion could be extended to considering the service professions with particular focus on professions such as elementary school education where women are the majority (most of the teachers are women) but do not have the power (most of the administrators are men) (Schmuck, 1987).

It can be argued that the discomfort some men had with the discourse of the class and their accompanying sense of marginality could support the eventual development of insight into the experiences of consistently marginalized people. However, the barriers to this awareness are great, especially those subtle, internalized barriers to recognizing privilege. For example, even in their acknowledged discomfort, these men retained the privilege of *choosing* to repress their ideas—choosing not to talk.

In discussions after the course was completed, one man came to realize that truly marginalized people cannot afford to shut down. Marginalized people must be at least bicultural—competent in their own culture by life experience and competent in the contingencies of the dominant culture for survival. His experience of marginality was temporary and incomplete. He retained the privileged option of shutting down, of not attending. The experience of being *oppressed* by a culture that neither recognizes nor values one's way of being in the world is quite distinct from the experience of *malaise* that results when those who have dominated begin to understand the insensitivity and harm of their domination and privilege.

The nuance in his belief that he had come to understanding marginality provides another topic with multiple paths into exploring the distribution of status and value in Western culture. High-status professions and individuals need not be sensitive to other cultural groups. Low-status professions and individuals must know the dominant culture to be able to gain access to valued commodities—to survival within the culture as a whole.

The graduate classroom is a powerful place for addressing these vast and complex issues of dominance and marginalization as they relate to the social service professions and the individuals composing them. Yet, even with our best pedagogical efforts, not all students left this class with a sense of having gained from it. Consistent with the tone indicated above, this man left quite disenchanted. The contrast of his experience with that of others in the class was reflected in one woman's final journal entry.

> The . . . piece about the ending that I am puzzling over is the response of someone I walked out to the parking lot with. He claimed the class was "awful," and with that label, seemed to feel there had been very little of substance for him . . . Does "awful" imply that he found value in none of these things? . . . I felt such a clash with this man. . . . Two people sat through the same . . . days of talk and events and emerged with opposite opinions. How alien I must feel to him, and how alien he feels to me. How could his upbringing, or his maleness, or his education, or his job, or his life circumstances be so different that he was not moved by the human connection which seemed to me to be the thread which wound through it all? And he stated his opinion so firmly, with what seemed to me an implied "that was a waste of time," a dismissal, a belittling. Of the class. But was it also of me? Since I loved it? Where did he get his sureness? From male privilege? . . . Do we truly occupy the same world? The entire class about diversity, about so many ways of seeing a thing, about so many meanings, and I am reduced to thinking either he is nuts or I am? I feel somewhat shaken by the difficulty of difference. It scares me because misunderstandings and different interpretations are rampant in our world. How do these differences get resolved? Right at this moment I feel pretty pessimistic about world politics. About anything more than fleeting peace in random places.

This student's writing revealed her orientation toward relationship and her astonishment at her male classmate's expressed aversion and disconnection. She was caught in the all-too-familiar wave of having the legitimacy of her experience thrown into question. Her questions about the implications of this disparity for larger social interactions are compelling. With the absence of emphasis on nurturing relationship, the likelihood of human connection and community is greatly diminished. At the same time, the intensity of this man's reaction is evidence of his being moved by the content and process of the course. He may have experienced the class's work on acknowledging women as discounting, even damning, of familiar and valued masculine ways of being and knowing. His response was strong, as were the responses reflected in each student's journal writings. That strength of reaction can be read as evidence of our success in posing the questions and shaking the cultural structures that maintain practices which devalue, discount, and attempt to ignore the feminine characteristics central to professional functioning. Because of the immediacy and pervasiveness of these issues, we continue committed to bringing students into overt dialogue and struggle with their role in the cultural valuation of the genders and, by unavoidable extension, other social groupings.

Implications for Graduate Instruction

The traditions of academia provide an environment that is simultaneously available for "free exchange of ideas" and hostile to any ideas that challenge the integrity of its traditions (Aisenberg and Harrington, 1988; Bateson, 1990). In the humanities (McConnell-Ginet, Borker, and Furman, 1980; Spender, 1989) as in science (Harding, 1991; Keller, 1985) introducing the voices and perspectives of women into the disciplines has met with resistance. The entry into academe of women themselves has often carried the tacit condition of their demonstrated acceptance of traditions authored and maintained by the academic patriarchs (Aisenberg and Harrington, 1988; Keller, 1983). In this context, the challenges to bringing attention and credibility to feminine ways of knowing and being are magnified.

Academics who elect to take on these challenges face substantial and subtly institutionalized pressures to retreat. Most subtle among these pressures is the hostility of traditional academic culture to self-reflection. Instruction that affirms and raises the status of culturally feminine ways of being and attends to the experiences and needs of the female population can only occur if the instructors themselves are clear on the implications of their privilege as it influences the epistemologies they apply to making meaning as scholars. Such clarity requires nondefensive and honest engagement in the self-reflective process of exploring personal biases. While criticism, evaluation, and educated judgments regarding objects of academic inquiry are central to scholarship, similar processing of personal ways of knowing and being in the world are historically without a place in the academy. Drawing again on the example of positivism, it would be inconsistent with the paradigm itself for the inquirer (the scholar) to acknowledge his or her subjectivity. This central paradigm of contemporary academe is grounded in the belief that pure truth is accessible through the implementation of objective and empirical methods—that these methods are so strong they override or render irrelevant any subjectivity on the part of the scholar. Given this belief, it is no wonder academics have found the notion of self-reflective scholarship oxymoronic.

The classroom experiences I have described above, along with growing evidence of the large portion of life experience that is overlooked with epistemologies like positivism, provide compelling evidence of the necessity of building self-reflection into the practice of social service professionals. This necessity assumes the value and practice of self-reflection among the faculty preparing these professionals.

Once adopted, self-reflection on the part of scholars is ongoing. This practice brings fresh understanding of the dynamic and constructed nature of both professional practice and its knowledge base. As we develop methods for considering and monitoring our own value structures and cultural assumptions, we become increasingly effective models for the students in our programs.

One of the most intensive and effective ways to develop these skills is through preparing and offering courses such as the one described above. Success in developing self-reflective skills rests in willingness to be a learner along with the student participants in the class—willingness to model learning as a legitimate way to function as a social service professional. Social service professionals are people who bring certain skills to a service delivery situation, while at the same time recognizing that no service will be rendered without collaboration among the deliverers and recipients. This relational and collaborative orientation can also be effectively modeled in the format of classes themselves. Relationship and collaboration are culturally feminine orientations. Sharing knowledge and its construction requires a level of surrender to the process of coming to know that is inconsistent with more instrumental, product-oriented masculine approaches to instruction. This pedagogical orientation thus stands in contrast with the traditional academic posture of instructor as the owner of knowledge determining who will have access, when and how. While feminine content can be introduced in more traditional academic formats, instructors who incorporate both feminine content and process into their courses will have the greatest effects.

Developing such courses requires engaging, personally and interpersonally, issues surrounding the devaluation of feminine activities and characteristics in our culture. This includes careful consideration of the impact of our own gender classifications on the ways we present the feminine characteristics of social service work. For example, the cues of the culture carried in the instructors themselves can influence the engagement of these issues.

In the course described above, we were two European-American women in our mid-thirties who chose to use a feminine format for much of the course. We were either contemporaries of or younger than most of the students in the class. We were (and are) of the dominant culture. We were privileged with education and careers. And, we were women. These facts met with the expectations commonly held by students that academic women be both authoritative and nurturant (Aisenberg and Harrington, 1988; Bateson, 1990). We had made clear, as part of our pedagogical process, our interest in students' experiences and feedback during the course. Consistent with our experiences in other classes and illustrating the experiences of many academic women, students readily expressed their discomfort with the content of the course, particularly as we dealt with issues of gender. Also typical, in our experience, was the attendant expectation that we do something to adjust the affective climate so that everyone felt better.

Given the traditions of the academy, it seems unlikely that two male instructors would be confronted similarly and held responsible for the affective discomfort of students. It seems unlikely that male instructors would be challenged for not representing the needs and experiences of the other gender in teaching a graduate course. These differences in the expectations students hold for male and female professors illustrate the subtle effects a professor's gender can have on the nature of presentation, discussion, and ultimate valuation of the feminine characteristics of the social service professions.

One way of taking instructional action based upon personal reflections regarding issues of gender involves making covert assumptions (our own and the students') overt and available as part of the text of the course. For example, I might ask course participants to consider the assumptions they make when they hear reference to a depressed person, a participant in Overeater's Anonymous, or a person accused of child sexual abuse. Each of these descriptors carries immediate gender associations—assumptions that may limit the extent to which the people themselves are seen. These assumptions have immediate implications for how the professional initiates a service relationship. To move class participants to a more substantial and personal level, I might find an opportunity to speak of the filters placed upon my own perceptions and sense of agency by being a woman raised in the South, by being the oldest of four daughters, by being a product of and participant in the academy. Offering my awareness of my own biases and willingness to explore them in order to improve my professional functioning provides a model to students for similar reflection.

I make this suggestion at the risk of it being cast off as another "touchy feely" approach to instruction. Such discounting attributions are commonly attached to relational approaches to learning that break with traditional pedagogy. Consistent with my practice of making the covert overt, I also encourage students to notice and learn from their resistance to the material in the course. Discounting as "touchy feely" approaches or ideas that are more relational (i.e., feminine) stands as a helpful example of resistance. When we are resistant to something, we are moved by that thing. When we are moved, we are in a unique moment. We can choose to shut down and reject the thing we resist or we can choose to explore and learn from our resistance. In choosing the latter, questions emerge for guiding exploration of resistance. What is it about that thing (idea, practice) that brings discomfort? What in my way of knowing is threatened so that I respond with judgment and resistance? These questions are as relevant for instructors as they are for students preparing to be social service professionals. They represent another step toward laying the pedagogical ground for full engagement of issues of gender as they influence our work.

Summary

To address seriously the status of feminine activities and characteristics we must enter into inquiry and dialogue, among ourselves and with our students, that challenge values and beliefs at the core of our ways of understanding the world. The epistemological cornerstones of gender are so deeply embedded in our notions of who we are individually and as a culture, that questioning them is necessarily unsettling. Because gendered valuations have profound implications for both responsive service provision and professional viability, these issues must be engaged actively in the preparation of social service professionals.

Perhaps the greatest barrier to dialogue and action on issues of gender is privilege. Because there is no immediate benefit to the dominant patriarchal culture in questioning its tradition, because to question that tradition would mean saying no to privilege, the challenge of amplifying feminine voices and advocating feminine activity is immense. This is nowhere more evident than in the traditions of academia. A primary task of instruction in the social services is to make clear the cost, to all people, of exclusive patriarchy. In a culture that has no room for the feminine, part of who each of us is as a human being is denied. In professions focused on the delivery of social services, the devaluation of the feminine corrodes the integrity of our work, leaving social service a set of impersonal performances with no relational base.

Given these challenges, raising the status of the feminine in our professions, and in our culture as a whole, is an urgent matter. We must enter the process committed to reflective, honest, and probing dialogue and remain engaged even as discomfort and resistance arise. As instructors of social service professionals, our participation in both dialogue and action (through pedagogical and curricular decisions) stands as an unavoidable and catalytic model for similar inquiry on the part of the people in our programs. To acknowledge and hold in high esteem the feminine characteristics of our work and ourselves is to make more whole and responsive the services we provide. Anything less is harmful to us all.

---

[1] Men may cook or weave or dress dolls or hunt hummingbirds but if such activities are appropriate occupations of men, then the whole society, men and women alike, votes them as important. When the same activities are performed by women, they are regarded as less important" (157).

[2] This fact underscores the necessity of recruiting more people of culturally and linguistically diverse groups into graduate professional programs.

12

Gender and Professional/Liberal Knowledge: Men's Perspectives

JAMES WALLACE

The experiences and ideas presented in this chapter make it appropriate to briefly revisit some of the issues of "political correctness" discussed in the introduction. During the past decade conservative scholars and pundits like Allen Bloom (1987), William Bennett (1984), and Dinesh D'Souza (1991) have accused college faculties and administrations of spinelessly knuckling under to pressure from activist women and minorities and of bastardizing and diluting the Western curricular canon in response. They note that many colleges and universities have added themes, materials, courses, and programs dealing with minorities, women, and the third world, and they claim that important understandings from the Western heritage have been degraded or squeezed out. Whatever the merits of their charges, these conservatives have succeeded in making the public aware of the "PC" issue, to the point that it has become part of the more general political dialogue.

Someone familiar with these issues, visiting core classes in Lewis & Clark's interdisciplinary studies program, might be struck by the absence of this form of the general curricular debate. When we established our core program in 1985 the faculty, with very little dissension, agreed that ethical, international, multicultural, and gender issues would be at the heart of our curriculum. This was partly because the undergraduate college—in which many of us taught—had already established a core program incorporating these elements. Because we teach aspiring and practicing professionals, for whom these are pressing issues, we had no difficulty agreeing that our graduate core program would make them central topics in our teaching. It may also be true that as the program has been implemented, those faculty for whom these issues are a priority have been those most likely to teach in the core program. Thus there have been forces tending to create, maintain, and intensify a "politically correct" curriculum.

So in some respects we have gone past the basic PC debate in our curricular development. As a group the faculty (in spite of some range in our politics) is committed to ethnic, national, racial, religious, and gender equity—as are most of our students. We spend little time, therefore, discussing whether or not such equity should be promoted; rather, we can move directly to questions of methodology and organizational structure. Given our ethical and political commitments, how can we best help professionals to deal creatively and constructively with the theoretical and practical issues of equality?

This does not indicate, of course, that as faculty and students we have transcended our past, evolved beyond stereotyping, or freed ourselves from residual prejudices and patriarchal views. But it does mean that we are committed to self-examination, individually and collectively, and that we seek to move toward equity, personally and professionally. We struggle in particular to promote gender equality through a clearer understanding of the effects that gender plays in constructing our world.

Given the demography of Lewis & Clark, it is not surprising that gender issues have received much attention during our first years as a graduate school. A majority of our administrators and faculty are women, and most of them have had some background in women's studies or gender studies. They are thus well prepared to teach courses dealing with gender issues.

The men who teach and have taught in our core program have in general had, however, considerably less experience with gender studies. Commitment to gender equality has not ensured that male faculty are fully prepared to teach new issues and new material. Men have had to move beyond their own professional specialties and work with topics and readings with which they were only partly familiar. We attempt to compensate for that lack of background by, whenever possible, pairing male and female faculty for team teaching and by joining people who have taught in the program with those who are new to it.

I first became personally concerned about this situation during the spring of 1989 when I taught with an experienced woman colleague[1]. I apprenticed myself to her and, as a newcomer to core, accepted her judgments concerning materials and strategies that she and other colleagues had used successfully before. She tactfully took the lead in many of the gender-related discussions, and I felt that throughout the term I was learning from her along with the students.

This experience led me to wonder how other male faculty had been inducted into gender-related teaching, so I decided to interview as many of them as I could on this topic. I was able to conduct interviews with ten of the sixteen men who had taught in the program up to that point. Seven were regular faculty of the graduate school or college; three were adjunct instructors, one of whom had taught full-time in the graduate school. (Since people have been very frank in interviews and informal discussions, I will not identify them by name or program. The interviews were conducted during the spring of 1990.)

I started with a list of questions that were important to me and added additional topics that were generated in the course of the interviews. Some of the interviews turned into dialogues as my colleagues and I shared and compared our common or disparate experiences. I felt that I was not just extracting information from them, but that we were co-constructing ideas about our experiences (Kegan, 1982, p. 4). We were using—partly intuitively—not a positivist "objectivity" model of research but one that Kathleen Barry calls an "intersubjectivity" approach (1992, p. 27). Interviewer and interviewee both became subjects of inquiry. The interviewing process was a source of real pleasure to me. I was able to have serious talks with men, some of whom I have worked with as long as fifteen years but with whom I have rarely had thoughtful extended discussions about curriculum, materials, and teaching strategies.

My informants had a range of experiences with core. Some, like me, had only taught once in the program; others had taught as many as five times in various courses. Most of the men had taught in teams with one woman; some had taught in teams of three with two women or with another man and a woman; one had conducted an off-campus core course by himself, never having taught in core before. Because of their own interests and backgrounds, men tended to teach in courses that stressed organizational issues; women more often taught in classes dealing with themes of adult development.

I asked each man what prior experience he had with gender issues or studies; what he had learned about gender issues from his team partner, from the materials, and from students; and finally, what effect, if any, the experience had on his teaching, other work, or personal life. I will organize my conclusions similarly.

Prior Experience with Gender Issues and Studies

The men I interviewed had a range of prior experience with gender issues. Three program graduates had been students in core classes and had found the experience meaningful enough so that they were glad to teach in the program. One of these came away from a core class impressed by the significance of "connected knowing," which he associated with feminine epistemology (Belenky et al., 1986, ch. 6). Some had participated in women's studies workshops and symposia; several had team-taught with feminist women in other courses or had used material dealing with family life; some had done research on professional ethics, which had included gender-related material.

Most had been concerned about gender issues but claimed little substantive knowledge. Some had become personally involved with gender controversies when wives and mates encountered discrimination and stereotyping. One reported that teaching in the graduate school, with a majority of women faculty, had sensitized him to gender issues. He noted that "he had sat at tables on campus and watched men go deaf when women started to talk." Others noted that working in traditionally female public service occupations had given them an identification with women's issues. One had developed a "quiet zeal" for gender equity through observing discrimination in his experience in administration. Another "had a fundamental personal commitment to equality," but core teaching had given him his first chance to look analytically at the effects of gender in professional work. Some reported family, school, or religious environments that had prepared them to become feminists. Being a feminist, of course, means different things to different men and is expressed in a variety of ways: voting, joining, and contributing to feminist organizations and participating in activist groups. Male faculty mentioned their political support for the Equal Rights Amendment, for affirmative action, and for pro-choice legislation and candidates.

My generalization from these discussions is that all the men had some acquaintance with women's issues, that they were supportive of political expressions of feminism, and that they were ready to learn more about these issues. As one said, he was "ripe for gender studies." But most identified gender studies as women's studies; specific attention to men's issues from a feminist or broader gender perspective is only beginning to occur in our program.

Learning from Women Colleagues

Men learned from course concepts, materials, and students but testified that their greatest learning came through their women colleagues. They reported a variety of new or intensified insights: they had gained a better appreciation of the pressures that face women in society; learned about the functioning of women in organizations; received "conceptual clarity" on women's roles; achieved a better understanding of relationships between feminism, ethnic, and gay and lesbian issues; learned more about the history, politics, and sociology of gender; and seen the connections between critical theory and feminism. One said that he had learned through modeling male/female dialogue for students in core classes and by discovering that men's and women's traditional ways of knowing could be complementary.

Male faculty were grateful to their female colleagues for extending and deepening their previous knowledge of women's issues and for strengthening their commitments to feminism. Teaching with women faculty had helped intensify and personalize what had previously sometimes been rather abstract and theoretical understandings. But lest I present too rosy a picture, it is important to remember that all of us experience the tension of keeping current with our own specialties as well as with the broader topics included in core. We also struggle with the persistence of old habits derived from our lives in patriarchal society and our work in masculinized institutions. Our lives are no easier since the arrival of feminism, but they are more interesting, richer, and potentially more positive.

Learning from the Curriculum

Women faculty contribute to the education of their male colleagues partly through the materials they use in core classes and partly because of the structure of team teaching, which requires both instructors to be co-investigators. The curriculum evolves as ideas, themes, and materials are continuously dropped and added. Some materials have particularly influenced the way men faculty think about gender issues. The book most frequently cited was Carol Gilligan's *In A Different Voice* (1982), especially for its emphasis on a feminine ethic of care and connection. One said that "Gilligan helped explain to me who I am." Nell Noddings's book *Caring: A Feminine Approach to Ethics and Moral Education* (1984), and her seminar at Lewis & Clark in the summer of 1988, reinforced what some had learned from Gilligan. Several mentioned the videotape "A Jury of Her Peers" as an effective dramatization of the contrast between an ethic of justice and an ethic of care.

Eleanor Bowen's *Return to Laughter* (1964) had shown some men the challenges a female anthropologist faced learning about men's lives in a different cultural context. R. M. Kanter's *Men and Women of the Corporation* (1977) had depicted analogous struggles in American society as women worked in the masculine world of business.

Several mentioned *Women's Ways of Knowing* (1986) as a key book. One man said that the book "helped make clear to me why I felt comfortable to be in elementary school, surrounded by young children." One had found the book helpful when he assisted a colleague in organizing a gender-related course. Another saw the stages of women's voices described in the book as applicable to other groups as well as to women. Two men mentioned that Robert Kegan's *The Evolving Self* (1982), although gender is not the primary focus of the book, had helped them to understand the differing ways men and women move through the life cycle.

Anthropologist Barbara Myerhoff's *Number Our Days* (1978), and the film drawn from it, showed several men relationships between gender and ethnicity and dramatized the differing effects of aging on men and women. Myerhoff also underscored some of Gilligan's ideas concerning women's greater recognition of the need for connectedness, as well as the pain that some men created for themselves by clinging to patterns of excessive autonomy and individualism. This message was extended for one man by Pilisuk's and Parks's *The Healing Web* (1986), which shows persuasively the deep human need for strong social bonds. Several mentioned Tillie Olsen's short story "Tell Me A Riddle" (1976), which personalized and dramatized some of these issues.

Learning from Students

Some women students in the classes reinforced ideas that men learned from female colleagues. In papers, journals, and discussions, female students cited their own experiences with stereotyping and discrimination. They told of being demeaned, ignored, and rendered invisible by males in school and at work. Women cited specific instances of being discouraged from taking mathematics and science courses. Some women responded to core discussions and materials with a stronger realization that they were not alone, that their experiences had been culturally determined, not individually invited. Younger students in particular, especially those who had been previously exposed to gender studies, found their continuing education in this area to be enlightening, therapeutic, and potentially useful in their careers and personal lives.

While male faculty learned from students who liked and appreciated course content and materials, they gained insights also from those men and women who resented and challenged the gender emphasis of courses. Male instructors encountered what they called the stereotyped "hidebound old-boy mentality" and "football coach mentality" of some men. Some students in administrative programs thought that Lewis & Clark was "overplaying" gender issues. A few religious and cultural conservatives rejected the feminist orientation of the courses. Some male students adopted a "passive-aggressive" stance toward gender materials, tuning out when they were discussed.

But occasional women students resisted gender material as well. Some were described as "passively compliant," while others said they were tired of gender studies. Some women who had achieved administrative positions did not see gender as a personal issue and felt that organizations were not as biased as core courses suggested. Some claimed, in effect, "I've made it" and others frustrated by their experiences, said "I've given up on it." Others said, "We're beyond that; its old stuff." Both male and female students sometimes felt, "We've done that gender material before; I've had enough of this." Some, embedded in traditional approaches to learning, saw gender material only as academic content to be mastered. If they had studied it once and passed a test on it, some didn't see the need to consider it again. Their challenge to gender issues became entangled with their resistance to a new epistemology, which saw knowledge and understanding as socially constructed. Learning about gender involved some significant unlearning along with learning. Deconstruction of old paradigms had to occur reciprocally with the construction of new insights.

More interesting, and more potentially useful, were the responses of those whose priorities were different. Minority women who identified more with their race than with their sex sometimes resented the time spent on gender and the relative lack of attention to minority issues. Gay and lesbian students broadened our discussions as they contributed their specific experiences and insights to our dialogues.

Instructors had various explanations for this range of responses. Younger students, in preprofessional programs like teacher education and counseling psychology, sometimes responded more positively to gender issues, perhaps because they could see ways of applying feminist insights in their work with individuals. And young students were more likely to have had prior experience with gender issues in their earlier education.

(But going beyond interviews with male faculty at this point, dialogues with women colleagues show that male and female faculty have sometimes had different experiences with younger and older female students. One woman who has taught extensively in core classes, wrote: "I have found that older women are very responsive to issues of gender; they often feel validated in ways that young women cannot appreciate, and they are often angrier and exhibit more understanding. They are more complex in their approach to these issues. True, we do have women who say 'I have made it.' But I have seen young women catering to the men and being sucked into appeasing them even more quickly than the older women. Age, experience, and even class background confound student responses to gender. The more seriously instructors present these ideas, and the more they question the fundamental structures of a patriarchal western world view, the more resistance they encounter from both men and women—especially the men.")

Some instructors judged that the students in public administration and educational administration were more embedded in patriarchal organizations and were thus not optimistic about changing them. And students in these programs are usually older and perhaps less flexible about changing long-held beliefs and practices. One man suggested that courses dealing with adult development, which focused largely on individuals, were sources of optimism, while those dealing with organizations and bureaucracies were bases for pessimism. And if this is so, it would be true with gender issues as well as with other topics considered in the courses.

Impact of Teaching in Core on Gender Considerations

Since the men teaching in core were already committed (at least verbally) to gender equity, affirmative action, the ERA, and choice, none described significant political or ideological shifts from working in these courses. Rather, as was suggested above, they now felt themselves to be better informed about gender issues and to have clearer perspectives on how women view the world. One said that teaching in core had accelerated his education on gender and had made him more critical of the literature on the topic. He noted that, just as the civil rights movement had been helpful to whites as well as blacks, so gender studies were useful to men as well as women. One reported having a better understanding of the way women feel when they "have to make it in a world defined by men."

Several mentioned specific effects of teaching in core and particularly of the emphasis on gender. One, who was going through a family crisis while teaching in core, said that the readings, activities, and discussions in the class were a source of personal insight and support to him. Another reported that *Women's Ways of Knowing* (1986) had helped him assist a colleague in structuring a course she was going to teach. Several said that the ethic of care had influenced their thinking on moral issues. One school administrator implemented in his district a teacher training program dealing with gender expectations and student achievement. His commitment to hiring more women for administrative positions had been strengthened. One felt that he was now ready to take the lead in teaching gender and minority elements of the course instead of leaving them to a female partner. One said that teaching in an adult development course that included a gender emphasis had helped make him become a better teacher. He was more conscious of trying to empower students, gave students more control of the class, and experienced greater success. One noted that teaching core had helped him to see some of his residual stereotyping and had sensitized him to a greater range of differences among individuals.

Next Steps

All of my male colleagues were eager to talk about ways in which gender issues could be more effectively addressed in a professional program. While they feel better informed in this area, they need deeper and more varied experiences in dealing with these issues if they are to help students apply new insights to their organizations and bureaucracies. There is a desire to incorporate activities and materials dealing explicitly with men's experiences and with gay and lesbian issues as specific examples of the impact of patriarchal values and worldviews. Several wanted to find ways of dealing directly with student anxiety—both male and female—about gender issues. There is an increasing recognition that gender material is "affect-driven," and that our instruction must deal directly with the strong emotions that students and faculty bring to these dialogues. We need to draw on new insights and materials about male psychology as it is formed in patriarchal society. We must prepare students to deal with the inevitable changes in gender issues that will continue to evolve throughout their lives and careers.

But the point made most forcefully was that while we have made determined efforts to meet institutional commitments to gender studies, we have been much less attentive to issues of social class and to multicultural and international perspectives. One man said, "We have been strikingly obtuse about and disinterested in race and class issues." He added that we claim to be preparing professionals to work in multiethnic and working-class environments, but our courses and materials don't fully reflect that commitment.

This is a serious challenge. If we take a simplistic zero-sum approach to curriculum development, this would mean reducing the time spent on gender and increasing that given to minority and social class issues. But this need not be the case. We need to integrate information and theories that deal with gender, race, and class in ways that help our students see both differences and commonalities in the challenges faced by oppressed groups. We may be able to help move students from the pessimism sometimes intensified by professional education to a realistic optimism based on common strategies and collective action. We have failed when we have taught gender issues in isolation; we succeed when our students see the structural economic and political causes of oppression generally and find ways of helping various subjugated groups to work together for common goals.

We need to compensate for a demographic situation in which, like many professional programs, we have many women but few minorities. While we must include more information, ideas, and materials about minorities in our courses, this will continue to look hypocritical as long as we maintain our current demographic patterns. But changing these patterns will not be easy. The College has had the same difficulties as most institutions in attracting and holding minority students and faculty. But we must exert whatever force we have to develop and maintain a more diverse student body, faculty, and administration. And in the meantime we must create more meaningful encounters with minority professionals and clients in our various fields. In spite of demographics, this can be done. A recent critical issues seminar on Hispanic migrants succeeded in involving large numbers of vocal minority representatives. The strong voices of racial, economic, and sexual minorities were heard at the latest College Gender Studies Symposium (which serves also as a graduate critical issues seminar). We, along with others engaged in professional education, have an ethical responsibility to help our students struggle realistically and creatively with the intertwined dilemmas of gender, race, and class.

One blessing of gender studies is that its insights can be applied in other fields. The challenge we now face is to help our students extend to other areas the same sensitivity many now have on gender issues. We and they must be equally responsive to issues of class, race, handicap, nationality, ethnicity, language, and sexual identity as all of these relate to ethical dilemmas in our various professions. That should be challenge enough to last well into the next millenium.

Notes

1. The 1992-93 Lewis & Clark Faculty-Staff Directory lists among graduate administrators and instructors twenty-two females and twenty males. Many of the women and some of the men have participated in the college's annual Gender Studies Symposium and similar conferences elsewhere. Several women faculty have published articles and books on gender issues.

13

Learning about Organizational Cultures and Professional Competence

GORDON LINDBLOOM

Can a professional education program fail its students by concentrating too much on developing their professional skills? How can professionals be prepared to cope successfully with the many conflicting demands and influences they will encounter when they enter their domain of practice? Can they be prepared to preserve their sense of vocation and professionalism in the face of bureaucracy and burnout? Is it possible to prepare students to nurture their ideals when they feel surrounded by opportunism and ethical compromise? What vision of professionalism and professional effectiveness shapes our decisions about preparing students for public service?

These are central questions that emerged as the graduate faculty at Lewis & Clark College sought to define the common needs of students from five professional preparation programs. Our reflection on these issues led us to focus on the relationship between professionals and the human and organizational contexts in which they function. We began with the recognition that most professionals work in complex organizations. These structured social environments provide them with clients, colleagues, resources, and opportunities to practice their professions. They also bring with them rules, budget limits, program demands, and co-workers. These realities and a host of others intrude on the ability of professionals to follow their own best judgments. They are the environment that shapes the chances for success and satisfaction in their work. Yet our preparation programs have operated on a private practice model. We have educated our students as if they would be able to practice with freedom to pursue their own vision unhampered by these impinging forces. This denial

219

of the real conditions of professional practice leaves our students vulnerable to confusion, frustration, and disillusionment.

In the face of these realities we believed it was worth taking time from specific professional studies to give students tools that would help them move skillfully in their future work environments. For mid-career students, there would be a chance to bring new light to bear on their experiences and to offer them new ways of pursuing their professional practice. If it was not possible to solve all the problems of bureaucracy, burnout, and public criticism, at least we could prepare them to understand their work environments better and offer them tools for intelligent and affirmative responses to the challenges they bring.

In developing this vision we were stimulated and helped by Donald Schon's elaboration of the way professionals must move beyond the boundaries of their specific professional skills. He describes the "reflective practitioner, " who observes carefully and learns how to apply discretionary judgment in situations of ambiguity and "zones of indeterminacy" (Schon, 1983). We recognized that teachers, counselors, and administrators must constantly adapt their repertoire of skills to the specific clients and to the differing schools, agencies, and communities in which they work. This is an ongoing challenge throughout a public servant's worklife. In reflecting on this, it became apparent that we were not even calling this to the attention of our students, much less helping them acquire the abilities to cope successfully with their surroundings.

We felt that professionals can and should be participants who not only respond and cope but who purposefully influence those environments. In our graduate programs and others like them, little was being done to help students foster the kinds of epistemic, interpersonal, and organizational competencies necessary to proactive participation. Internships, practica, and supervised experience help prospective teachers and counselors become more cognizant of realities they face when they assume full responsibilities. But those experiences are usually focused on developing individual practitioner skills. Typically, little careful thought or systematic attention is given to helping them learn how to work cooperatively with a diverse group of colleagues and to perform critical organization-focused tasks in ways that could be described as competent and professional.

As our thinking has evolved, it has become clear that we were expanding the definition of professional competence and moving toward a new vision of professional effectiveness. Schon's work showed us the professionals who are skilled in their interpersonal and organizational environment. They are able to observe thoughtfully, to pursue inquiries, to formulate hypotheses, and to test them in action. Instead of dismissing experiences that do not fit the conceptual and procedural models they learned in graduate classes, they accept anomalies as important phenomena and potentially valuable sources of learning. Equally important is the more basic assumption that interacting intelligently and skillfully with one's professional environment is an integral part of one's professional repertoire and identity. This expands the definition of professional competence well beyond the traditional image of the individual practitioner applying specialized knowledge and skills to a well-defined set of problems. It recognizes the interdependence most practitioners have with other professionals and the patterned relationships within which they work together. It also adds the vision of self-directed learners who continue to develop repertoires of competencies for working effectively in their environments.

The Curriculum

This evolving vision was the basis for our efforts to develop a curriculum that would address these issues. As we made our first attempts to teach an organization-oriented course, we learned that the differing attitudes and experiences of our students presented major challenges. The fact that our ideas were well-grounded and well-intended did not mean that our students embraced them with gratitude and enthusiasm. Skepticism and resentment of this new requirement was common as students came to class. They did not understand why they should take valuable, expensive time away from preparing for their chosen vocation to learn about something as dull and abstract as organizations.

Our belief that they faced many common issues in their professional work environment simply did not ring true for them. Twenty-three-year-old teacher candidates felt little in common with teachers with years of experience, and vice versa. Neither felt any rapport with school principals. The lack of common ground seemed even more pronounced for counseling students and classmates who were career employees of the U.S. Forest Service or of local government. The differences in age, gender, work experience, and culture of the different preparation programs, gave students a realistic experience of the diversity of people and perspectives they could encounter on the job. But at this time, it was not a prominent concern for most of them.

On the other hand, members of the classes who had several years of work experience almost all immediately recognized the validity of the issues being raised. When they grasped the intent, many of them, especially teachers and school administrators, took this as a chance to investigate important questions they faced. Other groups of students, especially aspiring counselors and younger teacher candidates, found it harder to see any important personal benefits to be gained. As one twenty-five-year-old woman said, "I just want to teach kindergarten. I don't want to have anything to do with school politics or what administrators do."

These realities and the variability introduced by having many different instructors and classes with differing aggregations of students led us to adapt the course content, level of abstraction, and teaching strategies significantly. We eventually arrived at a set of concepts and methods that we referred to as an "eighty per cent common" course outline. This allowed instructors to vary readings, course content, and procedures within some bounds but gave a common foundation that we and students could recognize, becoming a course we called Organizational Cultures and Professional Life. In the ten 3-hour class sessions available to us, we sought to move through such topics as:

- Theories of organization as metaphors or images that convey differing assumptions about the nature of work, work relationships, and organizational effectiveness.
- The influence of organizational structure on relationships, communication, authority, and accountability.
- Work environments as organizational cultures.
- The nature of professions and their assumptions of expert knowledge and practice set by members of the profession rather than the organization that employs them.

There was a signifcant shift in the overall emphasis from earlier to later versions of the class. The first offerings took a more sociological, analytical approach. We used readings from Lipsky's work on the unresolvable conflicts between the goals of top-level policymakers and the implementation of policy by workers who were face-to-face with the clientele (Lipsky, 1980), as well as several readings on the nature and structure of professions. This emphasis on macro-organizational phenomena seemed abstract to students and not clearly related to their own experience and dilemmas. Consequently we shifted toward an approach that sought to use the best work of theorists and researchers, but to apply it to the more immediate realities that our teachers, counselors, and administrators encounter. The effort increasingly was to provide students with the tools to make sense of the specific environments of the schools, clinics, water bureaus, and audit divisions they knew as front-line participants.

Discussions of organizational theory, for example, deemphasized elaboration of the fine points of the ideas of Weber, the humanists, and others and focused on the differing assumptions about how people work together effectively. Similarly, in presenting the nature of organizational structures, the emphasis was on seeing their impact on day-to-day relationships and communications, authority, accountability, status, and how people come to identify personally with their roles. Examples from organizations typical of those in which students worked or hoped to work were displayed, described, and examined for the ways they affect the experience of their participants and our students. Students were asked to examine their own environments to identify structures they know and how they are influenced by them.

The content of the course took shape around two broad themes. The first was the general nature of organizational work environments. Here the main aim was to give students ways of making better sense of their own experience in organizations and better ways of understanding organizations themselves. This included attention to purposes of organizations, ways of thinking about organizations, organizational cultures, leadership, power, and authority. The second group of topics were common issues faced by people in organizations, including change, diversity, conflict, stress and burnout, and ethics. In all of these areas, our assumption has been that having an intelligent, perceptive understanding of these dimensions of personal experience is critical for developing effective strategies for working in them.

As this emphasis on making sense of work environments emerged it brought with it the need to include a problem-solving or proactive dimension. It was hardly a surprise to find that many of the students did not like the work environment they were in. Many of them faced frustrations and sometimes severe problems. To help students understand their difficulties better but give no attention to ways of seeking improvements seemed irresponsible and unresponsive. While the classes never became a forum for action-planning and preparation of change agents, strategies for healthy functioning received attention in most areas of the course.

The readings offered to students around these topics were a varying array of books, chapters, monographs, magazine articles, and journalistic pieces. To date we have found no one book that addresses the range of issues we wanted to include. Different instructors have had their own preferred selections in many of these areas, so no consistent set of readings has been defined. The need for brevity, focus, and accessibility to nonspecialists has been critical. Weighty academic consideration of theory and evidence has been of little value in these classes. Short overviews, case studies, and lively discussions have been much more effective in engaging students.

The most consistently used reading has been Eleanor Bowen's *Return to Laughter*, which is a novelized account of her work as an anthropologist in West Africa (1964). Her account focuses on her personal struggle to understand the relationships and beliefs of the traditional society she went to study. While this may seem remote from the concerns of teachers, administrators, and counselors, her vivid account of the inner life of that alien culture has served as a powerful analog and metaphor for students' efforts to understand the culture of their own work environments. They have consistently found it engaging and full of challenges to conventional wisdom. Instructors have found it full of examples of the issues of power, authority, membership, shared assumptions, and the strength of custom and conventional beliefs in a social group. It has consistently been the most popular of our readings and has fostered much critical thinking about the assumptions that students bring to their work relationships.

The other major issue in selecting readings has been that most have been written about schools and educators. A small number have been about public service agencies, It has been almost impossible to find such writing about mental health settings. As a result, our students from counseling and public administration have had to read materials which are directed to people in the schools. While some have been able to make the translation, others have said they find them irrelevant to their own vision of their future careers.

Process of Instruction

To pursue this vision of professionals who are competent in understanding and participating purposefully in their work environments, the processes of learning are no less important than the knowledge offered. Our goal was to shape the work of the classes to foster and validate the skills and habits of mind that are critical to reflective learning. The methods we employed in pursuit of this goal were journal writing, small-group discussion, and reflective essays.

Students come to these classes with much more experience in organizations than most of them recognize. As a consequence, they possess a substantial repertoire of knowledge and concepts about organizations that has the characteristics of folklore. It is unorganized, largely unexamined, and is commonly clustered around schemas such as bosses, politics, meetings, committee work, paperwork, and rules. These personal repertoires are heavily tinged with judgmental and emotional biases. If we are to move our students from unreflective and reactive modes of coping based on their personal repertoires, it is necessary to evoke these implicit personal paradigms. Our challenge has been to engage students in recognizing their own paradigms, to explore their uses and misuses, and to test the usefulness of other paradigms.

Alternative ways of understanding experiences are offered through readings and presentations. But the most powerful way of promoting this integration of personal paradigms with new perspectives is to share the process of examining one's experiences with other members of the class. Recognizing and sharing this personal learning in small groups offers the critical opportunity to learn how students with different experiences and training view issues from different vantage points. Our goal was to help students become thoughtful observers of their own paradigms and those of others and to see the values in contrasting points of view. This ability is essential to collaboration among professionals with differing training and differing organizational roles.

The main vehicle for personal reflection has been the personal journal. We ask students to explore their own experiences, thoughts, reflections, and modes of thinking through writing. To give them the freedom for such open-ended exploration, it is necessary to relax normal academic evaluation of content, style, and organization. While different instructors have experimented with alternative ways of asking students to approach this, typical assignments ask students to respond to assigned readings with their thoughts on the issues discussed or to briefly describe and reflect on their experience with the topic under discussion. For example, when the class issue has been conflict, we commonly asked students to describe and reflect on a conflict they had experienced at work or in an organizational setting. We asked them to use concepts from the readings and class presentations to aid them in their effort to make sense of that experience in new ways.

Most of the journal writing was to occur between class sessions, but there were times when students were asked to write in their journal during the class. We experimented with asking them to write their immediate thoughts and reactions to some class presentations. Here the purpose was to have them focus on their individual responses to issues that have been raised before discussing them with members of their small group. At other times we asked students to write at the end of a class session their responses to the entire class. We asked that they focus on those parts of the theme presented that were most important for them or raised the most important issues, or gave them new perspective. Here again, our intent was to encourage students to capture and explore the growing edge of their understanding so that it would be better defined in their thinking and be available to them for further reflection.

It soon became clear that the journals contained much better thinking if we proposed a specific focus for each week's between-class reflection. For example, rather than simply ask that students read about power in organizations and write about their thoughts on the topic in general, we found it more productive to ask students to reflect on specific ways they had experienced the use of power or had themselves exerted power. This proposed focus was not mandatory, however. Students were offered the option of writing to a different dimension of the issue if they felt that would be more beneficial to them. Students who accepted our offer to use the class as a context to work on issues they were facing frequently chose this alternative.

The contents of these journals have been used in several ways. Most often, students were asked to read or share the essentials of their written reflections in small groups. At times we would ask every one of the five or six members to read their material. At other times, we asked one person to share his or her writing as a stimulus for discussion by their small group. Instructors read journals at intervals, responding to the issues raised by the students. Evaluation was typically limited to verifying that the student had or had not engaged in the reflective process thoughtfully and seriously. The contents of the journals could become the basis for the reflective essays that were the main assignments for evaluation in the class. In some classes we planned the suggested weekly journal topics to lead toward the focus of the upcoming essay assignment. When we did so, the papers that resulted clearly showed the effects of accumulating, well-articulated thought.

The use of small groups for discussion and reflection has been a second critical element in the overall strategy of fostering reflective learning. Here students have the opportunity to give voice to their own views but also encounter and take into account experiences and views different from their own. Our intent has been to stimulate dialogue that would expand the context of student thinking and add to the repertoire of concepts and experience that they can use to make sense of future situations.

Since it is easy for any small group to talk but not seriously engage issues and each other's differing views, we have taken care in how we compose our groups. In a first class session we conduct a set of get-acquainted activities during which students can be introduced to most or all of the thirty students present. To form the collaborative groups that will continue throughout the term, we typically ask them to assemble in groups of five or six persons each. Each group is to contain members from the different professional preparation programs in approximately the proportions represented in the class as a whole. So, for example, if 30 percent of the students in the class are teacher-education candidates, a six-person group would include two persons in teacher-education programs. We also sought balance between administrators and nonadministrators, men and women, and sometimes levels of experience. We also ask that students not join a group with close friends. Within these guidelines students still usually have some choice. In most groups we have been able to arrange a reasonable degree of diversity of orientation and experience while respecting key individual needs and preferences.

The main use of the groups has been for reflective dialogue. Typically we ask students to discuss ideas presented in readings and class presentations. As suggested above, we frequently ask that they use reflections contained in their journals as the beginning point for a discussion that is intended to engage them in thinking about the concepts presented as they apply in members' experiences. For instance, in discussing the concept of organizational cultures, we might ask individual students to first observe and write about the customs, symbols, and values that have characterized an organization in which they have worked. And we would ask them to examine the influences these have had on their work and satisfaction. Comparing and contrasting such experiences in the group offers students an opportunity to understand their own experience better and to expand it substantially through learning of the experiences of other group members. The metaphors and constructs gained through this reflective, interpersonal process then become part of the student's repertoire.

As was true with the personal journals, we quickly found that the value of these discussions depended substantially on how we asked the participants to focus the dialogue. The discussions could easily become superficial and scattered if instructions were too general or did not call for an end result of some kind. Giving focus required that students understand the ideas from readings or presentations well enough to talk about them and to see some connections to their own experiences. It was important that there be continuity between the content of readings, presentations, and the focus we proposed. Planning for results such as a journal entry or preparation of a presentation to the class helped galvanize and focus attention on the issues.

The third strategy for promoting reflective learning was the assignment of reflective essays. Typically we asked students to write and produce three in the course of the term. These were not to be the library research papers so typical of graduate study, but syntheses of the students' understanding of major themes presented in the class, and an application of these to their own experiences. The first paper was commonly focused around the concepts of organizational culture and leadership. Often we asked students to use the stories from *Return to Laughter* as metaphor, first extracting themes or examples that illustrate the realities of culture and then comparing and contrasting their own experiences. In so doing, students were encouraged to draw on material in their personal journals and discussions in their small groups to bring together their own thinking.

The second reflective essay asked students to take one of the major themes, such as conflict or change, and examine their experience with it using the ideas drawn from the class. The third paper was often an extension in which students were encouraged to examine their own vision of their way of participating in their work organization, the issues this presented them, and how they might pursue growth in their ability to integrate their values and professional goals with the cultures and processes of the organizations in which they work.

In recent classes we have experimented with having the small groups serve as writers' groups. We asked the students to bring part of a draft of their next reflective essay to class. In the class session, we then asked them to join with one or two members of their small group to read their drafts. Listeners were instructed to first reflect their understanding of the writer's ideas and then to offer comments and suggestions. Writers receiving this feedback were encouraged to make as many notes as they wished to help with further work on their papers. For many students this process appeared to be surprisingly powerful. Most students took voluminous notes from this dialogue and reported that it helped them clarify and deepen their understanding of their own ideas in significant ways. The papers that resulted gave evidence of this expanded grasp of issues that were important to the writers.

We also experimented with alternative small groups created for a specific task. Asking people to form groups of persons with similar jobs (or work roles) seemed particularly valuable in working with issues like conflict and change. We call these "job-alike groups." Administrators had very different experiences from veteran teachers. Veteran teachers understood these matters differently from novice teacher candidates and counselors. For most class members, including those with years of experience, these issues were fraught with confusion, emotion, and ambiguity. Providing them an opportunity to meet with professional peers to discuss such matters helped them define and validate aspects of their experiences and perceptions more clearly than was possible in heterogeneous groups. The increased confidence in their own understanding appeared to improve their capacity to articulate their experiences and to reflect on them in dialogue and in writing.

In a typical class session we have attempted to sequence these elements in a developmental progression. At the beginning we connect the topics of previous weeks and the readings done for this session. This has been done by presenting a brief overview, by taking questions on the readings and attempting to clarify key issues, by having participants meet in groups to share their journal reactions to readings, and sometimes by asking students to begin the session by writing their thoughts at that time regarding the topic of choice. After this warmup we would make a presentation, usually a lecture by one of the instructors on the major topic and themes for that session. These presentations were commonly a mix of ideas, examples, and case studies intended to weave together the more abstract concepts of organizational theory with experiential views and patterns. For example, in talking about organizational structure, we would display structures common to organizations in which these students work, describe the rationales for them, and discuss the effects these patterns have on daily personal contacts, accountability, and communication and how isolated or involved and how powerless or how influential people feel. After the presentation, students are typically asked to convene their groups to discuss the topic by clarifying key elements of the presentation and then examining their own experience of these matters. This activity was commonly supplemented by another presentation or wrap-up discussion in the entire class. At the end of class, we commonly preview the coming topic and readings, attempt to link it to the material of the past and present, and suggest a focus for journal responses to the readings for the next session. On occasion we gave time for writing a journal entry in which students could collect their responses to the issues raised in this session.

What Have We Learned?

If scientific verification of the results of this experimental effort is not possible, a number of "soft" generalizations have repeatedly suggested themselves, sometimes with compelling force. The most obvious of these has been confirmation of our initial decision about the importance of organizational competence for professionals. The mem-

bers of our classes who brought a history of professional work experience with them almost universally confirmed this. Most of them could
readily describe numerous experiences with colleagues, superiors,
committees, and policies that created dilemmas of critical importance
for their work and their welfare. Among those class members with
little or no professional work background, confusion and uncertainty
were obvious about how to make sense of their prior experiences with
organizations, for example, as students in public schools and colleges.
And even when they had been given introductory internships in the
schools and public agencies they hoped to work in, they had few useful
guidelines for making sense of those settings or how to imagine what
lay ahead in full-time work. Their need to see and name critical
elements of their human environment at work confirmed the validity
of our purposes in a different way.

Our continuing confidence about the need to prepare professionals for competence in their work environment did not mean that
students always agreed with us or that we could successfully deliver
the learning experiences necessary to develop the range of abilities
required for effective collaboration and leadership. It has been in
these areas where questions, ambiguities, and mixed evidence have
continued to prompt us to try new approaches.

The general content of the course outlined above as the "80
percent" agreement has gained the confidence of instructors who have
worked in this course over time and in several classes. In every class
we have tried at least a few new readings, changed the order and
emphasis of the topics, and adapted the pace and depth to the students
in that particular class. Instructors have experimented with different
approaches, such as a political power analysis of organizational life or
using organizational simulations as a vehicle for learning. Experience
with those classes has led back to the general approach outlined in this
chapter. This is not to say that the curriculum is now fixed or that
those of us involved are fully satisfied. It does mean that emphasizing
the areas of structure, culture, leadership, power, change, conflict,
ethics, and the need for professionals to grapple thoughtfully with
them has continued to make sense to us and to evoke critical reflection
from our students.

Similarly, we have gained increased confidence in the validity of
the reflective approach to learning for these purposes. It is easy for our
students to learn to repeat standard concepts about organizations but
diligent and sometimes emotionally demanding effort is required to
use these concepts to illuminate their own experiences. For example,
they can readily grasp central types of structural theory, but when we

ask them to describe which of those apply to their own work environments and how they affect the assumptions people make in their work relationships, most students struggle to develop an articulate understanding of the structures with which they have direct experience. And they need time and assistance to accurately name the ways these beliefs and assumptions shape their everyday experience. Few things could be more clear than this lesson that standard didactic approaches to organizational theory and practice do not provide insight and integrative learning unless substantial time and effort are devoted to connecting and integrating new concepts with previously unexamined areas of personal experience.

From this flows a crucial and unresolved question. How much new understanding and integration of this kind can we ask and expect our students to master in a one-term class with 30 hours of contact time? As instructors we can build in a large amount of rich content, but we do so at the risk of superficial understanding by our students and little chance that they will apply it in useful ways. If our goals are to help students develop new ways of understanding that can be firmly grounded in their experience, then we must go at a pace that challenges but does not overwhelm them. In practice, this has led us to identify and emphasize a few key concepts in each area. With skillful inquiry and successful integration as our goal, we have often concluded that "less is more." Fewer concepts, carefully chosen, give students better chances of putting them to use now and in the future.

No aspect of these classes has been more challenging than the wide range of age, experience, and interest presented by the students. Forty-three-year-old divorced mothers of teenaged children who want to counsel other women in transition find themselves in a small group with twenty-two-year-olds who want to teach deaf children. Veteran teachers find themselves in dialogue with park department employees. Our hope has been that this would provide the occasion for students to understand the different perspectives each one brings to common dilemmas and to recognize this as a critical dimension of life and effectiveness in any organizational setting. While a percentage of our students have been able to grasp this, many seem not to see this common ground. Instead, they have sought partners with compatible interests and experience.

This diversity has sometimes made it difficult to select and present material that is accessible and relevant to all the students in the class. Trying to address students with a mid-range of experience, for example the teacher with seven years' experience in the schools, has often meant leaving inexperienced members of the class confused and wondering what any of this has to do with them. At the same time it has left those with more organizational experience bored at the apparent simplicity and obviousness of the content. Presenting case studies and problem situations has been our most successful means of letting students with different levels of experience address common issues with their differing perspectives. But this has fallen far short of creating the common framework for dialogue that engages all students of differing backgrounds. Classes in which the coincidences of enrollment provided a more limited range of experience have achieved a level of common dialogue more readily than those with more diverse membership.

We have no means of making a definitive determination of what students take away from this experience. Our intent is to foster learning that is open-ended, unfolding, and incomplete. Since the interests, goals, and experiences of our students vary widely, what constitutes the most valuable learning for each student depends on how much of what is offered in class can be integrated into their thinking and how well they apply this now and in the future. Within these broad bounds, some of our goals appear to have been only partially achieved while others have been met to a significant degree.

Goals that have been only partially met include helping students to grasp the extent to which their differing roles, training, and experiences mean that they approach issues from different vantage points. When we have concentrated attention on this reality, we have noted a limited understanding of, for instance, why administrators, teachers, and counselors often differ regarding how much uniformity and how much individualization is acceptable in the way teaching and other services are provided within an organization. This slowness to understand is obviously influenced by a natural reluctance to acknowledge that one's own views are not the only legitimate perspective. Further, acknowledging that other views have legitimacy may require giving up a substantial degree of control over one's activities. Achieving greater success on this theme would require more persistent attention beginning early in the course and following through in several topic areas.

Embracing the legitimacy of diverse views and interests is the necessary basis for effective collaboration, use of diverse talents, and constructive response to conflict. Affirming these beliefs is needed but is not sufficient for competent organizational participation. Learning how to use specific pro-social skills, group procedures, and facilitative structures is necessary to collaborate successfully with one's colleagues, whether they are peers, superiors, or subordinates. The definition of these necessary tools for effectiveness has not been a part of the "80 percent" curriculum, and has seldom been outlined in the course. This is mainly due to the limits of time and the capacity of our students to absorb new ideas. Whether the coverage of other material should be reduced to provide more emphasis on these skills or whether it is best to leave their acquisition to other learning settings is not clear. I have now taught an experimental course that focuses specifically on the concepts and practices necessary for successful collaboration. The experience with one section indicated that there were advantages to this approach if students were prepared to embrace those goals. But experience with more groups is necessary to develop optimal approaches to the content and method of this new direction.

The goals of giving students a greater awareness of the influence of their organizational environment appear to have been substantially achieved. Almost all of our students have demonstrated a more perceptive understanding of some dimension of their organizational experience and have been able to write about it in increasingly articulate ways. Even for students with the least experience and most limited interest, participation in the class appears to have sensitized them to these realities and given them the beginnings of competence for making sense in the future.

Many of the more experienced students have not only recognized the validity of these goals but have welcomed the opportunity to use the class to examine an issue of special concern to them. One school principal chose to retrace the risky process by which he had discovered key elements of the culture of his current school and the ways he had tried to cope proactively with the threats and opportunities it provided. His goal was to assess how much he had learned, what successes and failures he had with this process, and what approaches might serve him well as he continued. A woman teacher who was considering becoming an administrator undertook a review of the successes and failures she had in working with two principals. Her goal was to identify more clearly what patterns of behavior and attitudes had made one working relationship satisfying and the other frustrating. A counselor who was in severe conflict with a supervisor analyzed that relationship with the help of paradigms presented in the class and used the results to make a decision about the next step in her career. Another analyzed the patterns of intergroup relations in the staff of a child-care organization to determine why consistency of treatment and improvements in treatment approaches were hard to bring about.

Individual efforts of this kind occurred in every class. While many students formulated their purposes gradually in the first half of the class, most succeeded in finding a theme of personal concern and a way to work toward improved ways of understanding that experience. In every class, anonymous written evaluations included comments such as, "This class made it possible for me to understand the situation I faced" or "This class came at just the right time for me. It helped me figure out what I want to do next in my career." In one notable term, twelve of the seventeen students I evaluated had used their class and papers to work out a solution to a major dilemma they were confronting in their work life.

This kind of evidence was heartening. It was only partially supported, however, in standardized course evaluations. These were typically mixed and provided average ratings lower than those received by the same instructors in their standard professional courses. Several factors may contribute to this. The course was not part of their vision of core professional preparation in their own field. An undertone of resentment at being required to take this nonstandard course was voiced quite often and seemed to be a lightning rod for many of the frustrations of graduate study. The approach to learning was unfamiliar, ambiguous, and may well leave most students without the same sense of completion they get in more standard courses. We have also noted a consistent pattern of lower rankings for team teaching as opposed to individually taught courses.

Rigorous evaluation of the learning acquired in this class would involve much more than the end-of-term course evaluations filled out by students, the assessment of learning represented in their writing, and our own collected observations as instructors. We would need to follow these students into their work settings to determine: first, whether they were able to articulate a useful understanding of events and conditions that they previously would not have understood; second, whether they choose to actively reflect and learn more about these phenomena; and third, to determine to what extent they used new insights from this learning to respond more effectively to specific experiences that confronted them. Conducting an evaluation of this kind is a substantial challenge demanding talent, resources, and significant commitment.

What we as a faculty have learned is substantial. We are now experimenting with new variations on this course. In one we are combining it with an emphasis on personal and professional development. In another the central focus is on developing the understandings and skills needed to implement collaboration between professionals and collaborative decision making in the organization. We expect to learn new lessons from these that will increase our understanding of ways to make this learning more accessible and relevant to our students.

A widening social consensus is calling for democracy in the workplace, decentralization in bureaucracies, and empowerment of people at all levels of organizational life. These aims grow out of humane values and the need for greater effectiveness in our public and private institutions. In developing the graduate classes described here we have begun to define a new vision of professional competence that reflects these aims. In working with our students we have been learning about how we can help them take steps toward acquiring this added dimension of professional effectiveness. We expect to continue to learn together.

14

The Evolution of a Graduate School: The Effects of Developing a Liberal Arts Core

CAROLYN L. BULLARD

The argument of this book is that the conscious commitment to address the issues and dilemmas of professional practice from a liberal arts perspective should have a positive impact on professional practice. If this is the case it should be apparent in the graduate school of professional studies at Lewis & Clark College. When the various programs were drawn together into the graduate school, the faculty was given a mandate to develop for its students a core curriculum based in the liberal arts. The discussions that created the core program became the framework for the dialogue that developed the school.

How that dialogue affected the development of the school will of necessity be an individual story for each participating member. The secretary who was on the front lines listening to the students' evolving perceptions of the core would have a different story from the faculty member who was deeply involved in the core's development. The student who was integrating the ideas explored in the core classes would tell a different story from the administrator who had to see that each piece of core was successfully staffed. I, too, have my own story as dean of the school during most of its transition years. I tell my story because I think it presents a good case study of the impact of liberal arts education on professional practice. My story is two-fold—my perceptions of how the evolution of a core program based in the liberal arts affected the school and how it affected me as a practicing professional in that school.

I see the impact of the liberal arts on our practices in the graduate school in three different areas. First, when we began to examine our practices we quickly found ourselves asking questions of meaning and purpose. Then to understand how meaning and purpose were played out in our professional lives, we had to try to understand how organizations worked. Finally, to make better sense out of meaning and purpose and of organizations, we had to ask an even more basic question: what constitutes knowledge? I will discuss each of these areas in turn.

Meaning and Purpose

All individuals must create for themselves the meaning of their own lives. Some see their lives as part of some grand design and take meaning from that. Others take meaning from their relationships and their families. Still others develop meaning from their activities, from good works, from meeting the needs of others through social actions.

The development of the core forced us to ask the question of meaning in the particular context of professional practice. This became a critical question in the 1980s because the professions for which we were preparing our students were under severe criticism. The decade began with sweeping attacks on teaching, with efforts to move the schools away from the liberalism of the 1960s and 1970s to a more prescriptive notion of education. The decade ended with education taking the blame for the sagging national economy. Government service became an anathema in the 1980s (Johnson, 1991).

The question of meaning became most salient for us as we began the development of the graduate school. Lewis & Clark College had graduate programs for a number of years, but the institution had always had an uneasy relationship with them, partly because of its own changing sense of mission. During the middle of the century the college had mandated public service as part of its mission. The College's emphases had been mixed, providing traditional liberal education alongside professional preparation in areas such as business and education. However, as the college moved into the 1980s it began to define itself as a high quality, liberal arts institution with an increasingly ambiguous relationship with its professional programs. The institution partly resolved this problem in 1984 by moving its graduate programs and undergraduate teacher education program into a separate graduate school. The complete demise of professional education was prevented in part as the graduate school expressed a willingness to develop a liberal arts core program whose purpose was to demonstrate the value of liberal arts education as a part of professional preparation.

There is no doubt that this change led to a crisis of meaning and purpose for members of the graduate programs. Some faculty members had long-term collaborative relationships with undergraduate faculty and had contributed considerably to undergraduate curriculum and governance. Some graduate programs had protected themselves institutionally by keeping themselves away from the undergraduate faculty and its politics as much as possible. Now each graduate program was thrown into an organizational structure with others, none of which had a secure place in the institution. And the faculty was being asked to develop a curriculum whose primary purpose was to prevent the demise of the graduate programs. The unstable political environment led to a quick succession of three deans, I being the third.

Along with other members of the graduate faculty, I underwent a crisis of meaning—a crisis I experienced on two levels. I had to assist the graduate school in finding its own identity and I had to discover my own identity as a dean. What I did not expect, but what in fact did happen, was that my work in developing and teaching the core became the frame for both tasks.

The graduate school faculty was typical of many professional faculties. The training and background of many had not led them to think much about organizational meaning, particularly the meaning of their own institution. If you asked who their most important colleagues were, they would not name people within the institution, but professors at other institutions who were in the same profession. This sense of extra-institutional loyalty was exacerbated by the internal reward system, which placed high value on autonomous, individualistic performance. (This emphasis has reached its height in the undergraduate faculty where only teaching and scholarship are recognized in the tenure process. College service and professional contributions are not considered.)

The development of the core program forced us to ask ourselves what our meaning was as a faculty. If we were to develop courses based in the liberal arts that all students must take, we had to assume there was meaning in our work beyond our own narrow professional goals. Determining that meaning came about by first asking ourselves what our graduates did well and where they were having problems. What we discovered was that on the whole, no matter which program our graduates were from, they felt relatively well prepared to carry out the specific responsibilities of their jobs. New teachers knew how to teach and manage their classes. Counselors were relatively comfortable with the systems they were using with clients. Administrators were confident that they had an understanding of good management practices. But our graduates found their professional lives considerably messier than they had anticipated. Teachers stepped into schools whose organizational culture was at cross purposes with their own belief systems. Counselors, whose preparation had focused on providing the best therapeutic practices possible, found their time swallowed up dealing with organizational problems. Administrators found a public who refused to believe that any activity carried out by a public agency had any value. Principals found teachers who simply had no understanding of what the roles and limits of administration were. Differing cultural groups our graduates encountered seemed to be at war with each other. Crises in families were taking enormous tolls on graduates' professional lives. Their individual values were being subverted both by their families and their organizations. Our graduates were finding they were no longer honored by our culture but rather were questioned as to why they weren't in professions with more monetary and status rewards. Once we had asked the question, "how are our graduates were faring?" we found our meaning in preparing practicing professionals had changed. And once we had found this change of meaning for our students, we found that our meaning as an administrative unit had changed. We could no longer see ourselves as just a group of programs thrust together by political accident. We began to see that we had, together, the need to deal with serious issues of meaning.

As we began to explore these issues, we discovered that each of our professions had attempted to define them within the individual context of each profession. For example, the high stress experienced by educators of deaf children had often been expressed as an outcome of the high rate of failure in helping deaf children reach a level of literacy in English. Music teachers defined their stress as a result of being treated like outsiders in each school they were part of. Counselors defined their stress as a result of poor psychological functioning on the part of administrators responsible for their programs. Public administrators blamed their problems on the lack of flexibility built into bureaucratic systems.

Having the problems defined as closely related to the specific content of each profession prevented individuals from using models outside their own profession to define or solve the problems. Once we as a faculty were able to see the problems as universal rather than profession-specific, we began to see the role the liberal arts could play. After all, issues of values, community, role conflict, family functioning, transition and crises are the very substance of literature, anthropology, art, and even science. Many of our students had strong liberal arts backgrounds. Our task became one of helping our students use the liberal arts as a means of defining and dealing with their professional lives. Thus, the birth of the core program.

My problems as dean were remarkably similar to those faced by our graduates. My involvement in the core gave me a set of tools for understanding those problems and for understanding myself in the role of dean. The impact was powerful. I began to understand that if we did not have a common sense of purpose in the school we would have considerable difficulty solving our problems. Faculty members often take strong, moral positions regarding any professional or governance issue presented. Compromising on issues is often viewed as compromising on moral principles. Because of tenure, there is often little incentive for faculty members to move beyond moral stances in problem solving. Participating in the development and teaching of the core helped me understand the role values play in decision making (Harrison, 1972) and the importance of shared values supporting community building (Bellah et al., 1972). It also became clear to me that building a coherent community was critical to the school's survival. Moral posturing and uncompromising battling would be our undoing. Several activities were undertaken to build our community, including academic endeavors and social events, and consciously to build a rhetoric of our meaning as a school.

The other impact of the core was at a much more personal level. The transition from faculty member to dean was personally demanding in ways I simply had not anticipated. I had never conceived of myself in such a position. I had always been considerably troubled by issues of power, having viewed power negatively. I had equated power with aggressiveness, hidden agendas, and manipulation. The survival of the graduate school seemed to be dependent at least in part on my ability to play power politics successfully. I did not define myself as aggressive, manipulative, nor particularly wise in dealing with hidden agendas. It was only in reading the literature on women's moral structures and behaviors (Gilligan, 1982; Belenky, et al. 1986; Regan, 1990) and discussing these issues with students and my co-teachers in core that I began to understand that my view of how the work of organizations should be done was not simply an idiosyncrasy developed out of my own psychology. Rather, it was at least similar to the way many other women saw their roles as leaders. This validated my own way of relating to other leaders in the institution and has on the whole been successful.

Another problem in my transition to dean was that it changed my relationships with faculty. In the past they were my colleagues, but now I had no idea what our relationship was to be. I had developed friendships that had provided strong support for me as a professor. I was uncertain now where to get my support without risking either my role as dean or other people's roles in relation to the dean's office. While

I was deep in this transition I was teaching a core class. The students, my co-teacher, and I investigated the role of support networks in transitions and the impact of self-definitions in understanding our relationships with others. I found my way through this crucial transition and perhaps have learned ways to help others through their own.

Organizations

As I began to tackle the problems of the graduate school, I realized that understanding organizations was critical—and interesting! The paradigm that I had brought with me to Lewis & Clark as a professor was that organizations at their best were to be ignored. I understood I could not do my work without the organization, and it certainly was fun to complain about it, but beyond that it had little meaning for me.

As the faculty began looking at the problems presented by our graduates, it became clear that our understanding of organizations was just not adequate. We began to look at the formal organizations in which we work as carriers of their own meaning and purposes. We began to understand just how much our work organizations have taken over family and community functions. They provide for our sustenance, medical support, retirement, social lives, and even child care. As women have moved into the workplace these functions have moved even more dramatically out of the family and other community organizations. It became much clearer why so much emotional energy is invested in our workplaces.

This awareness affected how I thought we should function as a school. I became more committed to the notion that we should see ourselves as a community and recognize that we had problems as a community to solve. I was not particularly concerned that individualism would become too subordinate to the whole since the centrifugal forces in higher education are enormous. I became committed to the notion that we should develop a sense of supporting each other's well-being, not just in terms of one another as individuals, but in caring for the success of each others' programs and professional achievement.

It was important to me that our school become a good place us to work. Faculty members and staff spend many hours of their lives in the institution. Often there is little social life beyond people's work lives. It is important to me that individuals in the school experience satisfaction, support, and success. All should find their work enhanced by their colleagues, by their being a part of this organization. There are days when I feel we have experienced success in meeting this goal. On other days I am less certain. Nevertheless, the core helped me formulate these goals for the school and keep them in my mind as I influenced the school in whatever ways I was able. This is not to say that excellence is not a goal. Faculty members certainly have the drive to be excellent unless they are demoralized into cynicism. But it is not my desire to push individuals to rampant individualism as the path to excellence. Community support is a more desirable way to achieve our academic and professional goals.

Our look at organizations has provided us with better tools for understanding the events that have taken place around and within the graduate school. Our examination in the core of marginalized groups (Hooks, 1988; Folk-Williams, 1979; Mow, date unknown) has helped us understand the institution's behavior toward us and our responses in return. When the institution was in considerable turmoil over the college presidency, as a minority group with little power, we chose our battles very carefully. We understood there was a price to pay for "hunkering down" to avoid the fray. But each decision was discussed within the context of organizational functioning. The risks and costs were carefully calculated. The faculty was able for the most part to discuss the strategies involved at an organizational rather than personal level. This allowed the school to survive, even to grow, during very dangerous moments. It is worth noting, however, that some of the outcomes of "hunkering down" are yet to be seen.

The core has helped us view our problems as graduate programs in a liberal arts institution as a cultural issue as much as an academic and personal one (Schein, 1985). As a result we have worked to change the culture of the institution by carefully selecting the language with which we describe ourselves and the activities we chose to promote. We continually observe the undergraduate college of arts and sciences for academic moves that connect with our own purposes. While this may all sound a little cold-blooded and nonacademic, our deeper understanding of organizational functioning has helped us see that our difficulties do not come out of bad people doing bad things, but rather have to do with organizational histories and mythologies being passed from one individual to another. We are simply trying to influence the myth structure of the institution.

Frames of Knowledge

Perhaps the most pervasive influence of the core has been in our notions of what constitutes knowledge and our roles as participants in the development of knowledge. The core has provided a vehicle, a purpose, and a common language for sharing our notions of knowledge.

We did not originally strike out to look at the question of knowledge. Most of us came from a rather typical positivist view accompanied by a belief that there was a single knowable reality if we simply asked the right questions in the right way. Our movement toward incorporating other views of knowledge originally received impetus from the work of feminist writers. We first tackled the notion that the hierarchies of moral behavior described by writers such as Kohlberg (1981) did not resonate with everyone, particularly with many women. Some women would not consider an abstract principle of justice as the highest level of moral behavior, but rather looked toward relational principles as more relevant guides to moral decision making. This led us, like many, to question the notion of knowledge as abstract, hierarchical, and ultimately singular. We began to incorporate in our thinking the possibility of a "Rashomon" view of knowledge. Our explorations of readings such as *Women's Ways of Knowing* (Belenky, et al. 1986) and *The Reflective Practitioner* (Schon, 1983) have led us to accept the notion that our students have real and important knowledge that they bring to our classrooms and that our knowledge as practitioners is then constructed from the collective experiences of the participants. This has forced us to forge deeper, more honest connections between theory and practice.

This opening has led us down many paths. Our research courses have undergone distinct modifications. We now incorporate in our courses an ethnographic component, providing our students with tools to ask and answer questions important to them in their own work sites. We have changed the teaching in many of our classrooms to include the students' voices. This was initially a most difficult task. The first core classes in which we asked our students to share their experiences and reflective knowledge as part of our information base were met with indignation. The students declared they were here to learn from the professors and not from the other students. This view rarely is heard now.

Faculty members took writing courses to learn how to express their own voices, how to help their students incorporate their voices into their own writing, and how to use their writing as a special means for understanding and interpreting their experiences.

We were led to struggle with issues of diversity. Experiences are viewed and understood differently if the cultural lens is different. Our students, staff, and faculty are trying to sort out what our roles are in the face of diversity. Is our job as teachers to provide middle-class "American Dream" models of success and all the skills leading to that or is a possible and desirable way to allow diversity to continue without excluding those with different values and behaviors from opportunities? This is a particularly poignant issue for us in the graduate school since the institution is made up of nearly all white middle-class students and faculty. Yet our graduates deal with issues of diversity every day in their places of work. We must help our graduates untangle the question of whether their students' or clients' responses are a result of cultural or of gender differences or individual functioning. We struggle with the issues of the meaning of justice and fairness. Is justice simply a middle-class linguistic trick to keep the ruling class in its place?

We do not view these questions nor our responses as unique to our school. However, we have chosen to use the disciplines of the liberal arts as vehicles for examining these questions. Having worked together on the core, we find we have at least a common frame of reference for examining the issues. We are prevented from trying to deal with these issues simply within the framework of our own professional literature. We are now able to use each others' professional literature, material drawn from the liberal arts, and each others' experiences as a means for examining all these issues.

Conclusion

I have to admit that in my role I am much more cynical about the effects of the liberal arts on professional behavior on some days than others. Sometimes negative events and behavior seem to overwhelm the school, leading everyone to withdraw. Lackluster institutional support can be wearing on everyone. Arguments occur at rather regular intervals about the value of investing time in the liberal arts–driven core rather than on work specific to each individual profession. Nevertheless, there is no question that the core program has had a very strong impact on me as a dean. The development of the core helped me frame the issues of leadership, the meaning of organization, and the nature of professional education. I would have been a different kind of dean and the school would have been a different place if we had not pursued the questions of the meaning of our professional lives together. My own experience with the core leads me to the conclusion that the inclusion of the liberal arts as a means of pursuing the questions of professional practice leads to a better understood, more functional professional life. Whether it is a more satisfying life would be an outcome dependent on each individual. There are those who argue that knowing what we now know might lead to more discontent with the professional life than ever! However, for a period of my life, what I have experienced through the core has made my work richer and made me a better dean. As an individual it would be hard to ask for more.

Afterword:
The Search for Personal and Professional Meaning

KEN KEMPNER

Although a large number of professors in higher education might rather wear their robes to class, many faculty are attempting to escape such parochialism. In this book we have met the vanguard of these liberating faculty who, as Celeste Brody and Carol Witherell note in chapter 4, have a "new vision of what it means to be a professional within a community of inquirers."

At first glance, this book and the authors' voices may have appeared to be yet another case study of professional education. The story, as you have read, is much deeper, however. At its essence this book is not only about a program but about the authors' escape from the tyranny of the "culture of positivism" (Giroux, et al., 1981, p. 42). This tyranny is manifested most clearly in the marginalization of the individuals and ideas that do not match the traits of the dominant culture. These "others" are marginalized on the basis of their gender, race, class, ideology, and other characteristics that make one unsuitable for acceptance into the dominant culture. The voices of others are heard throughout these chapters as the authors report and consider the struggle to confront the vestiges of their institution's "past process" (Veblen, cited in Wallace and Brody, Introduction).

My purpose in this Afterword is not to evaluate the success of the authors' struggles but to reflect upon the place of the core program in the larger cultural context of defining knowledge and professional self. First, I consider the authors' escape from the parochialism of positivism. Second, I address the purposes of professional education and then discuss the consequences of implementing the core program. Finally, I consider the core program's meaning in relation to professional practice.

The Culture of Positivism

The "culture of positivism," as Giroux (1981) terms it, is the hegemony that objectifies knowledge. Within the confines of positivism scientists presume knowledge to be objective, indisputable fact, as opposed to an act of subjective, social construction (Berger and Luckmann, 1966). Because there is no place for passion or subjectivity in science from this perspective, positivism is an inherently conserving enterprise that Adorno characterizes as the "puritanism of knowledge" (cited in Aronowitz and Giroux, 1985, p. 130). For positivists knowledge is preserved fact that excludes the ideas and the individuals who do not adopt the objectivity of the dominant perspective. Arguments of exclusion and marginalization are considered irrational, subjective judgments that have no place in empirical science.

Keller (1985) argues that the positivistic, objectified view of knowledge is a male manifestation that bases scientific reality in conceptions of domination and power over nature. Privilege is secured by advocates of positivism who adhere to its objectivity and renounce the subjectivity of socially constructed knowledge. Keller (1985, p. 87) explains that the accordance of this privilege is not gender-free: "truth has become genderized." Similarly, Mary Henning-Stout, in chapter II, finds academic culture inherently "patriarchal." Faculty are fountains of knowledge whose role it is to transmit the culture to presumably ignorant students. Because the majority of these faculty are white men the voices of the other are not afforded equal credibility. Others do not possess the objective knowledge and "cultural capital" these faculty of privilege own (Bourdieu and Passeron, 1977). The role of the other is to absorb knowledge, fact, and the dominant culture, either to become privileged or less ignorant of the objective truth. Given this "central paradigm of contemporary academe," Henning-Stout observes that the "challenge of amplifying feminine voices and advocating feminine activity is immense."

In its rejection of subjectivity, the patriarchal culture of academe devalues knowledge not based on rationalistic assumptions that the truth is knowable. From this perspective the facts merely need to be gathered up and reported for the truth to emerge. The hegemony of positivist thought is so powerful, Henning-Stout observes, it renders "irrelevant any subjectivity on the part of the scholar." She explains further: "Given this belief, it is no wonder academics have found the notion of self-reflective scholarship oxymoronic." The scholars who engage in such reflection and the knowledge they derive are devalued by the patriarchal culture. To escape the tyranny of this positivistic and patriarchal culture, Henning-Stout proposes that the goal for the Lewis & Clark core program is "to make clear the cost, to all people, of exclusive patriarchy."

This "cost" of patriarchy and privilege, which Henning-Stout defines so well in her chapter, resonates throughout this book. Rather than simply transmit knowledge, the faculty of the core program struggle to break through the traditions of positivism and embrace a larger vision of knowledge, equity, and professionalism. The patriarchal model of academe survives its challengers, however, because it is a monopoly of privilege by the dominant few. Whereas Tayloristic forms of business are perishing in the current marketplace, Tayloristic forms of professional education thrive. Best (1990, p. 137) observes that while "outdated economic theories live, outdated business enterprises do not." Ineffective professional schools flourish because their survival is derived from privilege.

As the anachronistic model of economic production in the United States has fallen prey to the contemporary production methods of Japan, U.S. methods of knowledge production and dissemination are also in danger of becoming sterile. Whereas "detailed factual knowledge and highly developed analytical skills were once considered the earmarks of expertise," significant changes both in how work is organized and the nature of the work itself have changed the concept of expertise (Lynton, 1991, p. 15–16). That most faculty have lagged behind this understanding of the fundamental changes in the workplace is not surprising, since fountains of knowledge are not easily redirected. How this changing nature of the workplace and expertise should be reflected in professional education is, of course, the impetus for the Lewis & Clark core program and this book.

In chapter 2, Celeste Brody directs much of her attention to the concept of creating a professional "community," in opposition to the traditional focus of professional schools on expertise and specialization. Brody rejects professional models that objectify knowledge and isolate students into individual owners of knowledge. Rather than consider education an individual commodity to be owned, stored, and bartered at a later date for employment (Wexler, 1987), Brody encourages education to be a community endeavor. Because professionals work within socially constructed organizations, Brody explains that their professional education should give them "a model for their work life."

The graduate core program at Lewis & Clark exemplifies the quest for a model of community. Rather than "bank" knowledge in students' heads (Freire, 1970), the philosophy and pedagogy of the core program is to help students understand and reflect on their place within the larger social context. Whereas a majority of professors in academe continue to secure privilege by banking knowledge, professionals cannot afford such arrogance. Because social service professionals are immediately accountable to their constituencies, the faculty of the core program questions the relevancy of the present academic model for the reality of professional practice. At its root, the core program considers the predominant academic model of patriarchy to be especially problematic for those who have typically been marginalized in higher education—women and minorities.

How all professionals should be educated is, of course, the fundamental dilemma facing the core program and the authors of this text. Crucial to achieving a solution to this problem, as Brody and Wallace note in the Introduction, is recognition of the inherent tensions existing among professional knowledge, the social context, and the academy in which professionals are educated. The Lewis & Clark faculty conceived the core program as a model to seek balance among these tensions. Inherent in the creation of this model is the search for a commonly defined purpose and goal for professional education.

Purpose of Professional Education

According to Bledstein (1976, p. x), "By and large the American university came into existence to serve and promote professional authority in society." Having no official, aristocratic class, American universities were free to secure professional privilege. Not being landed gentry, Americans created and then attended universities as the route to class status and privilege. By controlling access to knowledge and to the professions, universities became the gatekeepers for class status and the creator of a "professional middle class" (see Wexler, 1987).

Although the educational role of many of its European ancestors was to transmit knowledge to the aristocracy, American universities had to struggle with balancing an education for life with one for work. Present institutional models do not acknowledge, however, that most students do have to work for a living. Rather than integrate the life of the mind with the life of work, in which almost all students will engage, the majority of institutions construct great barriers between an academic education and a professional one. Historically, the liberal arts fields have been considered more scholarly and, hence, more worthy than professional education. This model is derived from the classical conception of higher education for the privileged few. It is an institutional form developed for the education of nobles and priests. This is a classist, racist, and sexist model that excludes those individuals who are not free, by accident of birth, to afford such an education. Segregating life from work is only possible for aristocrats whose livelihood is supported on the backs of the underclasses. The vestiges of this anachronistic structure continue to be found in U.S. universities, as the authors of this book relate.

How to achieve a balance between an education of the mind and an education for the realities of work is the essential dilemma for the faculty of the core program. Rather than securing their own privilege by hiding in a traditional structure for professional education, the faculty sought to balance professional and liberal education. Rather than simply transmit knowledge, this faculty developed a community that honored and included those ideas and individuals marginalized from a classic, liberal arts education. Rather than segregate professional knowledge from academic knowledge, the faculty struggled to understand and integrate professional knowledge with the psychological, social, and cultural contexts in which this knowledge is applied. Following Gramsci's advice, they sought to "break down the wall between vocational and academic education" to bring students "to the threshold of work with a broadly based education in both aspects of school knowledge" (in Aronowitz and Giroux, 1985, p. 11).

The core faculty take seriously the concept of democracy. Their desire is not simply to transmit passive knowledge to their students but to create a democratic educational community for individual and social transformation. Within such a community knowledge is not static, but a living and developmental process in which both student and faculty are engaged in a critical pedagogy (Freire, 1970, Freire and Shor, 1987). The goal of the core faculty is to ground academic knowledge in the reality of the humanly constructed organizations in which professionals will find themselves. Such a grounding demands that democracy be effected between faculty and student, faculty and faculty, and student and student.

Traditional conceptions of higher education based on the ownership and transmission of knowledge perpetuate the patriarchal culture of academe by devaluing the other's knowledge, culture, and benefit to the democracy. Aronowitz and Giroux (1985, p. 49) explain: "Since critical thinking is the fundamental precondition for an autonomous and self-motivated public or citizenry, its decline would threaten the future of democratic social, cultural, and political forms." Because the Lewis & Clark core faculty understand this threat, it should be no surprise that they are guided by feminist and critical theories.

How the integration of liberal and professional education has been actualized in the core program is a thread that runs throughout the writings in this book. This discussion is not one engaged often, as Lynton (1991, p. 12) complains: "Rarely is there any discussion of ways in which liberal education can be provided within a professional school." Not only have the faculty of the core program discussed the "ways" of integrating liberal education, they have developed what Fay (1987, p. 33) calls a "theory of transformative action." Fay explains that a theory is not "critical" unless it proposes a plan of action or praxis that moves theory into action. True to the goals of critical science, the faculty of the core program have acted upon their theory of transformative action by asking both their students and themselves to reflect upon their pedagogy, their definitions of knowledge, and their mutual dialogue. "Critical science wishes its audience to reflect on the nature of its life, and to change those practices and policies which cannot be justified on the basis of this reflection" (Fay, 1987, p. 66). Similarly, the core program faculty wishes its students to reflect on the nature of their lives and their professional practice. To stimu-late this reflection Joanne Cooper (chapter 6) encourages the use of journals "if students are to reach some integration of personal and professional identity."

Achievement of the transformative goals of critical theory and action are possible, however, only by the participants themselves working from the inside out. As Lynton (1991, p. 12) explains, integration of liberal arts with professional education has typically been imposed from "outside." Unfortunately, external interventions typically dictate what package of liberal knowledge should be owned by the professional, rather than explore how such knowledge is integral to the students' ability to work within the external commu-nity. Lynton (p. 14) notes, as well, that if an integration between liberal and professional education is to be achieved, the professionals themselves need to understand that liberal education is "an integral component of professional competence" and in their "professional self-interest."

That a liberal education is in the students' professional self-interest is a perspective integral to the core program. Faculty and students in the program do indeed attend to what Lynton (p. 20) calls the "reciprocal relationship between the practice of a profession and its context." In fact, this is clearly the goal of the core program. In chapter 4 Brody and Witherell explain that with their students they draw upon the lessons from "critical and feminist theory, life-span psychology, anthropology and the humanities" to understand both "our daily lives and the institutions in which we work." For the core faculty and their students it is a journey of "self-discovery and meaning making," a search for their individual "voices." This is an especially important and liberating task for those individuals whose voices have always been the other in the dominant culture (Gilligan, 1982). This recognition of value in one's voice and one's identity is the transformative goal both for critical and feminist theorists and an integral component in the core program. The goal of professional education is transformation, not merely transmission, "acts of cognition, not transferrals of information" (Freire, 1970, p. 67). As Brody and Witherell explain: "We teach to change lives."

Changing lives critically and democratically is not easy. Lives can be altered externally, but real change must be internally motivated. In chapter 6, Cooper refers to a student's use of the Taoist metaphor, "waking the dragon within." In his journal the student used this metaphor to explain the role a teacher should play in stimulating students to awareness of their own potential through reflective writing. "Waking the dragon" is an apt metaphor for the goals of the professional core program. Waking students to the power and dignity of their own voices and to the voices of the other is the goal of the "authentic recognition" Shor and Freire (1987) seek for education. This recognition accords respect to the other and is integral to a nonpatriarchal education, the goal of integrating liberal arts into the professions at Lewis & Clark.

Waking the dragon is risky, however. Critical reflection is quite uncomfortable for those not wishing to be disturbed. All the faculty were not enamored with the purposes, goals, and methods of the core program. The sanctity of individual programs and faculty independence were immediately jeopardized with initiation of the core program.

Consequences

Once the dragon was disturbed at Lewis & Clark the initiators of the core program did their best to control the anxiety of the faculty, especially the most reluctant ones. A strategy during the formative stages of the program's development was to conduct a faculty retreat on the evaluation of the program. I assisted in designing this evaluation and in facilitating the retreat with another faculty member and several consultants. The purpose of the retreat was to discuss the philosophy of the core, present findings from the evaluation, and to consider future plans for the core. In retrospect, I am not entirely certain I would agree again to help wake the dragon. The retreat was not altogether a pleasant experience, but, fortunately, time seems to have exhibited a healing effect.

Becoming part of a community, the antithesis of academe, was painful for many of the faculty. As Carolyn Bullard notes in chapter 14, "We could no longer see ourselves as just a group of programs thrust together by political accident." The faculty were accustomed to the meaning of their individual programs, but making sense of professional education across programs was a question not all the faculty would have chosen to entertain.

Participation in the core program compelled faculty, many for the first time, to consider interdisciplinary contexts, sources of knowledge, faculty development and organizational culture—the themes of this book. These themes challenged many of the faculty members' conceptions of self and of profession. The core program asked them to share, question, and create knowledge—a difficult task for those who saw their role as the transmitters of culture. In Bullard's assessment of the core, she notes its "most pervasive influence" has been questioning what constitutes knowledge and the faculty's role in the development of this knowledge. She explains, "The core has provided a vehicle, a purpose, and a common language for sharing our notions of knowledge."

The core plays a significant role in encouraging faculty to develop what Ault terms a "common interpretive framework"—personal reflection that considers the "functioning of a democratic citizenry" (chapter 9). If the goal of the core is to help students understand the inherent tensions between professional knowledge and the context of their practice, the faculty must speak from a common framework. As the authors throughout this book affirm, this framework is one based on community. While most of the faculty speak from this framework, not all could make the transition from a patriarchal conception of academe to one of community.

Even though participation in the core program required a commitment greater than simply sharing syllabi, Rusch (1989) did find that only three out of the thirty faculty she interviewed had "serious" reservations about the viability of the core program. She noted in her assessment of faculty perceptions during the formative stages of the core that concerns were not only philosophical ones. Reconceiving graduate education is costly both in time and money. Many faculty perceived professional education as a threat to the resources for undergraduate education, the primary mission of Lewis & Clark College. Rusch found, as well, that support of the core program was not politically wise for some faculty members. Tensions over the core existed not only between liberal arts and professional faculty but among the professional faculty themselves. Some professional faculty found that the core threatened their ability to induct students into the "guild" of the profession. These faculty did not gladly give up their precious course hours to the core.

In addition to concerns regarding time and money, Rusch found that not all the faculty in 1989 understood well the intended outcomes of the core nor did they have mutual ownership in the community of learners. Rusch recommended increased attention be given to: communications among faculty, administration and program support, instructional and program development, and continued evaluation of faculty and students. In the subsequent years each of these issues has been critical in developing community among the faculty.

In addition to Rusch's formal assessment, the faculty has continually reviewed the student evaluations of core courses to understand the consequences of the program. For example, in 1989 Brody prepared a summary from the student evaluations of the basic core classes and from additional written feedback on the overall core program. The majority of the students were positive in their assessment of core courses and reflected on the climate of "openness and trust." Brody grouped the concerns students expressed into the following areas: curriculum, variations in pedagogy, classroom climate, course readings, grading, and team teaching. Based on her findings Brody recommended core classes be limited to thirty students, the requirements of the core be reconsidered (i.e., number of courses, hours per course, content), and further evaluation of current and former students regarding the nature of the core and the courses be conducted. The success the core program has in preparing students for their professional practice and for their membership in the democracy will be the ultimate determinants of the core's effectiveness.

The Meaning of Professional Education

The transformative process described here is a quest worthy of the adventures recounted in great novels or blockbuster movies. We can literally picture our heroes waking the dragon and then narrowly escaping the clutches of positivism. They save the villagers by building communities that liberate the voices of the others while overcoming sexism and racism. Throughout this adventure the faculty, along with their students, demonstrate their wisdom by engaging in self-reflection and pondering how to live their lives.

Although a great adventure is a metaphor based typically on overpowering some foe, we might better think of the "journey" of the core program, as Brody and Wallace describe it, as an intellectual adventure whose goal is integration, not domination. Rather than conquer and possess knowledge, the faculty conceive the goal of professional education as a transformative one. Education is not a commodity to be owned, but a liberating influence. Freire (1970, p. 71) explains that this liberating concept of education is based on individuals' ability "to perceive critically the way they exist in the world with which and in which they find themselves." Similarly, the goal for the core faculty is to have students understand themselves and their professional practice in relation to the psychological, social, and cultural context in which they work. By engaging in such reflective action the students confront not only the fundamental question of how they should live their individual lives, but, as Morgan notes (chapter 1), how *we* should live our lives.

Rather than possess knowledge only for the self, the goal of the core program is to have students conceive of knowledge for the collective. Although individualism is an inherent characteristic both of the American culture and the educational system (Bellah et al., 1985), the core program focuses on knowledge and behaviors that emphasize the welfare of the group. A more collectivistic orientation is distinguished from an individualistic one based on the cultural attitudes toward cooperation, competition, and perceptions of self (Hofstede 1980; Triandis 1989). Individuals do not exhibit only individualistic or collectivistic behaviors, but exhibit varying degrees of individualism and collectivism on the basis of their gender, age, race, ethnicity, personality, and culture. The goal for the core program is to increase students' awareness of their orientations, the effect of the larger culture, and the organizations in which they find themselves.

In chapter 2 Brody contends that a responsibility of higher education is to create structures that offer students a model of collective behavior and of community. Through this experience, Brody notes, students will not only become better organizational citizens, but more able to understand the meaning and purpose of their professional practice. This life-developmental task of understanding the meaning of one's work and one's place in the larger cultural context is central to the experience of the core program.

A professional program whose goal is to build community and to engage students in self-reflection requires faculty commitment to such goals. Perhaps the most formidable barrier to enacting a professional core is having a faculty whose "unbridled passion for specialization and higher prestige" (Cuban in Brody, chapter 2) is greater than their sense of community. Because the reward structure for faculty at major research universities, in particular, is based on ownership of specialized knowledge and not on community, a professional core may only be possible in certain institutions. Although the effect of Lewis & Clark's size and private status on the core is not specifically explored in this book, we are left to wonder how probable the success of a professional core might be in a large, public institution. In institutions where faculty are fountains of knowledge and education is simple transmission of culture, could a professional core ever be established and succeed? A principal outcome of the professional core is that it offers a model of community not easily duplicated in traditional institutions of higher education. Other attempts at integrating liberal arts into the professions have been successful, but few have attempted a transformation on the order of Lewis & Clark's core.

The journey to which the authors of this book introduce us is by no means over. The search for meaning is a continuous one, both for students and for faculty. Students are always graduating, faculty are continually aging, and the cultural context is forever changing.

Not only is the core program a model of community, it is a model for life. Much of its success can be attributed to the faculty's passion for seeking the meaning of their professional and personal lives. The core program attempts to be transformative and liberating, a nonpatriarchal education where teacher and student are engaged in mutual learning. When professors understand that education is a search *with* students for meaning, there is no arrogance over ownership of esoteric, temporal knowledge. The Lewis & Clark faculty's quest for personal and professional meaning with their students is perhaps the greatest gift the core program has to offer.

References

Aisenberg, N., and Harrington, M. (1988). *Women of academe: Outsiders in the sacred grove.* Amherst: University of Massachusetts Press.

Allen, Paula Gunn. (1986). *The sacred hoop: Recovering the feminine in American Indian traditions.* Boston: Beacon Press.

Alpert, J., and Conoley, J. C. (1988). Mainstreaming psychology of women with school psychology. *Professional School Psychology,* 3:1–3.

Amin, S. (1989). *Eurocentrism.* New York: Monthly Review Press.

Apple, Michael W. (1992). Educational reform and educational crisis. *Journal of Research in Science Teaching,* 29(8):779–89.

———(1993). *Official Knowledge.* New York: Routledge.

———(1986). Curriculum, Capitalism and Democracy: A Response to Whitty's Critics. *British Journal of Sociology of Education,* 7(3).

———(1986). *Teachers and texts.* New York: Routledge and Kegan Paul.

Aptheker, Bettina. (1989). *Tapestries of life: Women's work, women's consciousness, and the meaning of daily life.* Amherst: University of Massachusetts Press.

Arendt, Hannah. (1959). *The human condition.* New York: Doubleday.

Argyris, Chris, and Schon, Donald (1974). *Theory in practice: Increasing professional effectiveness.* San Francisco: Jossey-Bass.

Aronowitz, Stanley, and Giroux, Henry. (May 1988). Review of *The closing of the American mind,* by A. Bloom and *Cultural literacy* by E. Hirsch. *Harvard Educational Review.* 52:172.

———(1985). *Education under siege.* New York: Bergen and Garvey.

Aslanian, C. B., and Brickell, H. M. (1980). *Americans in transition: Life changes as reasons for adult learning.* New York: College Entrance Examination Board.

Baier, Annette C. (1987). Hume, the women's moral theorist? In Kittay, E. F. and Meyers, D. T. (Eds.). *Women and moral theory.* Lanham, MD: Rowman and Littlefield.

259

Baldwin, James. (1962). *The fire next time.* New York: Dell Books.

Baldwin, Christina. (1977). *One to one: Self-understanding through journal writing.* New York: M. Evans and Co.

Barry, Kathleen. (1992). Toward a theory of women's biography: From the life of Susan B. Anthony. In Teresa Iles, *All sides of the subject: Women and biography.* New York: Teachers College Press.

Bateson, Mary Catherine. (1990). *Composing a life.* New York: Plume.

Baumrin, B., and Freedman, B., eds. (1982). *Moral responsibility and the professions.* New York: Haven Publications.

Belenky, Mary; Clinchy, Blythe; Goldberger, Nancy; and Tarule, Jill. (1986). *Women's ways of knowing: The development of self, voice and mind.* New York: Basic Books.

Bellah, Robert; Madsen, Richard; Sullivan, William; Sideler, Ann; and Tipton, Steven. (1985). *Habits of the heart: Individualism and commitment in American life.* Berkeley: University of California Press.

Bellah, Robert; Madsen, Richard; Sullivan, William; and Tipton, Steven. (1991). The good society. *America* 165(4).

Bellah, R.; Madsen, R.; Sullivan, W. M.; Swidler, A.; and Tipton, S. M. (1991). *The good society.* New York: Alfred A. Knopf.

Benhabib, Seyla, and Cornell, Druceilla, eds. (1987). *Feminism as critique.* Minneapolis: University of Minnesota Press.

Benjamin, Martin. (1990). *Splitting the difference: compromise and integrity in ethics and politics.* Lawrence: University Press of Kansas.

Bennett, William J. (1984). *To reclaim a legacy: A report on the humanities in higher education.* Washington, D.C.: National Endowment for the Humanities.

Berger, P.L. and Luckman T. (1966). *The social construction of reality.* Garden City, NJ.: Doubleday.

Berthoff, Ann. (1981). *The making of meaning.* Portsmouth, NH: Boynton Cook.

Bloch, E. (1986). *Natural Law and Human Dignity.* Translated by Dennis J. Schmidt. Cambridge, MA: MIT Press.

Best, N.E. (1990). *The Celebration of Work.* Lincoln, NE: The University of Nebraska.

Bloom, Allen. (1987). *The closing of the American mind.* New York: Simon & Schuster.

Bly, Robert. (1990). *Iron John.* New York: Harper & Row.

———(1988). *A little book on the human shadow*. San Francisco: Harper & Row.

Bolman, Lee G., and Deal, Terrence E. (1991). *Reframing organizations*. San Francisco and Oxford: Jossey-Bass.

Bourdieu, P., and Passeron, J.C. (1977). *Reproduction in Education, Society and Culture*. Beverly Hills, CA: Sage Publications.

Bowen, Eleanor. (1964). *Return to laughter*. New York: Doubleday.

Brody, Celeste, and Witherell, Carol. (1987). Individual and societal perspectives on adulthood. Course syllabus. (Available from the authors at Lewis & Clark College, Graduate School of Professional Studies, Portland, OR 97219).

Brody, Celeste, and Schmuck, Patricia. (1992). Individual, ethical and organizational development. A course syllabus. Unpublished paper. Portland, OR: Lewis & Clark College.

Brookfield, Stephen. (1990). Using critical incidents to explore learners' assumptions. In Jack Mezirow and Associates. *Fostering critical reflection in adulthood*. San Francisco: Jossey-Bass.

———(1986). *Understanding and facilitating adult learning*. San Francisco: Jossey-Bass.

Browlee, Paul A. P. (August 1992). Speech to the Association of American Colleges, University of Rochester, in Faculty News, University of Hawaii Professional Assembly.

Bruffee, Kenneth J. (1985). *A short course in writing* (3rd ed.). Boston: Little, Brown.

———(1984): Collaborative learning and the "Conversations of Mankind," *College English*, 46(7): 635–652.

Bruner, Jerome. (1986). *Actual minds, possible worlds*. Cambridge, MA: Harvard University Press.

———(1983). *In search of mind: Essays in autobiography*. New York: Harper & Row.

Buber, Martin. (1965). *Between man and man*. New York: Macmillan.

Campbell, Richmond, and Sowden, Lanning, eds. (1985). *Paradoxes of rationality and cooperation*. Vancouver: University of British Columbia Press.

Canfield, Dorothy. (1945). Sex education. Reprinted from *Four-Square*. New York: Harcourt, Brace and World.

Chickering, Arthur. (1981). *The modern American college*. San Francisco: Jossey-Bass.

Chomsky, Noam. (1989). Necessary illusion: *Thought control in democratic societies.* Boston: South End Press.

———(1988). *Manufacturing consent: The political economy of the mass media.* New York: Pantheon Books.

———(1987). *On power and ideology.* Boston: South End Press.

Chronicle of Higher Education (December 4, 1991; January 22, 1992).

Clinchy, Blythe M. (1990). Issues of gender in teaching and learning. *Journal on excellence in college teaching,* 1:522–567.

Cohen, Elizabeth. (1986). *Designing groupwork: Strategies for the heterogeneous classroom.* New York: Teachers College Press.

Coles, Robert. (1988). *The call of stories: Te aching and the moral imagination.* Boston: Houghton Mifflin.

Commission on Minority Participation in Education and American Life. *One-third of a nation.* Washington, D.C.: American Council on Education.

Connelly, F. Michael, and Clandinin, Jean. (1990). Stories of experience and narrative inquiry. *Educational Researcher,* 19(4):2–13.

Cooper, J. L.; Prescott, S.; Cook, L.; Smith, S.; Mueck, R.; and Cuseo, J. (1990). *Cooperative learning and college instruction: Effective use of student learning teams.* Long Beach, CA: Institute of Teaching and Learning.

Cooper, J. L., and Muech, R. (1990). Student involvement in learning: Cooperative learning and college instruction. In *Journal on Excellence in College Teaching,* 1:68–76.

Cooper, Joanne, and Dunlap, Diane (Autumn 1991). Journal keeping for administrators, *The Review of Higher Education,* 15(1):65–82.

Cooper, T. (1991). *An ethic of citizenship for bureaucrats.* Englewood Cliffs, NJ: Prentice Hall.

Cortes, C. A. (1990). Pluribus unum and the American future. *Today.* IV(3).

Cremin, Lawrence A. (1989). *Popular education and its discontents.* New York: Harper & Row.

Cross, Patricia. (1981). *Adults as learners: Increasing participation and facilitating learning.* San Francisco: Jossey-Bass.

Cuban, Larry. (1992). Managing dilemmas while building professional communities. In *Educational Researcher,* 21(1):4–11.

Cuseo, Joe. (1992). *Cooperative learning: A pedagogy for diversity.* In *Cooperative Learning and College Teaching.* 3(1):2–6.

D'Souza, Dinesh. (1991). *Illiberal education: The politics of race and sex on campus.* New York: Free Press.

Darder, A. (1991). *Culture and power in the classroom.* New York: Bergin and Garvey.

Darnnell, Rezneat M. (1976). *Impacts of construction activities in wetlands of the United States.* Tereco Corporation, College Station, Texas. U.S. Environmental Protection Agency [EPA] report 600/3-76-045.

Darwall, Stephen L. (1983) *Impartial reason.* Ithaca and London: Cornell University Press.

Denhart, Robert B. (1984). *Theories of public organization.* Monterey, CA: Brooks/Coles.

Dewey, John. (1930). *Human nature and conduct: An introduction to social psychology.* New York: Modern Library.

———(1938). *Experience and education.* New York: Macmillan.

———(1916). *Democracy and education.* New York: Macmillan.

Domhoff, W. (1986). *Who rules America now? A view for the eighties.* New York: Simon & Schuster.

DuBois, W. E. B. (1975). *Color and democracy: Colonies and peace.* New York: Kraus-Thompson.

Eisner, Elliott. (1979) *The educational imagination.* New York: Macmillan.

Elbow, Peter (1986). *Embracing contraries: Explorations in teaching and learning.* New York: Oxford University Press.

Etzioni, Amitai, ed. (1969). *The semi-professions and their organization.* New York: Free Press.

Fay, B. (1987). *Critical Science: Liberation and its limits.* Ithaca, NY: Cornell University Press.

Fishman, P. M. (1983). Interaction: The work women do. In B. Thorne, C. Kramarae, and N. Henley eds., *Language, gender, and society.* 89–101. New York: Newbury House.

Fleming, Reg. (1986a). Adolescent reasoning in socio-scientific issues, part I: Social cognition. *Journal of Research in Science Teaching,* 23(8): 677–87.

———(1986b). Adolescent reasoning in socio-scientific issues, part II: Nonsocial cognition. *Journal of Research in Science Teaching,* 23(8), 689-98.

Folk-Williams, J. (March 1979, April 1979). On being non-Indian. *Foundation News,* 15–20.

Foucault, M. (1977). *Power / knowledge: Selected interviews and other writings.* New York: Pantheon Books.

Frank, Anne. (1978). *Diary of a young girl.* New York: Random House.

Freire, Paulo. (1970). *Pedagogy of the oppressed*. New York: Herder and Herder.

Freire, Paulo, and Shor, I. (1987). *A pedagogy for liberation*. South Hadley, MA: Bergin and Garvey Publishers.

Fuentes, Carlos. (1988). In R. Simonson and S. Walker. *Multicultural literacy*. Saint Paul, MN: Gray Wolf Press.

Gabelnick, Faith; MacGregor, Jean; Matthews, Roberta S.; and Smith, Barbara L. (1990). *Learning communities: Creating connections among students, faculty and disciplines*. San Francisco: Jossey-Bass.

Galeano, E. (1988). In R. Simonson and S. Walker. *Multicultural literacy*. Saint Paul, MN: Gray Wolf Press.

Gannett, Cinthia. (1992). *Gender and the journal*. Albany: State University of New York Press.

Garcia, R. I. (1991). *Teaching in a pluralistic society: Concepts, models, strategies* (2nd ed.), New York: Harper Collins.

Gauthier, David. (1986). *Morals by agreement*. Oxford University Press.

Gibbard, Allan. (1990). *Wise choices, apt feelings*. Cambridge, MA: Harvard University Press.

Gilligan, C. (1982). *In a different voice: Psychological theory and women's development*. Cambridge, MA: Harvard University Press.

Gilligan, C.; Lyons, N. P.; and Hanmer, T. J., eds. (1990). *Making connections: The relational worlds of adolescent girls at Emma Willard school*. Cambridge, MA: Harvard University Press.

Gilman, Carol P. (1988). The home (1903). In J. Donovan (ed.), *Feminist theory: The intellectual traditions of American feminism*, 45-48. New York: Continuum.

Giroux, Henry. (1992). Educational leadership and the crisis of democratic government. *Educational Research* (May 1992), pp. 4 11.

———(1988). *Schooling and the struggle for public life: Critical pedagogy in the modern age*. Minneapolis: University of Minnesota Press.

Giroux, H., et al., eds. (1981) *Curriculum & Instruction: Alternatives in Education*. Berkeley, CA: McCutchin.

Gless, D. J., and Smith, B. H. (1992). *The politics of liberal education*. Durham, NC: Duke University Press.

Gomez-Pena, G. (1988). In R. Simonson and S. Walker. *Multicultural literacy*. Saint Paul, MN: Gray Wolf Press.

Goodsell, Anne; Maher, Michelle; Tinto, Vincent; Smith, Barbara L.; MacGregor,

Jean. (1992). *Collaborative learning: A sourcebook for higher educa-tion.* University Park, PA.: National Center on Postsecondary Teaching, Learning & Assessment.

Gowin, D. Bob. (1981). *Educating.* Ithaca: Cornell University Press.

Graduate School of Professional Studies. (1986). *Graduate catalog.* Portland, OR: Lewis & Clark College.

Graff, Gerald. (1992). Teach the conflicts. In *The politics of liberal education.* Darryl J. Glass and Barbara Herrnstein Smith (eds.). Durham, NC: Duke University Press.

Gramsci, A. (1971). *Selections from prison notebooks.* New York: International Publications.

Graves, Donald. (1983). *Language and children's learning.* Portsmouth, NH: Heinemann Press.

Grumet, Madeleine R. (1991). The politics of personal knowledge. In *Stories lives tell: Narrative and dialogue in education.* New York: Teachers College Press. 67–78.

———(1987). Pedagogy for patriarchy: The feminization of teaching. *Interchange* 12, 165–184.

Gudmundsdottir, Sigrun. (April 1991). The narrative nature of pedagogical content knowledge. Paper presented at the annual meeting of the American Educational Research Association, Chicago.

Habermas, J. (1973). *Theory and practice.* Boston: Beacon Press.

Hardin, Garrett. (1968). The tragedy of the commons. *Science,* 162(1);243–48.

Harding, Sandra. (1991). *Whose science? Whose knowledge?* Ithaca: Cornell University Press.

———(1987). *Feminism and methodology.* Bloomington: Indiana University Press.

Hargeaves, A. (1992). Cultures of teaching. In I. Goodson and S. Ball (eds.), *Teachers' lives.* Boston: Routledge & Kegan Paul.

Harris, A.; Ingraham, C.; and Lam, M. K. (in press). Teacher expectations for female and male school-based consultants. *Journal of Educational and Psychological Consultation,* 4.

Harrison, Benjamin, ed. (1992). *Environmental assessment: Tualatin River National Wildlife Refuge.* Portland, OR: U. S. Fish and Wildlife Service, Region 1.

Harrison, R. (1972). Understanding your organization's character. *Harvard Business Review.* 50(1) January-February: 119–28.

Haskell, Thomas L., ed. (1984) *The authority of experts: studies in history and theory.* Bloomington: Indiana University Press.

Hastings Center (1987). *The professions: The public interest and the common good.* by B. Jennings, D. Callahan, and S. M. Wolf. Hastings-on-the Hudson, NY: Hastings Center.

Heilbrun, Carolyn. (1988). *Writing a woman's life.* New York: Ballentine Books.

Held, Virginia. (1987). Feminism and moral theory. In Kittay, Eva Feder, and Meyers, Diane T. (Eds.) *Women and moral theory.* Lanham, MD: Rowman and Littlefield.

Hirsch, E. D. (1987). *Cultural literacy.* New York: Houghton Mifflin.

Hollingsworth, Sandra. (1992). Learning to teach through collaborative conversation. In American *Educational Research Journal,* 29(2): 373–404.

Hooks, B. (1990). Yearning: *Race, gender, and cultural politics.* Boston: South End Press.

————(1988). Straightening our hair. *Z Magazine* (September 1988), 33–37.

Hoshmand, L. T., and Polkinghorne, D. E. (1992). Redefining the scientist-practice relationship and professional training. *American Psychologist,* 47(1):55–66.

House, David B. (1991). *Continuing liberal education.* New York: National University Continuing Education Association, Macmillan Publishing Co.

Hughes, Robert. (1993). *The Culture of Complaint: The Fraying of America.* New York: Oxford University Press.

Hummel, R. (1987). *The bureaucratic experience* (3rd ed.). New York: St. Martin's Press.

Ignatieff, M. (1984). *The needs of strangers.* New York: Viking.

Jacobs, Harriet. (1861). *Incidents in the life of a slave girl.* Cambridge, MA: Harvard University Press.

Johnson, David, W.; Johnson, Roger, T.; and Maruymama, G. (1983). Interdependence and interpersonal attraction among heterogeneous and homogeneous individuals: A theoretical formulation and a meta-analysis of the research. *Review of Educational Research,* 53: 5–54.

Johnson, David W.; Johnson, Roger T.; Smith, Karl A. (1991). *Active learning: Cooperation in the college classroom.* Edina, MN.: Interaction Book Company.

Johnson, H. (1991). *Sleepwalking through history: America in the Reagan years.* New York: Norton.

Kant, Immanuel. (1963). *Lectures on ethics*. Indianapolis: Hackett Publishing Company.

Kanter, R. M. (1977). *Men and women in the corporation*. New York: Basic Books.

Keen, Sam. (1988). The stories we live by. *Psychology Today,* 22(12): 46–47.

Kegan, Robert. (1982). *The evolving self. Problems and process in human development*. Cambridge, MA: Harvard University Press.

Keller, E. F. (1985). *Reflections on gender and science*. New Haven: Yale University Press.

———(1983). *A feeling for the organism: The life and work of Barbara McClintock*. New York: Freeman.

Kelly, George. (1955). *A theory of personality*. New York: Norton.

Kersey, S. N. (1981). *Classics in the education of girls and women*. Metuchen, NJ: Scarecrow Press.

Kittay, Eva Feder and Meyers, Diane T., eds. (1987). *Women and moral theory*. Lanham, MD: Rowman and Littlefield.

Klein, Edward and Erickson, Don, eds. (1988). *About men*. New York: Pocket Books.

Kohlberg, Lawrence. (1981). *The philosophy of moral development*. San Francisco: Harper & Row.

Kuhn, Thomas. (1970). *The structure of scientific revolutions* (2nd ed.). Chicago: University of Chicago Press.

Larson, M. (1977). *The rise of professions: A sociological analysis*. Berkeley: University of California Press.

Lewin, Kurt. (1948). *Resolving social conflicts*. New York: Harper's.

Lieberman, Ann. (1992). The meaning of scholarly activity and the building of community. *In Educational Researcher,* 21(6): 5–12.

Lipsky, M. (1980). *Street-level bureaucracy: Dilemmas of the individual in public service*. New York: Russell Sage Foundation.

Lorde, Audre. (1984). *Sister outsider*. Freedom, CA: Crossing Press.

Louis, M.R. (1990). Acculturation in the workplace: Newcomers as lay ethnographers. In B. Schneider (ed.), *Organizational climate and culture,* 85-129. San Francisco: Jossey-Bass.

Lukinsky, Joseph (1990). Reflective withdrawal through journal writing. In Jack Mezirow and Associates. *Fostering critical reflection in adulthood*. San Francisco: Jossey-Bass.

Lusted, D. (1986). Why pedagogy? *Screen.* 17(5):2–14.

Lynch, J. (1989). *Multicultural education in a global society.* Colham, Bristol: Falmer Press.

Lynton, E. A. (1991). *New Priorities for Universities: Meeting Society's Needs for Applied Knowledge and Competent Individuals.* San Francisco: Jossey-Bass.

Lyons, Nona. (1990). Dilemmas of knowing: Ethical and epistemological dimensions of teachers' work and development. In *Harvard Educational Review,* 60(2):159–80.

———(1983). On self, relationships and morality. *Harvard Educational Review* 53:125–45.

MacPherson, C. B. (1962). *The political theory of possessive individualism.* New York: Oxford University Press.

Maine, Neal. (1992). Ecology centers in the public schools. *The Ecological Society of America: News from the Education Section,* 3(1):11–13.

Mander, J. (1991). What You Don't Know About Indians. *Utne Reader* (November–December 1991).

Mann, Lawrence R. (1988). The prospects for general education in university professional education. In Ian Westbury and Alan Purves (Eds.). *Cultural literacy and the idea of general education.* Chicago: National Society for the Study of Education.

Marshall, Stephanie P. (1992). We must help create a learning community. In *Update,* 34 (6). Alexandria, VA: Association for Supervision and Curriculum Development.

Martin, Jane Roland. (1987). Transforming moral education. *Journal of Moral Education,* 16, no. 3.

———(1985). Becoming educated: A journey of alienation or integration? *Journal of Education,* 167(3).

McConnell-Ginet, S.; Borker, R.; and Furman, N., eds. (1980). *Women and language in literature and society.* New York: Praeger.

McPhee, John. (1989). *The control of nature.* New York: Noonday Press.

Mead, George H. (1934). *Mind, self and society.* Chicago: University of Chicago Press.

Mead, M. (1972). *Twentieth century faith, hope, and survival.* New York: Harper & Row.

Means, R. (1992). Public lecture on Native Americans at the Colorado State University.

Memmi, A. (1967). *The colonizer and the colonized.* Boston: Beacon Press.

Merton, Thomas. (1990). *The seven story mountain.* San Diego: Harcourt Brace Jovanovich.

Metzger, Deena. (1986). *Circles of stories.* Parabola, IV(4). Original work published in 1969.

Meyers, Diane T. (1987). The socialized individual and individual autonomy: An intersection between philosophy and psychology. In Kittay, Eva Feder and Meyers, Diane T. (eds.). (1987). *Women and moral theory.* Lanham, MD: Rowman and Littlefield.

Meyers, J. (1988). School psychology: The current state of practice and future practice of the specialty. *Professional School Psychology, 3,* 165–76.

Mezirow, Jack, and Associates. (1990). How critical reflection triggers transformative learning. In Jack Mezirow and Associates. *Fostering critical reflection in adulthood.* San Francisco: Jossey-Bass.

Miller, Alan. (1985). Cognitive styles and environmental problem solving. *International Journal of Environmental Studies, 26,* 21–31.

Miller, G. Tyler, Jr. (1991). *Environmental science: Sustaining the Earth* (3rd ed). Belmont, CA: Wadsworth.

Miller, Janet. (1990). *Creating spaces and finding voices: Teachers collaborating for empowerment.* Albany: State University of New York Press.

Milne, A. A. (1970). *The house at pooh corner.* New York: Dell.

Morgan, D. (November 1987). Varieties of administrative abuse: Some reflections on ethics and discretion. *Administration and Society,* 19:267–84.

Morrison, Tony. (1987). *Beloved.* New York: New American Library.

Mow, Shanny. (undated). How do you dance without music? Unpublished manuscript. Portland, OR: Lewis & Clark College.

Murphy, Richard. (1979). You scratch my back I'll scratch yours. *In Unit VI: Marine ecology.* Los Angeles: Institute for Marine and Coastal Studies, Sea Grant Program, University of Southern California.

Myerhoff, Barbara. (1978). *Number our days.* New York: Simon & Schuster.

National Endowment for the Humanities Fellowships: Guidelines & Application forms (1986).

Nagel, Thomas. (1970). *The possibility of altruism.* Oxford: Oxford University Press.

National Commission on Excellence in Education. (1983). *A nation at risk*. Washington, D.C.: Government Printing Office.

Noddings. (February 1988). An ethic of caring and it's implications for instructional arrangements. *American Journal of Education*, pp. 215–30.

Noddings, Nel. (1986). Fidelity in teaching, teacher education, and research for teaching. *Harvard Educational Review*, 56(4):496–510.

———(1984). *Caring: A feminine approach to ethics and moral education*. Berkeley: University of California Press.

Norris, C. (1991). *Deconstruction: Theory and Practice*. New York: Routledge.

Nosow, S. and Form, W., eds. (1962). *Man, work and society*. New York: Basic Books.

Nussbaum, Martha C. (1990). *Love's knowledge: Essays on philosophy and literature*. New York and Oxford: Oxford University Press.

Olsen, Tillie. (1976). I stand here ironing. In *Tell me a riddle*. New York: Dell Books. Original work published 1956.

Orians, Gordon H., ed. (1986a). *Ecological knowledge and environmental problem solving*. Report of the National Research Council's [NRC] Committee on the Application of Ecological Theory to Environmental Problems. Washington, D. C.: National Academy Press.

———(1986b). The place of science in environmental problem solving. *Environment*, 28(9):12–41.

Ostrom, Elinor. (1990). *Governing the commons: The evolution of institutions for collective action*. Cambridge, MA: Cambridge University Press.

———(March 1987). Institutional arrangements and the commons dilemma. Paper presented at the Annual Meeting of the Public Choice Society, Tucson.

Ozick, Cynthia. (May 1986). The moral necessity of metaphor. *Harper's Magazine*, pp.64–65.

———(1983). Usurpation (Other People's Stories). In *Bloodshed and three novellas*. New York: E. P. Dutton/Obelisk. Original work published 1976.

Palincear, Annemarie S.; Stevens, Dannelle D. L; and Gavelek, James R. (1988). Collaborating in the interest of collaborative learning. Paper presented at the annual meeting of the American Educational Research Association, New Orleans.

Parenti, M. (1991). *Make-believe media: The politics of entertainment*. New York: Saint Martin's Press.

Parfit, Derek. (1984). *Reasons and persons.* Oxford: Oxford University Press.

Pepi, David. (1985). Making nature satisfy. In *Thoreau's method: A handbook for nature study.* Englewood Cliffs, NJ: Prentice Hall.

Piaget, Jean. (1954). *The construction of reality in the child.* New York: Basic Books. Originally published in 1937.

————(1952). *The origins of intelligence in children.* New York: International Universities Press. Originally published in 1936.

Pilisuk, Mark, and Parks, Susan Hilliard. (1986). *The healing web: Social network and human survival.* Hanover, NH: University Press of New England.

Porty, Amelie Oksengerg, ed. (1980). *Essays on Aristotle's ethics.* Berkeley: University of California Press.

Pradl, Gordon. (1990). Collaborative learning and mature dependency. In M. Brubacher, R. Payne, and K. Rickett (eds.), *Perspectives on small group learning.* Oakville, Ontario, Canada: Ribicon Publishing.

Quality Education For Minorities Project. (1990). *Education that works.* Cambridge: M. I. T. Press.

Ramirez, M., and Castaneda, A. (1974). *Cultural democracy: Bicognitive development and education.* New York: Academic Press.

Rawls, John. (1971). *A theory of justice.* Cambridge, MA: Harvard University Press.

Regan, H. B. (1990). Not for women only: School administration as a feminist activity. *Teachers College Record, 91*(4), 565–77.

Reisman, Marc. (1986). *Cadillac desert.* New York: Penguin Books.

Rogers, Carl. (1961). *On becoming a person.* Boston: Houghton Mifflin.

Rohr, J. (1989). *Ethics for bureaucrats.* New York: Marcel Dekker (2nd ed.).

Rorty, Richard. (1979). *Philosophy and the mirror of nature.* Princeton, NJ: Princeton University Press.

Rosaldo, R. (1990). *The Stanford Observer.* Stanford University, CA.

Rowe, Mary Budd. (1978). *Teaching science as continuous inquiry:* New York: McGraw-Hill.

Rusch, Edith. (1989). External evaluation on the Core Program. Lewis & Clark College. Unpublished report.

Sadker, M., Sadker, D., and Kline, S. (1991). The issue of gender in elementary and secondary education. In Grant (ed.), *Review of Research in Education, 17*:269–334. Washington, D.C.: American Educational Reearch Association.

Sapon-Shevin, Mara. (1990). Cooperative learning: Liberatory praxis or hamburger helper? How we collude in our own disempowerment. A paper presented at the annual meeting of the Amerian Educational Research Association, Boston.

Schaef, Anne W. (1981). *Women's reality: An emerging female system in a white male society.* San Francisco: Harper & Row.

Schein, E. H. (1985). *Organizational culture and leadership.* San Francisco: Jossey-Bass.

Schlesinger, Arthur, Jr. (1992). *The disuniting of America: Reflections on a multicultural society.* New York: Norton.

Schmidt, M. R. (1992). Alternative kinds of knowledge and why they are ignored. *Proceedings of the fifth annual symposium of the public administration theory network,* Chicago, pp. 75–86.

Schmuck, P. A., ed. (1987). *Women educators: Employees of schools in western countries.* Albany: State University of New York Press.

Schmuck, Richard, A., and Schmuck, Patricia, A. (1992). *Small group processes in the classroom* (6th ed). Dubuque, IA: Wm. C. Brown Publishers.

Schon, Donald. (1988). Coaching reflective teaching. In Peter Grimmett and Gaalen Erickson (eds.). *Reflection in teacher education.* New York: Teachers College Press.

———(1987). *Educating the reflective practitioner.* San Francisco: Jossey-Bass.

———(1983). *The reflective practitioner: How professionals think in action.* New York: Basic Books.

Sharan, Yael, and Sharan, Shlomo. (1992). *Expanding cooperative learning through group investigation.* Albany: State University of New York Press.

Shor, Ira, and Freire, Paulo. (1987). *A pedagogy for liberation: Dialogues for transforming education.* South Hadley, MA: Bergin and Garvey.

Shor, Ira. (1986). *Culture wars: School and society in the conservative restoration, 1969–1984.* Boston: Routledge and Kegan Paul.

Sidgwick, Henry (1966). *The methods of ethics.* New York: Dover.

Slavin, Robert. (1989). *School and classroom organization.* Hillsdale, NJ: Earlbaum.

Smith, Barbara L. and MacGregor, Jean. T. (1992). What is collaborative learning? In Anne Goodsell, Michelle Maher, Vincent Tinto with Barbara L. Smith, and Jean MacGregor (eds.). *Collaborative learning:*

A sourcebook for higher education. University Park, PA.: National Center on Postsecondary Teaching, Learning & Assessment.

Sophocles. *Antigone.* (1990) New York: Oxford University Press.

Spender, D. (1989). *The writing or the sex?* Elmsford, NY: Pergamon.

Stafford, Kim. (1987) *Having everything right: Essays of place.* New York: Penguin Books.

Stanford Observer. (April-May 1988, November-December 1990).

Starr, P. (1982). *The social transformation of American medicine.* New York: Basic Books.

Strauss, Levi. (1968). *Liberalism: ancient and modern.* New York: Basic Books.

———(1959). *What is political philosophy?* Glencoe, IL: Free Press.

Sullivan, W. and Bellah, R. (1987). The professions and public philosophy: the perspective of the common good. Paper presented to Lewis & Clark Graduate Faculty, February 13, 1987.

Swartzlander, Susan, Pace, Diana, & Stamler, Virginia Lee. (1993). "The Ethics of Requiring Students to Write About Their Personal Lives," in *The Chronicle of Higher Education.* pp. 131-32. (February 17, 1993).

Tannen, D. (1991). *You just don't understand.* New York: Ballantine.

U.S. Bureau of the Census. (1992). *Statistical abstract of the United States.* Washington Press, Government Printing Office.

Urban, Wayne J. (1988). Review of The Closing of the American mind, by A. Bloom. *Journal of American History,* 75:869 (December 1988).

Veblen, Thorstein. (1918). *The theory of the leisure class.* New York: Heubsch. First published in 1899.

Vygotsky, Lev. (1978a). *Mind in society.* Cambridge, MA: Harvard University Press.

———(1978b). *Thought and language.* Cambridge, MA: MIT Press.

Wallace, J. and Loudin, W. (1991). Qualities of collaboration and the growth of teachers' knowledge. Paper presented at the annual meeting of the American Educational Research Association, Chicago.

Weiler, Kathleen. (1988). *Women teaching for change: Gender, class and power.* South Hadley, MA: Bergin and Garvey.

Wexler, Philip. (1987). *Social analysis of education: after the new sociology.* New York: Routledge, Kegan Paul.

Witherell, Carol. (1991). The self in narrative: A journey into paradox. In Carol Witherell and Nel Noddings (eds.). *Stories lives tell: Narrative and dialogue in education.* New York: Teachers College Press.

Witherell, Carol and Noddings, Nel, eds. (1991). *Stories Lives Tell: narrative and dialogue in education.* New York: Teachers College Press.

Young-Eisendrath, Polly, and Hall, James. (1991). *Jung's self psychology: A constructivist perspective.* New York: Guilford Press.

Zeichner, Kenneth, and Gore, Jennifer. (1989). Teacher socialization. In W. R. Houston, M. Haberman, and J. Sikula (eds.). *Handbook of research on teacher education,* 329-348. New York: Macmillan.

Contributors

Charles R. Ault, Jr., coordinates Lewis & Clark College's Master of Arts in Teaching (M.A.T.) program for new science teachers and instructs elementary teachers in courses on science and mathematics. He holds his Ph.D. from Cornell University and has a special interest in problem solving in earth science and environmental education. For several years he has concentrated his research interests on the development of children's understanding of time, energy, and matter as revealed in the context of task-centered interviews.

Celeste M. Brody is visiting assistant professor of education at Lewis & Clark College in Portland, Oregon, where she coordinates the graduate core program and the Northwest Cooperative Learning Institute. She earned her Ph.D. from Ohio State University in curriculum and instruction. Her areas of specialization include instructional theory, adult development, and teacher cognition, and they reflect her concern for the preparation, growth, and continuing development of teachers at every level of education. Her research interests include narrative expressions of collaborative relationships among teachers and the study of collaborative contexts for understanding the complexities of human learning and growth.

Carolyn Bullard is former dean of the graduate school of professional studies at Lewis & Clark College, and professor of Special Education: Deaf and Hard-of-hearing. She has taught deaf children in both residential and day school programs. She received her master's degree from Columbia University and her Ph.D. from the University of Washington. Her research has focused on instructional practices and the language development of deaf children.

Joanne Cooper is assistant professor of educational administration at the University of Hawaii at Manoa. She teaches courses in higher education with a specific focus on qualitative research, multicultural education, and community colleges. Dr. Cooper holds a Ph.D. in educational policy and management from the University of Oregon. Her research interests include the uses of journalkeeping for professionals and the study of organizational culture and change.

Jack Corbett is associate professor of public administration at Lewis & Clark College where he teaches courses in policy analysis, natural resource management, organizational theory, and comparative public policy. He holds a Ph.D. from Stanford University and has taught at several universities in the United States, Canada, and Mexico. He was a senior Fulbright lecturer in Mexico City and has served as policy consultant to federal agencies and nonprofit organizations. He has authored articles and book chapters on water and land management issues in Mexico and Canada, as well as Hispanic political and cultural issues in the United States.

Ken Donald is a native Osage-Ponca. He holds an M.S.W. degree from Portland State University and an M.S. in school psychology from Lewis & Clark College. He currently serves as a school psychologist for the Beaverton School District in Oregon. His special interests are in working with minority youth and youth with emotional, behavioral and/ or economic problems.

Mary Henning-Stout is associate professor at Lewis & Clark College where she coordinates the school psychology training program in the department of counseling psychology. She received her Ph.D. from the University of Nebraska and maintains her research interests in gender issues in the practice, training, and research of school psychology.

Ken Kempner is associate professor of education at the University of Oregon where he specializes in leadership and higher education. He is the author of numerous chapters and articles on community colleges, higher education, international and comparative education, program evaluation, and qualitative research methodology.

Robert Klein is assistant professor in the education department at Springfield College, Massachusetts. He teaches courses in growth and development, adult development, group processes in the classroom, and multicultural foundations of education. He taught in the Lewis & Clark College graduate core program in 1989. Dr. Klein earned his doctorate in teaching, curriculum, and learning environments from Harvard University. His research interests include adult development and group processes.

Gordon Lindbloom has a Ph.D. from the University of Oregon and is a counseling psychologist and associate professor in the counseling psychology program at Lewis & Clark College. He is active in clinical practice and in supervising graduate students in counseling. He has worked for twenty years with school staff groups and with other public and private organizations to help them improve their effectiveness through improved collaboration and conflict resolution. His interests include stress and anxiety disorders, work stress, conflict and cooperation in work settings, and counseling for couples and families. His current research is on the interpersonal conflicts experienced by school principals.

Ruth Lundblad completed her master's degree in special education for the hearing impaired at Lewis & Clark College. She is a writer, a mother of four children, and a teacher of the hearing impaired.

Douglas F. Morgan is professor of public administration and director of the master's program in public administration at Lewis & Clark College in Portland, Oregon. He received his Ph.D. degree in political science from the University of Chicago. His articles on administrative ethics have appeared in various journals and books.

Nel Noddings is professor of education at Stanford University, where she teaches courses in philosophy of education, ethics, and feminist studies. In addition to three books, *Caring: A Feminine Approach to Ethics and Moral Education, Women and Evil,* and *Awakening the Inner Eye: Intuition in Education* (with Paul Shore) she is author of more than sixty articles and chapters on various topics.

Zaher Wahab is professor of teacher education at Lewis & Clark College. An Afghan-American, Dr. Wahab is a graduate of Stanford University (M.A. and Ph.D.). Professor Wahab has written and lectured extensively on various aspects of countries he has visited, notably Sweden, South Korea, Portugal, Costa Rica, Nicaragua, Japan, and China. His professional, intellectual, and civic concerns include issues of race, class and gender, political economy, ethics, comparative studies, and critical educational/social theory.

James M. Wallace has his Ed.D. from Harvard University. He is an educational historian who writes on the relationships between education and journalism, education biography, the history of teaching, and professionalization. He recently published *Liberal Journalism and American Education,* 1914–1941. (Rutgers University Press, 1991.) He has an active interest in alternative education and was involved in starting two alternative schools in Portland, Oregon, where he is professor of teacher education at Lewis & Clark College.

Terrence R. Whaley is a recent recipient of a Spencer Fellowship for the project, "Literary reconstruction in the social sciences." He received his Ph.D. from the University of Chicago in philosophy and education and is a regular presenter at annual conventions of the American Educational Research Association. He has published articles on Dickens, George Eliot, Matthew Arnold, Thomas Huxley, and, most recently, Aristotle and postmodern criticism. Terry is a teacher of secondary English in the Seattle public schools and an adjunct faculty in Lewis & Clark College's graduate core program.

Carol Witherell is associate professor of education and director of teacher education programs at Lewis & Clark College in Portland, Oregon. A former teacher of primary grades, she received her Ph.D. in educational psychology from the University of Minnesota. She has served on the faculties of Santa Clara University, Colgate University, the College of William and Mary, and Wesleyan University, where she has taught moral development and ethics in education; child, adolescent, and adult development; and educational psychology. Carol is the co-editor (with Nel Noddings) of *Stories Lives Tell: Narrative and Dialogue in Education,* published by Teacher's College Press.

Index

"Action Learning and Reflection in the Workplace" (Marsick), 114
Activities: male-associated, 189, 193; valued, 189; women's, 191–193
Actual Minds, Possible Worlds (Bruner), 73
Affirmative action, 3, 135, 214
Answer-seeking, 8, 67, 187
Antigone (Sophocles), 36
Ault, Charles, 9, 68, 147–167, 254
Authority, 93; and collaborative learning, 56; professional, 21; of teachers, 56
Autobiography, 75, 96–97
Autonomy, 17, 82, 212; moral, 25; overvaluation of, 70

Bacon, Francis, 13
Banks, James, 5, 6
Barry, Kathleen, 209
Behavior: collective, 256; economic, 150; feminine, 190; institutional, 243; moral, 244; negative, 99; and official policy, 35
Belenky, Mary, 50, 73, 74, 77, 78, 97, 244
Beliefs: distortions of, 89; evaluation of, 90; expression of in stories, 40; making explicit, 42–43; repeated patterns of, 41; socially justifying, 54; uncovering, 47
Bellah, Robert, 5, 6, 36
Bennett, William, 2, 5, 6, 135, 207
Bicultural education, 141
Bilingual education, 3
Bloom, Allen, 2, 5, 6, 207
Bly, Robert, 99
Bowen, Eleanor, 211, 224, 228
Brody, Celeste, 1–10, 11, 12, 29–47, 49–68, 69–87, 247, 249, 252–253, 256

Browlee, Paul, 116
Bruffee, Kenneth, 53
Bruner, Jerome, 5, 6, 71, 73
Buber, Martin, 74
Buchanan, Patrick, 6
Bullard, Carolyn, 10, 188, 237–246, 254
Bureaucracy: decentralization in, 235; depersonalized nature of, 114; expectations in, 2; limits of decision-making in, 36; survival in, 35

Cadillac Desert (Reisman), 36
Call of Stories (Coles), 36
Canfield, Dorothy, 95
Caring: A Feminine Approach to Ethics and Moral Education (Noddings), 73, 211
Castenada, Alfredo, 144
Change: agents, 97, 138; in communities, 55; developmental, 95; openings for, 55; of outcome, 153; reflection on, 67; resistance to, 32; social, 97
Chronicle of Higher Education, 134
Class: equity, 34; professional understanding of, 68; social, 57
Clients: demands of, 13, 18; diversity of, 50
Coles, Robert, 5, 6, 36, 130
Collaboration, 202
Collegiality, 45, 51, 64
Comer, James, 5, 6
Communication: of concepts, 155; and developmental perspective, 95; improving, 94; patterns, 95; process of, 120; in relationships, 119; skills, 94; ways of, 79; in writing, 106, 107
Community: among teachers, 29; changes in, 55; within classrooms, 59;

279

commitment to, 30–31, 46; contexts of, 30–34; of discourse, 65; and interdisciplinary studies, 29–47; language of, 54; learning, 38; networks, 73; of peers, 51, 54; professional, 249; program goals for, 33–34; shared norms in, 58, 59–60; significance of, 40; standards of judgment, 26; values in participation in, 33

Compensatory education, 3

Competition, 70

Concept, 157; definition, 155; of democracy, 251; of felt significance, 164–165; in science, 157–160; shared meaning, 155; systems, 156

Confidentiality, 60

Conflict, 76; and collective knowledge, 63; moral, 2, 22; moral principle and self-interest, 151–152; in organizational life, 36; resolution, 51; teaching, 5

Conservatism, 5, 6; effect on education, 2, 135–136; social, 2

Continuing Liberal Education (House), 103

The Control of Nature (McPhee), 151

Conversation. *See* Dialogue

Cooper, Joanne, 9, 67, 103–116, 252

Corbett, Jack, 9, 68, 169–186

Co-teaching, 11, 30, 37–46; conditions supporting, 39–40; constraints of, 43–46; defining, 38–39; equality and dominance in, 45; gender balance in, 45, 91; goals of, 38; leadership in, 44; multiple partners in, 44-45; narratives in, 41; scheduling, 35; trust in, 39

Cremin, Lawrence, 10

Crews, Frederick, 5, 6

Cuban, Larry, 29

Cultural: democracy, 141; diversity, 33, 194; identity, 73; norms, 71; relationships, 141; sensitivity, 170; values, 36

Culture: dominant, 192, 198–199, 247, 253; gender practices, 190; organizational, 65, 137, 219–235; patriarchal, 204, 248, 249, 251; of positivism, 247, 248-250; of power, 136; as process, 141; professional, 51; professional understanding of, 68; stories in, 82

Curriculum: construction, 9; core, 31-33, 39, 46, 237-246; development, 216; interdisciplinary, 31-33; internationalization in, 175-177; issue-oriented, 9-10; "living," 40, 41; patriarchal, 3; reform, 169; traditional, 3

Decision-making: equality in, 64; limits in bureaucracies, 36; moral, 244; and personal values, 113; values in, 241

Democracy: concept of, 251; cultural, 141; equality of, 15; multicultural, 144-145; in workplace, 235

Detachment, 70, 75

Development: adult, 50, 51-53, 67, 71, 89-102; cognitive, 32; curriculum, 216; human, 35, 82, 94; intellectual, 32; of knowledge, 243; of leadership, 59; learning as, 32; moral, 52, 67; personal, 4; professional, 36, 174; psychological theory of, 94-96; of shared norms, 59; societal, 73

Dewey, John, 1, 5, 6, 7, 10, 50, 187

Dialogue: across professions, 49-68; among different professions, 12; classroom, 9; and collaboration, 41; connection to narrative, 41, 74; educational, 139; and ethical ideal, 74; on gender issues, 204; journals as, 105; nature of, 86; of professional life, 53-58; promoting, 89; reflective, 34, 67, 103, 227; self, 105; social context for, 54

Diary of a Young Girl (Frank), 103

Diversity, 7, 32, 134, 138; cultural, 33, 194

Donald, Ken, 9, 67, 78-82

d'Souza, Dinesh, 2, 5, 6, 207

Ecology, 156, 161; Orians model, 162-163

Ecosystems, 149, 156, 160-162

Educating (Gowin), 164

Education: attacks on, 2-3; bicultural, 141; bilingual, 3; "choice" in, 3; compensatory, 3; conservatism in, 2, 5, 6, 135-136; and culture, 1; defining, 10; as end in itself, 28n3; experiential, 72; gender studies, 3, 5; global, 5; government intervention in, 3;

human rights, 141-142; intergroup, 142; internationalization of, 68; language, 142; liberal, 3, 5, 10; minority groups in, 133, 134-136, 216; multicultural, 3, 5, 136-144; and racism, 134-136, 136; special, 33; traditional, 3, 53; transfusion model, 5, 6

Education, professional, 2, 33; collaborative learning in, 50-58; continued development in, 4; gender issues, 195-201; internationalization of, 169-186; liberal arts in, 13-27; and liberal education, 10; meaning of, 255-257; and multiculturalism, 133-145; purpose of, 250-253; status hierarchy in, 19-20, 24-25; stories in, 69-87

Egoism, 123-124, 131

Elbow, Peter, 59

Elitism, 1

Empathy, 78, 118

Environment: changing, 1; collaborative, 42; degradation of, 147, 169; problem-solving in, 147-167; for reflection, 91-92; symmetry of interactive processes in, 154; work, 222

Equity: class, 34; ethnic, 208; gender, 5, 7, 34, 208, 214; race, 208

Ethic(s): of care, 68, 72, 117-131, 211, 215; codes of, 21, 22; deontic, 119; gender relations, 117; Judeo-Christian, 135; Kantian, 119, 121; objective reasons, 125-126; practical, 128-130; of principle, 68, 117, 119; professional, 21; subjective reasons, 125-126

Eurocentrism, 136, 139, 143, 144

The Evolving Self (Kegan), 73, 94, 212

Experience: in adult learning, 52; age, 57, 63; alternative understandings of, 225; common, 72; of feelings, 165; gender, 57, 63, 209-210; giving meaning to, 47; individual, 71; and knowledge, 40, 195; languages of, 51; life, 71; morally stimulating, 17; negative, 99; personal, 52, 159; professional, 52; reflection on, 110; sharing, 41, 56, 72, 90, 110, 155; social class, 57; student, 86; and theory, 17; validity of, 63

Feminine: activities, 189, 190; collaboration, 202; in public service professions, 189-205; status of, 190, 191-193; ways of knowing, 201

Feminism, 32; and collaborative learning, 50; and critical theory, 211; criticism of status hierarchy, 20; critiques of developmental psychology, 17; ethics of, 119; student resistance to, 196-201, 213; theory, 97

Frank, Anne, 103

Freire, Paulo, 74, 144, 253

Geertz, Clifford, 29

Gender: age responsiveness to issues, 214; balance in co-teaching, 45; dialogue on, 204; equality in decision-making, 64; equity, 5, 34, 208, 214; and ethnicity, 212; experience, 57, 63; identity, 73, 213; and interpretation of life events, 71; issues, 33; issues in professional education, 195-201; and life course, 97-98; perspectives in teaching, 37; and professional/liberal knowledge, 207-217; professional understanding of, 68; roles, 98; status, 189-205; stereotypes, 51, 99, 210, 212, 215; studies, 3, 5, 188; of teachers, 203

Gilligan, Carol, 5, 6, 73, 74, 77, 78, 117, 119, 120, 121, 122, 123, 124, 211, 212

Girard, Andre, 70

Government, intervention in education, 3

Gowin, D. Bob, 164, 165

Graff, Gerald, 5

Groups: ethical guidelines for, 60; facilitators in, 61; implicit-explicit process, 58, 62-63; interactive, 90; and journal writing, 100-101; large, 100; minority, 133, 134-136; personal disclosure in, 60; presenters in, 61; problem-solving in, 94; processors in, 61-62; roles in, 61-62; small, 58-59, 226; trust in, 72

Habits of the Heart: Individualism and Commitment in American Life (Bellah), 36

Hardin, Garrett, 151, 167

Harding, Sandra, 50
Harrington, Michael, 5, 6
Having Everything Right (Stafford), 75
The Healing Web (Pilisuk & Parks), 73,
212
Heinz dilemma, 119
Henning-Stout, Mary, 10, 187, 189-205,
248, 249
Hollingsworth, Sandra, 50
House, D.B., 103
Hughes, Robert, 6
Humanism, 68

Identity: bicultural, 144; ethnic, 73;
gender, 73, 213; personal, 103, 171;
professional, 103, 171; racial, 213;
value in, 253
In a Different Voice (Gilligan), 73, 119,
211
Individualism, 212; autonomous, 17;
ethical, 14, 21, 22, 27n2; Lockean, 16;
overvaluation of, 70
Interaction: of different perspectives, 37;
ecosystem, 154; with natural systems,
148; social, 50; unreflective, 197
Interdisciplinary studies, 29-47; common
issues in, 34-37; content in, 45;
leadership in, 44; program goals in,
33-34
Internationalization, 169-186; academic
units interests in, 172-173; central
administration interests in, 172;
curriculum in, 175-177; exchanges in,
178-179; faculty interests in, 173-174;
field experience in, 179-180; hosting
in, 177-178; implementation, 175-180;
interdisciplinary concerns in, 171; in
language and area studies, 170;
student interests in, 174; subject and
disciplinary competency in, 170-171

Jacobs, Harriet Ann, 96
Journals, 67, 91, 103-116, 227, 252; adult
use of, 68; class, 105; dialogical, 75,
105; ethical guidelines for, 60;
learning, 114; personal, 225-226;
personal disclosure in, 60; as
reflective practice, 103
Judgment: acceptance of, 112; commu-

nity standards, 26; as decision based
on valuing, 163; discretionary, 220;
ethical, 1; moral, 2; and personal
disclosure, 60; professional, 219-220;
rejection of, 112; of significance, 165
Jung, Carl, 98, 99-100
Justice, 72, 244

Kant, Immanuel, 122
Kanter, R.M., 211
Keen, Sam, 85
Kegan, Robert, 50, 71, 73, 82, 94, 95, 98,
212
Kelly, George, 50
Kempner, Ken, 10, 188, 247-257
Klein, Robert, 9, 67, 89-102
Knowing: connected, 210; logicoscientific
mode, 71; narrative mode, 71, 74, 79;
paradigmatic mode, 71; teachers'
ways of, 46; ways of, 5, 30, 56, 60, 71,
74, 79, 94; women's ways of, 97, 201,
211
Knowledge: as abstract, 244; abuse of, 1-
2; applied, 19-20; authority of, 55;
banking, 249-250; constructed, 46, 54,
97; controlling access to, 250; critical,
20; defining, 188; development of,
243; ecological, 149; esoteric, 19; and
experience, 195; frames of, 243-245;
liberal, 207-217; and life experience,
40; new, 55; objective, 248; as
objectivity and generalizability, 71;
passive, 20, 251; pedagogical, 41;
personal, 89, 201; process of acquisition, 42; professional, 18, 19-20, 207-
217, 251; puritanism of, 248; received,
97; shared, 41; social construction of,
32, 50, 54, 56, 213, 248; specialized,
19, 21; subjective, 97; tacit, 20;
teachers as transmitters of, 5;
teachers' beliefs about, 42; theoretical, 19-20; traditional, 8, 28n3, 55, 56,
67; validation of, 20
Kohlberg, Lawrence, 17, 119, 121, 124,
244
Kuhn, Thomas, 50

Language: of community, 54; of critique,
138; education, 142; foreign, 170;

interdisciplinary, 139; of opposition, 120; professional, 54; as social construction, 138; specialized, 51

Laughter, 116

Learning: about gender, 210-214; adult, 51-53, 92; collaborative, 31, 32, 42, 49-68; communicative, 90; communities, 38, 49; competitive, 51; cooperative, 49, 86; from curriculum, 211-212; as development, 32; experiential, 59, 60-61, 73, 86, 87; interactive, 31; journals, 114; love of, 103, 116; new, 87; personally relevant, 103; reflective approach, 230; responsibility for, 59; social construction of, 54; social contexts, 53; social interaction in, 50; from students, 212-214; styles, 52, 59, 87; theoretical, 60-61; from women colleagues, 210-211

Lectures on Ethics (Kant), 122

Lewin, Kurt, 50

Liberal arts: and moral conflict, 22; in professional education, 13-27; redefinition of, 137-141

Liberal education, 3, 5, 10, 237-246; and civic responsibility, 15, 16; goals of, 103; and knowledge of human condition, 22; meaning of, 14-18; self-critical capacity of, 23; traditional elements of, 16-17; transformation of, 15-16

Lindbloom, Gordon, 10, 188, 219-235

A Little Book on the Human Shadow (Bly), 99

Lundblad, Ruth, 9, 67, 82-85

Lyons, Nona, 50, 117

McPhee, John, 150-151

Maine, Neal, 161

Marginalization, 198, 199, 243, 247, 248, 250, 251

Marsick, Victoria, 114

Mead, George Herbert, 49

Mead, Margaret, 189

Meaning: co-constructing, 46; of concept, 155; developmental changes in, 95; of experiences, 47; imposition of in schools, 141; making, 50, 52, 71, 76, 82, 94; personal, 50, 247-257; policentric patterns of, 17; profes-

sional, 247-257; of professional education, 255-257; shared, 41, 155; social, 50; social construction of, 50

Men and Women of the Corporation (Kanter), 211

Merton, Thomas, 103

Miller, Janet, 50

Morgan, Douglas, 9, 11, 13-27

Mulcahy, Joanne, 193-194

Multicultural education, 3, 5, 136-144; instructional dimensions, 142; insufficiency of, 142

Multiculturalism, 68, 133-145

Myerhoff, Barbara, 73, 79, 92, 212

Narratives: from anthropology, 92-94; autobiographical, 96-97; connection to dialogue, 41, 74; oral tradition in, 78, 79; power of, 36, 41; and professional education, 69-87; of self, 41; of teaching, 41; as texts, 41

National Defense Education Act, 170

A Nation at Risk, 2

Noddings, Nel, 5, 6, 73, 74, 76, 78, 117, 119, 126, 127, 211

Number Our Days (Myerhoff), 73, 79, 92, 93, 212

Olsen, Tillie, 73, 77, 78, 83, 212

One to One (Baldwin), 107

Oppression, 138

Organization(s), 242-243; complex, 14, 21-22, 219; conflicts in, 29; culture of, 65, 219-235; group dynamics in, 93; influence on relationships, 222; loyalty to, 11; mores in, 2; nature of, 35, 70; patriarchal, 214; professionals in, 188; socially constructed, 249; survival in, 35; theories of, 222, 223; women in, 210-211

Orians Model, 162-163

Overspecialization, 38

Ozick, Cynthia, 82

Paradox: of community, 31; integration of, 74; of nature of life, 82; in professional education, 21-22

Parks, Susan Hillier, 73, 82, 212

Patriarchy, 204, 208, 211, 214, 248, 249, 251

Pedagogy: for adult development, 51-53; critical, 141; reflecting on, 40
Pepi, David, 164, 165
Piaget, Jean, 50
Pilisuk, Mark, 73, 82, 212
Pluralism, 133, 135, 137
Political correctness, 6, 207, 208
Positivism, 192-193, 201, 247, 248-250
Power, 93; allocation, 49; collective, 85; of connection, 75; culture of, 136; exercised by professionals, 21; of narrative, 36, 41; over nature, 248; political, 19; relationships, 139; of stories, 82; of technology, 33
Practice, professional: collaboration in, 50; competing values in, 29; criticisms of, 18-22; epistemological debate, 19-20; ethical dilemmas in, 11, 34; and interpersonal problems, 114; legitimacy of, 13-14; moral tensions in, 11, 25, 26; nature of reality of, 18-19; ontological debate on, 18-19; organizational dimensions of, 22; and organizations, 219-235; paradox in, 21-22; and personal life, 70, 113-115, 139; purpose of, 21-22; reflective, 37; requirements of, 50-51; self-interest in, 127; sociological perspective, 19; teleological debate, 21-22; use of narrative in, 36
Prisoner's dilemma, 152
Privacy, 60, 110, 111
Problem-solving, 72, 90, 223; across disciplines, 35; cooperative, 60; environmental, 147-167; group, 60, 94; and specialized language, 51; team, 51; technical approaches, 11
Professional: authority, 21; codes of ethics, 21, 22; community, 249; competence, 219-235; decision-making, 113; development, 174; ethics, 21; identity, 103, 171; judgment, 219-220; knowledge, 251; meaning, 247-257; relationships, 111-112; self, 188; skills, 25, 220
Psychology: counseling, 33; developmental, 17

Question-posing, 8, 67, 187

Race: and discourse of multiculturalism, 134-136; equity, 34, 208; professional understanding of, 68
Ramirez, Manuel, 144
Reason, 2
Reflection, 61-62, 100; about change, 67; and adult development, 89-102; creating, 56; critical, 89, 94; and dialogue, 67; on experience, 110; as healing process, 113; on one's own life, 60; personal, 159; process of, 98; promoting, 90; on reality, 74; in writing, 112
The Reflective Practitioner (Schon), 90, 244
Reisman, Marc, 36
Relationships: caring, 74; client-practitioner, 21; collaborative, 37, 38, 39; cultural, 141; faculty, 40; gender and ethnicity, 212; hierarchical, 37; and human service professions, 190; interpersonal, 97; interracial, 97; pedagogical, 141; power, 139; preservation of, 121; professional, 111-112, 114; role-bound, 114; team, 41; as texts, 40; theory and practice, 24-25; working, 50
Relativism, 58
Repression, 99, 100
Return to Laughter (Bowen), 211, 224, 228
Rights, human, 136, 141-142
Rogers, Carl, 100
Rorty, Richard, 50, 54
Rousseau, Jean Jacques, 191

Schlesinger, Arthur Jr., 3
Schon, Donald, 90, 220, 244
Science, ecological, 147-167
Self-analysis, 100
Self-disclosure, 42
Self-expression, 100
Self-interest, 26, 117-131; legitimating, 187; and moral principle, 151-152
Self-narratives, 41
Self-reflection, 59, 201, 202
The Seven Story Mountain (Merton), 103
Shadow effect, 99-100
Sharan, Yael and Shlomo, 50

Shor, Ira, 2, 74, 253
Silence, 97
Skills: basic, 23; communication, 94;
    conflict resolution, 51; critical
    thinking, 137; feminine, 187; group,
    64; interpersonal, 187; leadership, 91;
    professional, 25, 220; reflective, 91,
    94; self-reflective, 202; social, 49;
    writing, 23
Social: bonds, 212; change, 1, 97; class,
    57; conservatism, 2; constructivism,
    12, 49, 50, 53, 58, 65; interaction, 50;
    justice, 34; meaning, 50; networks,
    73; skills, 49; transformation, 138, 251
Society: men's role in, 98; patriarchal,
    211, 215; specialized knowledge needs
    of, 19
Sophocles, 36
Stafford, Kim, 75
Stereotypes, 208; age, 51; ethnic, 51;
    gender, 51, 99, 210, 212, 215; race, 99
Stories, 92, 130; and expression of
    beliefs, 40, 41-42; personal nature of,
    40; power of, 82; in professional
    education, 69-87; students', 76-86

Teachers: authority of, 56; beliefs of, 42;
    gender of, 203; sense of community
    among, 29; as transmitters of
    knowledge, 5; vulnerability to
    criticism, 55
Teaching: and adult developmental
    needs, 51-53; collaborative, 5, 32. See
    also Co-teaching; competing values
    in, 29; of conflicts, 5; connected, 195;
    and construction of knowledge, 46;
    and cross-cultural perspectives, 37;
    gender-related, 37, 208; in interdisci-
    plinary programs, 36-37; moral
    dilemmas in, 30; narratives of, 41;
    reflective skills, 91, 94; risk taking in,
    39; styles, 39; team, 5, 32, 38, 208
Team teaching, 5, 32, 38, 208. See also
    Co-teaching
Tell Me a Riddle (Olsen), 73, 83, 212
Thinking: abstract, 17; critical, 32, 68,
    103, 137, 140, 142, 251; dichotomous,
    6; ecological, 150; as internalized

conversation, 53; mastering, 54; as
    mode of inquiry, 34; reflective, 187
Tragedy of the commons, 147-167
"The Tragedy of the Commons" (Hardin),
    151-152
Trust, 42, 72, 73; building, 64; in co-
    teaching, 39
Truth: genderized, 248; as intersection of
    multiple perspectives, 40; regimes of,
    140

Values, 70; based on salary, 192; choices
    among, 11; competing, 11, 29;
    cultural, 29, 36; in decision-making,
    241; in identity, 253; implicit, 35;
    individual, 113; male-associated, 190;
    overt, 35; patriarchal, 215; shared,
    241; traditional, 169; uncovering, 47;
    of women's work, 190, 191
Veblen, Thorstein, 1, 2
Voice: finding one's, 74; value in, 253
Vygotsky, Lev, 50

Wahab, Zaher, 9, 68, 133-145
Wallace, James, 1-10, 188, 207-217, 256
Weiler, Kathleen, 50
Whaley, Terrence, 9, 68, 117-131
Witherell, Carol, 9, 67, 69-87, 247, 252-
    253
Women's Ways of Knowing (Belenky),
    73, 77, 97, 212, 215, 244
Work: collaborative relationships in, 50-
    51; cooperative, 220; developmental
    challenges in, 2; environments, 222;
    meaning-making in, 52; women's, 190
Worldview: adult, 52; Eurocentric, 136,
    139, 143, 144; integrated, 17;
    patriarchal, 214, 215
Writing, 32; as communication process,
    106, 107; for critical inquiry, 59; fear
    of, 106-109, 115; intrusive, 110;
    journal, 91, 100-101, 103-116;
    mastering, 54; as mode of inquiry, 34;
    reflective, 112; skills, 23